Austere Realism

Representation and Mind
Hilary Putnam and Ned Block, editors

Austere Realism

Contextual Semantics Meets Minimal Ontology

Terry Horgan and Matjaž Potrč

A Bradford Book
The MIT Press
Cambridge, Massachusetts
London, England

MIT Press books may be purchased at special quantity discounts for business or sales promotional use. For information, please e-mail special_sales@mitpress.mit.edu or write to Special Sales Department, The MIT Press, 55 Hayward Street, Cambridge, MA 02142.

This book was set in Stone Serif and Stone Sans on 3B2 by Asco Typesetters, Hong Kong, and was printed and bound in the United States of America.

Library of Congress Cataloging-in-Publication Data

Horgan, Terry, 1948–.
Austere realism : contextual semantics meets minimal ontology / Terence E. Horgan and Matjaž Potrč.
    p. cm.—(Representation and mind series)
Includes bibliographical references and index.
ISBN 978-0-262-08376-8 (hardcover : alk. paper)
1. Ontology. 2. Realism. 3. Semantics. I. Potrč, Matjaž. II. Title.
BD311.H67   2007
149′.2—dc22   2007032259

10   9   8   7   6   5   4   3   2   1

To the memory of our mothers, Helmi McCorkle and Branka Jurca

Contents

Preface

This book grows out of our collaborative philosophical interaction with one another during the past decade. Matjaž spent the academic year 1996 as a Fulbright Scholar in Terry's department at the University of Memphis. Philosophy of psychology was his main interest, which led to a conference in Ljubljana, Slovenia on Horgan and Tienson's 1996 book *Connectionism and the Philosophy of Psychology* and to the publication of the conference proceedings in Potrč 1999b. Discussion spread to other areas of philosophy, including metaphysics, vagueness, and the origins of analytic philosophy and phenomenology—which led to a conference on vagueness in Bled, some of whose papers are collected in Horgan and Potrč 2000, 2003, and to a conference on origins whose proceedings are collected in Horgan, Potrč, and Tienson 2002. Our conversations about metaphysics, which continued over several years on different occasions of Terry's visiting Slovenia, led to four coauthored papers (Horgan and Potrč 2000, 2002, 2006a, 2006b) and then to this book. The book contains material adapted from these papers and also from Barnard and Horgan 2006; Horgan 1993b, 1998b, 2001b, 2002; Horgan and Timmons 2002; and Potrč 1999a. We thank the editors of the journals in which these papers appeared for their kind permission to adapt material from them. Other papers and books containing ideas that are echoed in this book include Horgan 1986a, 1986b, 1991, 1995a, 1995b, 1996, 2000; Potrč 2000, 2002b, 2002d, 2003, 2004a; and Potrč and Strahovnik 2004a, 2004b, 2005.

We are grateful to a number of friends and collaborators for helpful discussion about these matters over the years. Special thanks to Robert Barnard, Wilhelm Baumgartner, David Chalmers, Jonathan Dancy, Norman Gillespie, Mitch Haney, Helen Daly, Rafael Hüntelmann, Jenann Ismael, Dale Jacquette, Barry Loewer, Michael Lynch, Cole Mitchell, Laurie Paul,

Maria Reicher, Mark Richard, Steve Schwartz, Jonathan Schaffer, Herman Stark, Vojko Strahovnik, Danilo Šuster, Tadeusz Szubka, Bill Throop, John Tienson, Mark Timmons, Armando Verdiglione, and Timothy Williamson. Helpful critical papers about work of ours reflected in this book include Lynch 2002; Reicher 2002; Szubka 2002; Tienson 2002; Williamson 2002; and Richard 2006. Our thanks too to Hilary Putnam, who in 1986 directed a very enjoyable NEH Summer Seminar on "Philosophical Problems about Truth and Reality" at Harvard, replied in Putnam 1991 to Terry's seminar essay containing an early articulation of ideas in the present book (Horgan 1991), replied to Matjaž's Pecs, Hungary realism presentation in 2003, and in 1986 urged Terry to write a book on these themes; better late than never.

Introduction

Austere realism is a philosophical position comprising both ontological and semantical theses. Metaphysically, it claims that the right ontology—whatever exactly it might be—is *austere* in the sense that it excludes numerous putative objects, properties, and relations that are posited in ordinary belief and discourse, and it also excludes many that are posited in scientific theorizing. Semantically, it claims that numerous statements that are normally considered true, and that initially appear to have ontological commitments incompatible with an austere ontology, are indeed true but do not really incur such ontological commitments.

Blobjectivism is a specific version of austere realism. Ontologically, it claims that the world contains no real parts, but that this world is nevertheless structurally rich and dynamical. There are old movies featuring a kind of object coming from space, the Blob, with the distinguishing property of engulfing each particular entity and incorporating it into its all-encompassing mass.[1] This is not how we conceive the cosmos, because it presupposes the previous independent existence of the many. The Blob is supposed to be a kind of amorphous mass. We prefer to call our world *the blobject*. This implies that we are speaking of an object, and that this object has a relevant structure, namely the highly articulated structure of our world, to which it is identical. The name *blobjectivism*, as a position in metaphysics that takes the blobjective object as its starting point, captures well our preoccupation and intentions in using the term blobject.[2] The term 'blobjectivism' is useful in yet another manner: it indicates a metaphysical position that is both a form of metaphysical realism—the blobject is objectively real—and is strongly monistic. The blobject is *objectively real*, but lacks any objectively real *parts*.

We maintain that austere realism and blobjectivism, despite their initial air of implausibility, are not contrary to common sense, but actually are in deep agreement with it. The aim of this book is to argue for austere realism, and for the blobjectivist version of it, in a way that shows the compatibility between these positions and reflective common sense.

Austere realism consists of several ontological theses and several semantic theses; blobjectivism embraces all of these and adds more specific ontological claims of its own. This combination of ontological and semantic dimensions is where their strength comes from, as we intend to demonstrate. In order to aid in articulating the theses of austere realism and blobjectivism, and for other purposes as well, let us first introduce some useful terminology. Thought and language employ features that can usefully be called *positing apparatus*—features like names, quantifiers, and predicates in natural language, and thought-constituents that are the analogues in thought of such natural-language constituents. What we will call *positings* are affirmations in thought or language that employ positing apparatus in the manner that conforms with a nonnominalistic variant of Quine's well-known criteria of ontological commitment (Quine 1960)—a variant of the Quinean criteria that not only construes a statement's constituent names and existential quantification as incurring ontological commitment to *individuals* answering to those names and quantifiers, but also takes the statement's constituent predicates as incurring ontological commitment to *properties* answering to these predicates.

In order to avoid awkward circumlocution about positing apparatus and positings in thought and language, we will often simply speak of *posits*. Such talk, as employed here, is meant to be understood as deliberately bracketing the issue of ontological commitment. For example, the statement "Numbers are posits of Smith's ontological theory" is to be understood as being noncommittal about whether or not there really are such entities as numbers. This statement can be roughly paraphrased by a statement like "Smith's ontological theory includes theses that employ positing-uses of the category 'number'."[3]

Using the language of posits, the ontological and semantic theses of austere realism can be given the following preliminary formulation (to be refined and elaborated later in the book):

Ontological Theses

1. There is a mind-independent, discourse-independent, world.

2. The right ontology excludes most of the posits of everyday belief and discourse, and also many of the posits of mature scientific theories.

Semantic Theses

1. Truth is correspondence between language and thought on one hand, and the world on the other.

2. Numerous statements and thought-contents involving posits of common sense and science are true, even though the correct ontology does not include these posits.

3. Truth, for such statements and thought contents, is indirect correspondence.

Blobjectivism embraces these generic ontological and semantic theses of austere realism, and also the following additional ones:

Blobjectivist Ontological Theses

3. There is really just one concrete particular, namely, the whole universe (the blobject).

4. The blobject has enormous spatiotemporal structural complexity and enormous local variability—even though it does not have any genuine parts.

The first ontological assumption and the first semantical assumption of austere realism both are strongly endorsed by reflective common sense, and both deserve to be taken as default positions when one inquires about ontology and truth. Although each has been challenged in philosophy— the ontological assumption by "global irrealists" about metaphysics, and the semantic assumption by (for instance) advocates of minimalist/ deflationist or epistemic theories of truth—we will largely take for granted these two assumptions throughout the book—as does reflective common sense. (We will critically engage such views briefly in chapter 5, however.)

The remaining ontological and semantic theses require substantial further articulation, which they will receive in the course of the book. For now, let us just emphasize how deeply intertwined are the ontological theses 2–4 with the semantical theses 2 and 3, within the package-deal position we will defend. We maintain that an austere ontology, even blobjectivist ontology, is actually consistent with numerous commonsense and scientific beliefs about the world. This is so because truth, for such beliefs, is an indirect form of correspondence that does not require the world-itself to contain individuals or properties corresponding to the positing apparatus employed in those beliefs (or in the statements that express them).

Serious metaphysical inquiry, we maintain, ought to pay great respect to deeply held commonsense beliefs and to reflectively compelling commonsense modes of reasoning. Philosophical theorizing should accommodate common sense as much as possible; also, if and when it departs from common sense, it should explain plausibly the sources of whatever commonsense beliefs (or modes of reasoning) it rejects. Much of this book will be organized around a three-stage dialectical progression involving common sense—a reflective intellectual journey along a road leading toward austere realism. The first stage—the *thesis* stage, in Hegelian terminology—delineates various ontological and semantical claims that common sense initially and naively is inclined to embrace, when it begins to go reflective about matters of ontology and semantics. These claims together comprise what we will call *simple common-sense metaphysical realism*—for short, *simple realism*. The second stage—the *antithesis*—reveals a number of deep problems that arise for simple realism—problems that emanate fairly directly from common sense itself, as it becomes yet more carefully reflective about matters of ontology and semantics. The third stage—the *synthesis*—is a set of conclusions about matters of ontology and semantics that also emerge out of common sense itself, after it has become persistently reflective about the problems that emerge at the antithesis stage. These conclusions constitute a *refined* form of commonsense realism—namely, austere realism.

The first six of this book's seven chapters will be devoted to articulating and defending austere realism—first by arguing for this position via the three-stage dialectic described above (chapters 1–4), and then by providing further arguments in favor of the view (chapter 5) and addressing and replying to several important objections that can be raised against it (chapter 6). This portion of the book will stand on its own; one could accept its conclusions even if one refrains from following the fork in the road that subsequently leads to the specific species of austere realism we ourselves favor, namely, blobjectivism. Thereafter (chapter 7) we will mount an argument for the theoretical preferability of blobjectivism over other candidate versions of austere realism; in the course of doing so we will address various questions and challenges that arise for blobjectivism specifically.

Considerations of philosophical method will figure prominently in the course of the argument, and they will be made explicit at various stages as we proceed. We take this to be especially important because of the stress we put on the contention that reflective common sense can, and does, motivate conclusions about ontology and semantics that initially seem deeply repugnant to common sense itself. We will be arguing not only (i) that commonsensical *reasoning* leads one to austere realism when such reasoning is applied to the problems that confront simple realism, but also (ii) that the semantical component of refined realism actually vindicates commonsense *beliefs* employing commonsense posits. Reflective common sense can be brought to realize, we maintain, that the truth of most commonsensical beliefs is a matter of indirect correspondence to the world (rather than direct correspondence), and hence—odd though this sounds at first—that such beliefs do not actually incur ontological commitments to their own posits.

1 | Simple Realism: The Naive Approach to Truth and Ontology

We now turn to the position that presents itself as being straightforwardly opposed to the claims of austere realism, namely the position naively adopted by common sense in respect to what there is and what constitutes truth. As the dialectic of commonsense metaphysical realism later unfolds, it will become clear that ultimately there is no strong tension between austere realism and reflective common sense. But at the very beginning of discussion, such an opposition looks quite natural. The reflective mode will then lead toward refinement in commonsense thinking about ontology and truth, as common sense comes into tension with itself (the antithesis stage) and then overcomes this internal tension (the synthesis stage). But at the beginning stage, when common sense reflects naively on matters of ontology and semantics, it arrives at a position sharply at odds with austere realism—the position we are here calling simple commonsense metaphysical realism.

This chapter will initiate the dialectical progression by spelling out the ontological and semantic theses of simple realism, and by underscoring the incompatibility between these theses and austere realism.

1.1 The Ontological and Semantic Theses of Simple Realism

When common sense goes reflective about truth and ontology, how does it construe its own ontological commitments? What does common sense believe to be really there? How does it conceive of truth and its connection to ontology? It initially arrives at a naive view about these matters. The term 'naive' captures the fact that this position is common sense's *initial* position, at the beginning of ontological inquiry. This term also indicates that there is more to come: the naive position is only the first stage of what will evolve into a three-stage dialectic, as commonsense reflective investigation into ontology and truth progresses. Here then are the ontological and semantic theses of simple realism.

Ontological Theses

O1. Metaphysical realism: There is a mind-independent, discourse-independent world.

O2. Naive commonsense ontology: The right ontology includes many of the posits of everyday belief and discourse and many of the posits of mature scientific theories. Also, when there are multiple items falling under a given posit-kind, such multiplicities conform well to the counting practices that are routinely employed for that posit-kind.

Semantic Theses

S1. Correspondence conception of truth: Truth is correspondence between language and thought on one hand, and the world on the other.

S2. Abundance of truth: Numerous statements and thought-contents involving posits of common sense and science are true—including numerous counting-statements about such posits.

S3. Naive construal of correspondence: Truth is a direct mapping between thought/language and the world.

S4. Naive construal of ontological commitment: Commonsense beliefs and statements are ontologically committed to their posits.

Common sense is deeply committed to a world that exists independently apart from how it is conceived or described by humans or other thinking creatures; this is *metaphysical realism*, thesis O1. Common sense is also deeply committed to two ideas about truth. First is the idea that a thought or statement is true just in case it *corresponds* to the world; this is the correspondence conception of truth, thesis S1. Second is the idea that numerous beliefs and statements that are normally thought to be true, in everyday thought and discourse and also in science, really *are* true (including numerous beliefs and statements about how many objects of a given kind there are at, or within, a given location or within a given region); this is semantic thesis S2. These three deeply held beliefs will remain in place as the reflective dialectic of common sense progresses through its successive three stages.

Semantic thesis S3, which construes truth as a *direct* form of correspondence between thought/language and the world, is typically elaborated along the following lines (with the formal language of predicate logic as a model). A logically atomic thought/statement is true just in case (1) there are objects $o_1, \ldots, o_n$ in the correct ontology that are respectively denoted by the respective singular constituents of the thought/statement, (2) there is a monadic or polyadic relation R in the correct ontology that is expressed by the predicative constituent of the thought/statement, and (3) R is jointly instantiated by $o_1, \ldots, o_n$ (in that order). Likewise, the thought/statement is false just in case (1) there are objects $o_1, \ldots, o_n$ in the correct ontology that are respectively denoted by the respective singular constituents of the thought/statement, (2) there is a monadic or polyadic relation R in the correct ontology that is expressed by the predicative constituent of the thought/statement, and (3) R is *not* jointly instantiated by $o_1, \ldots, o_n$ (in that order). A nonatomic thought/statement is true (or false), roughly, just in case (1) it is true (or false) according to a Tarski-style recursive characterization of the truth predicate, and (2) it meets condition (1) solely by virtue of the truth or falsity of certain logically simpler thought-contents or statements that either (a) are constituents of the original nonatomic thought/statement, or (b) are obtainable from such constituents by instantiating singular constituents for quantified-variable constituents.

Semantic thesis S4, pertaining to ontological commitment, fits naturally with S3. Since the truth of a thought/statement requires that the correct ontology includes the thought/statement's posits (and that these posits instantiate the properties and relations predicated of them by the thought/statement), beliefs and statements are thereby ontologically committed to their posits.

The second ontological thesis of simple realism, O2, spells out common sense's naive belief about what should be embraced by an appropriate ontology. Thesis O2 fits hand-and-glove, within naive commonsensical reflection, with the semantic theses S2–S4. For, thesis S3 says in effect that the correspondence that constitutes truth involves direct referential linkages between the positing/counting apparatus of language/thought on one hand (e.g., names, predicates, and quantifiers) and individuals and properties on the other hand. This means that in order for a thought or statement to be true, there must be items in the mind-independent, discourse-independent world (viz., individuals and properties) that directly answer to the thought/statement's constituent positing apparatus. Thus, the thought/statement is ontologically committed to its posits—thesis S4. So, when one naively reflects commonsensically about matters of ontology, taking one's commonsense beliefs and the well-confirmed claims of contemporary science as largely true (thesis S2), one initially concludes that the right ontology—whatever exactly it is—must include many of the posits of everyday belief and discourse plus many of the posits of mature scientific theories—and must include multiplicities of them that conform to routine counting practices. This is thesis O2.

1.2 Ontological Vagueness

When common sense initially dwells upon certain questions pertaining to the nature of its posits, it arrives at the verdict that these questions have no determinate answer. For instance, there are questions of synchronic composition: Which particles of matter are literally *parts* of some posited item (e.g., a living human being, or a building, or an automobile, etc.), and which particles of matter are merely inside it without literally being parts of it? When you sip a cup of coffee or inhale a breath of air, are those recently internalized coffee molecules and air molecules immediately parts of your body, or are they merely inside of it? If the latter, then at what point during the processes of metabolization do these molecules, and/or their own proper parts, become parts of your body? The commonsensical response is that *there is no precise fact of the matter* about such questions.

Certain questions about spatiotemporal boundaries evince the same commonsensical reaction. Consider an acorn that falls to the ground, germinates, and gradually grows into an oak tree. At what point during the growth process does the tree itself begin to exist? The commonsensical response is that the tree *has no precise initial temporal boundary*; rather, it comes into being gradually. At what point in time did *you yourself* come into being, during the process that commenced when sperm met egg in your mother's womb? The commonsensical answer is the same as in the case of the acorn and oak tree.

Analogous observations hold for virtually all the posits of both ordinary thought/discourse and of science. Thus, the initial commonsensical view is that all such posits are *vague* items—vague with respect to their synchronic composition, for instance, and also vague with respect to their spatiotemporal boundaries. (Common sense surely regards them as vague in other respects too—e.g., vague with respect to how an object's parts could change, or be rearranged, or be replaced, without the object itself ceasing to exist.)

The initial commonsensical view about ordinary posits, then, is that they are *vague* items. The vagueness in question does not reside in language or in thought, but rather in the items themselves. Thus naive common sense conceives its posits as *ontologically* vague—mind-independently real items about which there is no precise fact of the matter concerning their composition, their boundaries, or their capacity for persistence through change.

A way to make vivid simple realism's commitment to the ontological vagueness of its posits is to ask how common sense initially reacts to questions that pose versions of what Peter Unger (1980) called *the problem of the many*. Suppose for the moment that there are various ontologically precise objects, all of which are good candidates for being identical with Mount Whitney—say, precise mereological sums of matter that differ from one another only very slightly. The slight differences involve matters like precise spatiotemporal boundaries and precise synchronic composition. (For present purposes, it doesn't really matter whether or not these mereological sums are *totally* precise. They might be individuated via their composite molecules, for instance, and yet the spatiotemporal boundaries of a single molecule might remain somewhat vague or indeterminate.) Is one and only one of these objects the unique referent of the name 'Mount Whitney', and if so, then which one?

When common sense initially considers this question, it seems immediately obvious that if indeed there are all these precise objects, then no specific one of them qualifies as the unique referent of 'Mount Whitney'. For, there are numerous equally well-qualified candidates (perhaps *infinitely* many such candidates); nothing about the world itself could make it the case of any one of these candidates that it, and not any of its competitors, is Mount Whitney. Yet, common sense does not conclude from this that there is no such unique object as Mount Whitney, or that there are vastly many mountains (perhaps infinitely many) in the local vicinity of the erstwhile Mount Whitney. Rather, the initial commonsensical view is that there is just one Mount Whitney, and that *none* of these precise objects is identical to it. The real Mount Whitney is a vague object rather than being any one (or more than one) of these precise objects.

This commonsensical way of reacting to the problem of the many reveals the importance of incorporating commonsensical ways of *counting* into the formulation of simple realism. Hence the second part of the ontological thesis O2, asserting that multiplicities falling under a given posit-kind conform to the counting practices that are routinely employed for that kind. And hence too the second part of the semantic thesis S2, asserting that among the many posit-involving truths are numerous counting-statements involving the posits.

1.3   Scientific Posits

We take it that when common sense initially dwells upon matters of ontology, it considers theoretical science to be ontologically committed to its posits too. The semantic theses of simple realism apply to scientific claims, and not just to claims made in nonscientific terminology. So simple realism is also metaphysically realist about the theoretical posits of mature science—electrons, quarks, cells, quasars, black holes, and so forth.

There are those, we realize, who are metaphysical realists about various observable entities posited by prescientific common sense (e.g., middle-sized dry goods) but are metaphysical irrealists (or metaphysical agnostics) about unobservable theoretical entities posited by science. (See, e.g., van Fraassen 1980.) Such a metaphysical position, however, is not the one that common sense itself comes to when it initially goes reflective about ontology, since such a position is contrary to *simple* realism. Simple realism supposes that the claims of mature science are largely true, and thus asserts that the posits of mature science are real—are items in the correct ontology. Although atoms and quarks are not directly observable, they are no less real than things that are observable, such as middle-sized dry goods. Naive common sense says, "Observable things are obviously real, and so their unobservable microparts must be real as well."

There are also those, we realize, who are metaphysical realists about entities posited in mature scientific theories, but who are irrealists about certain posits of nonscientific thought and discourse—for example, about "socially constructed" entities like nations and corporations. There is something plausible about this line of thought, especially insofar as it is directed toward posits of everyday discourse that are not directly observable in the manner of middle-sized dry goods and whose putative existence is supposedly a matter of institutional decree (e.g., legal or contractual decree). We will address this plausible side of that position further below. But once again, such a position is contrary to the *naive* commonsense view —namely, simple realism—because it apparently requires some backing away from the semantical theses of simple realism in order to somehow accommodate ordinary claims about nations, corporations, and the like while eschewing genuine ontological commitment to such posits. Simple realism cleaves to the naive construal of correspondence, which considers truth as a direct kind of mapping between language or thought and the world. Simple realism also embraces the naive construal of ontological commitment, which applies to corporations and nations no less than to middle-sized dry goods.

1.4 The Conflicts between Austere Realism and Simple Realism

Simple realism clearly conflicts strongly with austere realism (and hence with blobjectivism), about both matters ontological and matters semantic. On the ontological side, there is no conflict concerning the first ontological thesis of simple realism, which is also a part of the austere realist position. But the second ontological thesis of austere realism clearly is in conflict with the second ontological thesis of simple realism. Austere realism denies, whereas simple realism affirms, that the right ontology includes numerous posits of both nonscientific and scientific thought and discourse— numerous entities that simple realism says are *real parts* of the whole cosmos.

When common sense goes ontologically reflective, its posits initially appear to be ontological commitments. This means that cats, cups, and stones appear to it as among what is ultimately real—as items in the correct ontology. Likewise, the posits of science appear to be ontological commitments. This means again that whatever completed physics claims to exist— atoms, quarks, strings, or waves—are also part of the correct ontology.

These ontological claims of simple realism are obviously in sharp conflict with the ontological theses of austere realism and of blobjectivism. Austere realism, as we shall explain, claims that the right ontology excludes virtually all the concrete particular posits of everyday thought and discourse— including cats, cups, and stones. Blobjectivism claims that there really is just one concrete individual—the entire cosmos—and that it does not have any real parts. Simple realism, however, holds that vastly many parts are real in an ultimate ontological manner. Blobjectivism also claims that the cosmos exhibits rich structural complexity and spatiotemporal local variability, despite lacking any genuinely real parts. Simple realism, however, construes structural complexity in terms of distinct parts and their various relations to one another.

On the semantic side, there is no conflict concerning the idea that truth is correspondence between discourse/thought and the world; both simple realism and austere realism affirm this, in their respective first semantic theses. But simple realism does not recognize any distinction between direct and indirect correspondence—a distinction that we will discuss at some length later in the book. Instead, simple realism construes truth as a direct mapping between language/truth and reality, a mapping that requires the posits of true thoughts/statements to be items in the correct ontology.

Austere realism, on the other hand, holds that numerous statements (and the thought-contents they express) are not really ontologically committed to their posits—that is, are not ontologically committed to individuals in the mind-independent world answering to the names, definite descriptions, and existential quantifications employed in these statements, and are not ontologically committed to properties and relations answering to the predicates employed in these statements. Austere realism holds that although the nature of the mind-independent world is indeed the basis for the truth of these statements (and the truth of the thoughts they express), truth is typically an indirect relation rather than the kind of ontology-implicating mapping that constitutes direct correspondence. More on this as the book unfolds.

2 | Problems for Simple Realism

In the previous chapter we introduced simple realism and started comparing it to austere realism (and to blobjectivism). In this chapter we will argue that when one considers carefully certain matters that arise in connection with questions of ontology, reflective common sense itself uncovers powerful reasons for repudiating simple realism—even though simple realism is the ontological-cum-semantic position that reflective common sense *initially* accepts when it considers questions of ontology and semantics. The upshot of this stage of our inquiry will be to leave reflective common sense deeply in tension with itself: on the one hand, common sense is still inclined to accept simple realism; on the other hand, common sense is aware of very deep problems that appear to render simple realism untenable.

2.1 Methodological Remarks

The main methodological maxim that will be honored in the present chapter is this: it is important to *follow commonsense reflection to where it leads*. This means not recoiling from the apparent consequences of a line of thought that seems guided by commonsensical modes of reasoning just because these apparent consequences might seem repugnant to naive common sense itself. It means not backing off from the inquiry when common sense begins to fall into internal tension with itself. For, the internal tension might very well be genuine.

2.2 Lightweight Posits

We will use the phrase 'metaphysically lightweight posit' in a deliberately vague way. Under this rubric we include "socially constructed" institutional entities like corporations, universities, nations, and multinational organizations (e.g., NATO). We also include various nonconcrete cultural artifacts, like Beethoven's Fifth Symphony (as distinct from concrete performances of it) and Quine's book *Word and Object* (as distinct from concrete tokens of it).

It is not plausible that institutional entities like corporations and universities are denizens of the world-itself, *over and above* entities like persons, buildings, land masses, items of office equipment, and the like. This ontological claim is not plausible because it seems to make it far too easy to bring new items into being. From a commonsense perspective, people certainly do produce things that did not exist before—for example, people produce consumer items in factories, they build houses, they paint pictures. But such ways of adding to the "furniture of the world" are acts of creation or production in a very literal sense: one actually fabricates a new physical object that did not exist before by suitably combining and connecting physical objects that *did* exist before. Nothing of the sort happens, however, when (for instance) several people who regularly meet for lunch on Tuesdays begin to refer to themselves as "the Tuesday lunch club," or when a group of people sign various legal documents declaring the existence of "the Winnemucca Widget Corporation." From a commonsense intuitive perspective, adding to the world's ontology requires literally *fabricating* some new thing, rather than just engaging in practices like adopting new ways of talking or signing pieces of paper.

Yet, when one considers whether it might be possible to "reduce" a putative entity like a university to these other kinds of entities—say, by identifying each university with some set of them (or some mereological sum of them), or by systematically paraphrasing statements that posit universities into statements that do not—there is no plausible reductive account remotely in sight. For, the project of systematically paraphrasing university-talk into statements that eschew all talk of universities looks hopeless; and the trouble with attempts to *identify* a university with some set (or sum) of buildings, persons, computers, and so on is that there are always numerous equally eligible candidate-sets (or candidate-sums), and there is no reason to identify the university with any one of these over against any of the others. Likewise, mutatis mutandis, for other kinds of institutional entities like corporations and nations and for nonconcrete cultural artifacts like Beethoven's Fifth Symphony and Quine's *Word and Object*.

To accept these conclusions is to acknowledge that common sense, as it becomes progressively more reflective about matters of ontology and truth, does not wholeheartedly endorse either the ontological thesis O2 of simple realism or the semantic theses S3 and S4. One is inclined to think that the world-itself does not contain entities answering to posits like universities, symphonies, or NATO. One is also inclined to think that everyday beliefs about such items are somehow true, even so.

Even if one accepts this, middle-sized dry goods still are apt to seem ontologically kosher, as are the posits of theoretical science (e.g., electrons and quarks). But there has now arisen a commonsensically felt need for a suitable semantic treatment of beliefs and statements positing entities like nations, corporations, and the like—a treatment that can allow for the truth of these statements even if the mind-independent world does not contain items corresponding to their metaphysically lightweight posits. And there are further arguments to come, whose scope is broader.

2.3   The Special Composition Question

Peter van Inwagen (1990) wields an important and powerful form of metaphysical argumentation that has been too little appreciated in philosophy. He poses what he calls the Special Composition Question (for short, the SCQ): "When do several objects jointly compose an object?" When one reflects carefully and commonsensically on this question, with van Inwagen as one's guide, one quickly finds oneself in the grip of a surprising and disturbing train of thought.

Van Inwagen considers several initially plausible candidate-answers to the SCQ. He argues that each has highly implausible consequences, namely, commitments to putative entities that are not genuine objects at all according to our usual ways of thinking and talking. (For example, the suggestion that *contact* among a group of objects is what makes them jointly compose an object entails the grossly counterintuitive result that when two people shake hands, a new compound object comes into existence that ceases to exist when their hands separate.)

Van Inwagen argues, by elimination-via-counterexample of various initially plausible potential answers to the SCQ, that the only acceptable answer is that several objects compose an object when they jointly *constitute a life*. On this basis, he concludes that the right ontology of physical objects includes only two kinds of material beings: (1) "simples," whatever these might turn out to be (e.g., electrons and quarks, perhaps), and (2) living organisms. Discourse that posits other kinds of concrete objects, he says, should be understood by analogy with talk about the motion of the sun through the sky: useful and informative, but not literally true.

Initially, one is apt to think that there *must* be some general answer to the SCQ that is more inclusive than van Inwagen's—or at least a class of more inclusive general answers pertaining respectively to various "sortal" concepts like *table, cloud, mountain, continent,* and so forth. But pessimism quickly sets in once one actually tries to formulate such and answer. If you feel optimistic on this matter, we invite you to give it a try—and also to read van Inwagen's book. We predict that your optimism will not persist.

Two important theoretical desiderata are in play in van Inwagen's discussion of the ontology of material beings: (1) finding a systematic, general, answer to the SCQ, and (2) adopting an ontology that conforms reasonably well to our pretheoretic beliefs, and our scientifically informed beliefs, about what kinds of physical objects there are. Van Inwagen argues very persuasively that these desiderata are deeply in tension: they cannot both be satisfied. But he also assumes, without explicit argument, that insofar as the two desiderata conflict, satisfying (1) is theoretically more important than satisfying (2).

Now, it might well be asked whether one *should* attach more theoretical importance to obtaining a general and systematic answer to the SCQ than to "saving" tables, chairs, and other objects that one pretheoretically considers robustly, mind-independently real. If so, why? We submit that the answer to the first question is affirmative, and here is why. An adequate metaphysical theory, like an adequate scientific theory, should be systematic and general and should keep to a minimum the unexplained facts that it posits. In particular, a good metaphysical or scientific theory should avoid positing a plethora of quite specific, disconnected, sui generis, compositional facts. Such facts would be ontological oddities; they would be metaphysically queer. Even though explanation presumably must bottom out somewhere, it should bottom out with the kinds of "unexplained explainers" we expect to find in physics—namely, highly general, highly systematic, theoretical laws. It is just not credible—or even intelligible— that it would bottom out with specific compositional facts that themselves are utterly unexplainable and which do not conform to any systematic general principles. Rather, if one bunch of physical simples compose a genuine physical object, but another bunch of simples do not compose any genuine object, then there must be some reason *why*; it couldn't be that these two facts are themselves at the explanatory bedrock of being.

There cannot, then, be a body of specific compositional facts that are collectively disconnected and unsystematic and are individually unexplainable. Such ontological arbitrariness is not possible in the world-itself—the world whose constituents are van Inwagen's concern. In Horgan 1993b this is called *the principle of the nonarbitrariness of composition* (NAOC). This principle is fundamental and highly plausible and is a very compelling general constraint on metaphysical theory construction. It generates the requirement that an adequate metaphysics of concrete particulars be one for which there is a general and systematic answer to the special composition question. This requirement has very strong weight in metaphysical theory-construction, enough to trump the desideratum of preserving the posits of common sense and science.

So the upshot so far is that the need to provide a systematic and general answer to the SCQ, together with the great difficulty of providing such an answer that also pretty much includes all and only the kinds of physical objects that are posited in ordinary and scientific discourse, makes it very likely that the right ontology of concrete particulars will have to be one that posits either many fewer, or else many more, kinds of concrete particulars than those that are usually posited in science and in common sense.[1] *Common sense itself appreciates this fact*, when common sense reflects on the SCQ. One candidate ontology that provides a systematic and general answer to the SCQ is van Inwagen's own, comprising only physical simples on the one hand, and living organisms on the other. Other eligible ontologies, including ontological blobjectivism, will be considered in chapter 7.

Needless to say, however, the commonsensical realization lately mentioned is in substantial tension with simple realism. Naive common sense not only believes that ordinary middle-sized dry goods (for instance) are mind-independently real objects, but also believes that mind-independently real objects do not compose without restriction into *additional* mind-independently real objects. Naive common sense recoils, for example, at the idea that there is some genuine denizen of reality denoted by a definite description like 'the mereological sum of the Eiffel Tower, George Bush's left little finger, and Mount Everest'. Yet the apparent moral of the SCQ—a moral to which common sense itself gets driven when one reflects on this question—is that naive commonsense ontology cannot be right: either there are many more mind-independently real objects than naive common sense recognizes (objects such as the intuitively repugnant mereological sum lately mentioned), or there are many fewer.

Let us try making clear the impact of this discussion for the tension that arises for simple realism. As common sense becomes ontologically reflective, it appreciates that an adequate ontology will need to be one for which there is a systematic general answer to the SCQ. (Common sense, when it goes ontologically reflective, appreciates the principle of NAOC for ontology.) On the other hand, commonsensical reflection leads, by elimination of plausible candidate answers, to the conclusion that very probably, there is no systematic general answer that captures pretheoretic judgments about when a bunch of physical things collectively constitute another thing. A deep tension ensues between these two concurrent beliefs. In slightly different words, when common sense goes ontologically reflective, it requires there to be a systematic, general answer to the SCQ. Yet it also realizes that evidently no such answer conforms well to common sense's own ways of positing objects.

2.4 The Boundarylessness of Vagueness

Vagueness is ubiquitous in language and thought, both in everyday discourse and science. Moreover, many of the concrete particulars and properties posited in everyday discourse and science are vague. For example, many posited particulars are vague with respect to their spatiotemporal boundaries, or vague with respect to their synchronic composition. Likewise, many posited properties and relations are vague with respect to their range of actual and potential instantiation. But when one attends carefully to the nature of vagueness, some striking implications emerge: namely, that vague objects and vague properties/relations are logically impossible (contrary to simple realism)—and hence either (1) thought and discourse involving vague posits are systematically false, or else (2) truth, for vague thought and discourse, cannot conform to simple realism's conception of correspondence. Here we will set forth the reasoning leading to these conclusions. For clarity of exposition, we will segment the discussion into subsections.

2.4.1 Boundarylessness

We begin by discussing vagueness as a generic phenomenon. The points we will make in this subsection apply both to vagueness in language and thought (i.e., semantic vagueness) and (if such there be) to vagueness in the world (i.e., ontological vagueness). An essential aspect of any form of vagueness is *sorites susceptibility*: for any vague constituent of language or thought, and for any putatively vague object, property, or relation, there is a *sorites sequence* directly involving that item. A sorites sequence is a progression of statements, or of states of affairs (actual or possible), that generate a sorites-paradoxical argument. For example, here is a sorites sequence for the vague predicate 'bald' and for the putative vague property *baldness* (with 'B(i)' symbolizing 'A man with i hairs on his head is bald'):

$$B(0), B(1), \ldots, B(10^7)$$

Here is a corresponding sorites-paradoxical argument:

$$(n)[B(n) \supset B(n + 1)]$$

$$B(0)$$

Therefore, $B(10^7)$

The claim is that there will always be such a sorites sequence for any vague linguistic expression, any vague concept, or any putatively vague object, property, or relation.

A second essential attribute of genuine vagueness is what Mark Sainsbury (1990) calls *boundarylessness*. This feature, which obtains with respect to a sorites sequence, involves the simultaneous satisfaction by the sequence of the following two conditions:

The Difference Condition: Initially in the sorites sequence there are items with a specific status, and every predecessor of an item with this status has the same status. Eventually in the sequence there are items with the polar-opposite status, and every successor of an item with this status has the same status. No item in the sequence has both the initial status and the polar-opposite status.

The Transition Condition: There is no determinate fact of the matter about status-transitions in the sorites sequence.

Examples of polar-opposite statuses are baldness versus nonbaldness, heaphood versus nonheaphood, satisfying the predicate 'is bald' versus satisfying the predicative expression 'is not bald', truth versus falsity.

The Transition Condition needs further conceptual unpacking. It involves, essentially, two conceptual aspects or dimensions, one individualistic and the other collectivistic:

The Individualistic Same-Status Principle (ISS Principle): Each item in the sorites sequence has the same status as its immediate neighbors.

The Collectivistic Status-Indeterminacy Principle (CSI Principle): There is no correct overall assignment of statuses to the items in the sequence.

The ISS Principle is so called because it involves items in the sequence considered one at a time—each considered in relation to its immediate neighbors. The CSI Principle is so called because it involves the items in the sequence considered collectively. Both principles are essentially involved in the idea of boundarylessness—the idea of absence of sharp boundaries.

Suppose, for instance—contrary to the ISS Principle—that there is some item in a sorites sequence that does not possess the same status as one of its immediate neighbors. Then there is a sharp status-transition between these two items, a sharp boundary—which goes contrary to the very idea of boundarylessness (i.e., absence of sharp boundaries). The status-transition might not be from the initial status to its polar-opposite status, of course, because there might be one or more intermediate statuses—for instance, an in-between status one might express as "indeterminate whether bald or not bald." But the point is that a sharp status-transition of *any* kind would violate boundarylessness, even if the transition involves some intermediate status between the original status and its polar opposite.

Suppose now—contrary to the CSI Principle—that there is some correct overall assignment of statuses to all the items in the sorites sequence. Then, given that any sorites sequence must satisfy the Difference Condition, there are bound to be sharp status-transitions between certain successive items in the sequence—because eventually there are items that have the polar-opposite status of the initial items, and no item can have both the initial status and its polar-opposite status. But again, sharp status-transitions of any kind would violate boundarylessness, which is essential to vagueness.

So the ISS Principle and the CSI Principle are both aspects of boundarylessness: they both figure as conceptual dimensions in the notion "no fact of the matter about status-transitions." And boundarylessness is itself the very essence of vagueness.

But if this is so, then vagueness also involves a certain specific kind of logical incoherence: namely, the *mutual unsatisfiability* of various principles that are all essential aspects of vagueness. For instance, the Difference Condition and the ISS Principle cannot be jointly satisfied, because the only way for the ISS Principle to be satisfied by a sorites sequence would be for all items in the sequence to have the same status—contrary to the Difference Condition. Also, the ISS Principle and the CSI Principle cannot be jointly satisfied, given that some items in the sequence have some status or other (as required by the Difference Condition); for, satisfaction of the ISS Principle would require statuses (indeed, the same status) for all the items in the sequence—contrary to the CSI Principle.

2.4.2 Vagueness in Language and Thought

We turn now from generic features of vagueness to semantic vagueness— that is, vagueness in language and thought. This is a genuine phenomenon, despite the mutual unsatisfiability of the ISS Principle and the CSI principle. Semantic vagueness is possible because these two principles do exert a form of *normative governance* over semantically correct use of vague discourse and semantically correct thought-content. Such governance requires that these two status principles must be *adequately respected in affirmatory practice* (even though the status principles are not mutually satisfiable). Semantically appropriate affirmatory practice is itself a matter of conformity with certain mutually obeyable *practice standards*, in particular, the following two prohibitory ones:

> The Individualistic Status-Attribution Prohibition (The ISA Prohibition): Never attribute a specific status to an item in a sorites sequence and also attribute a different, incompatible, status to its immediate neighbor.

> The Collectivistic Status-Attribution Prohibition (The CSA Prohibition): Never affirm any determinate overall assignment of statuses to the items in a sorites sequence.

These two practice-standards are mutually obeyable in semantically correct judgmental/affirmatory practice—and, moreover, are mutually obeyable along with correctly assigning statuses and polar-opposite statuses to *some* items in a sorites sequence.[2] Thus, semantically correct judgmental/ affirmatory practice remains possible on the part of agents who think and speak using vague concepts and vague language—even though the ISS and CSI Principles are not mutually satisfiable by the respective items in a sorites sequence.

What constitutes normative governance of judgmental/affirmatory practice by the ISS and CSI Principles? Such governance consists in two correlative facts. First is the fact that these two status principles are *respected in practice* by agents who make judgments and affirmations in accord with the ISA Prohibition and the CSA Prohibition. That is, when an agent's practice conforms to these two practice standards, the agent thereby avoids status assignments that are in conflict with the ISS Principle or the CSI Principle.

This feature of competent judgmental/affirmatory practice does not by itself, however, constitute normative governance by the ISS and CSI status principles. For, if vague concepts and terms had sharp but *unknowable* transition-boundaries, then a semantically competent agent would be required to conform in judgmental/affirmatory practice to the ISA and CSA Prohibitions anyway, but for epistemic reasons rather than semantic ones: the agent would never be epistemically warranted in affirming any sharp transitions or any overall status-assignment—even though some overall status assignment, containing sharp status-transitions, would be *semantically* correct. (Normatively correct judgmental/affirmatory practice is subject to epistemic standards, not just purely semantic ones.)

So a second fact, also partly constitutive of what it is for the ISS and the CSI Principles to normatively govern proper judgmental/affirmatory practice, is that there do not exist any sharp transition-boundaries. (The nonexistence of such boundaries is an essential aspect of the notion of boundarylessness—as the term itself indicates.) Thus, the two prohibitory practice-standards are grounded not epistemologically, but rather semantically: not in ignorance of sharp boundaries, but rather in the ISS and CSI Principles themselves. These status principles are semantically "in force," even though they cannot be mutually satisfied by the respective items in a sorites sequence. They are in force in the sense that it would be semantically incorrect—rather than epistemically incorrect—to engage in judgmental/affirmatory practice that violates them. That is, it would be semantically incorrect to assign statuses to items in a sorites sequence in ways that conflict with the ISS Principle or the CSI Principle. Such status-assignment practice would be semantically incorrect *because* that assignment would be in violation of the ISS Principle and the CSI Principle.[3]

A crucially important feature of the ISA Prohibition and the CSA Prohibition, of course, is that they can indeed be consistently obeyed in practice—and, moreover, can be consistently obeyed while also assigning statuses to some items in a sorites sequence and also assigning polar-opposite statuses to other items. The trick is that in order to exhibit semantically correct judgmental/affirmatory practice, one must refrain from undertaking to assign statuses to *all* the items in the sequence—and one must also refrain from ever assigning a specific status to some item and also assigning some different status to an immediate neighbor.

In short, although the Difference Condition must actually be *satisfied* by vague discourse, its satisfaction consists in semantic governance by two mutually *un*satisfiable semantic-status principles. This governance is a matter of the way the semantic-status principles undergird mutually obeyable affirmatory-practice standards, notably the two prohibitory ones just stated. Vague discourse that obeys these practice standards thereby respects the semantic-status principles as well as possible, given their mutual unsatisfiability—and well enough. Satisfaction of the Transition Condition itself, for vague discourse and vague thought-content, consists in affirmatory practice that respects the status principles in this way—and that does so because of the semantically normative force of status principles themselves, rather than because of ignorance of sharp boundaries. There are no sharp boundaries.

The considerations lately set forth all emanate from reflective common sense itself, when one attends carefully and commonsensically to what is involved in the idea of boundarylessness. Given the uncontestable Difference Condition pertaining to a sorites sequence, evidently the only way to avoid what has just been said about the ISS and CSI Principles and about the ISA and CSA Prohibitions would be to reject the Transition Condition and adopt a treatment of vagueness that posits sharp semantic transitions in sorites sequences—which commonsensically seems deeply contrary to the very nature of vagueness itself. For instance, "epistemicism" holds that there is always a sharp transition between truth and falsity in any sorites sequence of statements, although the location of this transition is unknowable by finite creatures like ourselves (Sorensen 1988; Williamson 1994). Similarly, "classical supervaluationism"—the version of supervaluationism that is formulated in a metalanguage governed by classical logic and classical two-valued semantics—holds that there are always two sharp transitions in any sorites sequence of statements: a sharp transition between statements that are true and ones that are neither true nor false, and another sharp transition between the latter and statements that are false.[4] Both epistemicism and classical supervaluationism seem *grossly* implausible commonsensically, because the very essence of vagueness seems to be boundarylessness—that is, the absence of sharp transitions.

So when one reflects carefully and commonsensically on boundarylessness as an essential feature of vagueness, one comes to appreciate that vagueness essentially involves a certain form of logical incoherence—namely, the normative governance of affirmatory practice by mutually unsatisfiable semantic-status principles. This specific kind of incoherence, which we will call *weak* logical incoherence, needs to be distinguished from a stronger and highly malevolent kind of incoherence that we will call *strong* logical incoherence—namely, rampant commitment to individual statements that are logically contradictory, such as statements of the form $\Phi \ \& \sim\Phi$.[5] It is important to appreciate that weak logical incoherence does not necessarily bring strong logical incoherence in its wake. As long as one assiduously obeys the ISA and CSA Prohibitions, one's use of vague discourse will not force one to embrace contradictory statements. In practice, such prohibition-obeying usage will in effect quarantine the weak logical incoherence of vagueness, rather than allowing it to metastasize into strong logical incoherence.

2.4.3 The Impossibility of Ontological Vagueness

The ideas just set forth concern vague discourse and vague thought-content. (The relevant practice-standards concern affirmatory practice, both in language and in thought.) However, when one asks whether there could be such a phenomenon as *ontological* vagueness—that is, whether the correct ontology could include vague objects and/or vague properties and relations—the situation is very different. Vague entities would have to exhibit an ontological form of boundarylessness—they would have to satisfy the condition that there is "no determinate fact of the matter" about transitions in a sorites sequence. But what could constitute the satisfaction of this Transition Condition, in the case of ontological vagueness? When one reflects carefully and commonsensically on this question, one can find no intelligible analogue of the key idea appealed to in the case of vague language and thought—namely, the idea that semantic governance by mutually satisfiable semantic-status principles is a matter of affirmatory *practice* being subject to mutually *obeyable* status-attribution prohibitions. Rather, evidently the putative vague entities would have to directly satisfy both the ISS Principle and the CSI Principle. Since this is impossible, evidently so is ontological vagueness.

Let us underscore this jarring conclusion by formulating in a slightly different way the reasoning that forces itself upon reflective common sense concerning the issue of ontological vagueness. The *world* cannot be logically incoherent, even in the weak way: it cannot satisfy ontological analogues of mutually unsatisfiable semantic standards. For example, there cannot be a genuine property H (for 'heaphood'), and a sequence of sand conglomerations each of which has one fewer grain than its predecessor, such that (i) initially in the sequence there are instances of H (with each predecessor of an H instance being an H instance), (ii) eventually there are non-H instances (with each successor of a non-H instance being a non-H instance), and (iii) for each pair of successive piles in the sequence, either both are H instances, or both are non-H instances, or both are neither. For, the only way to satisfy condition (iii) would be for all the piles to have the same status vis-à-vis H. But vagueness involves boundarylessness essentially, and boundarylessness involves weak logical incoherence essentially. Hence there cannot be ontological vagueness—and in particular, there cannot be vague objects, vague properties, or vague relations.

So, upon attending carefully to the nature of vagueness, reflective common sense finds itself forced to the radical-looking conclusion that ontological vagueness is impossible, and hence that the correct ontology cannot contain any vague objects, properties, or relations. Needless to say, this conclusion flies directly in the face of simple realism's ontological thesis O2. For, virtually all the putative objects, properties, and relations posited in commonsense thought and discourse—and very many of those posited in scientific theorizing as well—are vague. They are vague with respect to spatiotemporal boundaries, for instance, and also with respect to composition (both synchronically and diachronically). Thus, the impossibility of ontological vagueness means that none of these posits are included in the right ontology—which directly contradicts thesis O2. Reflective common sense is thus now in profound internal tension, and it has brought itself under intense pressure to back away from thesis O2.

The impossibility of ontological vagueness also calls seriously into question simple realism's semantic theses S3 and S4. If indeed truth is a direct mapping between thought/discourse and the world (thesis S3), so that commonsense beliefs and statements are ontologically committed to their posits (thesis S4), then the vastly many thoughts/statements that common sense considers true and that posit vague objects, properties, and relations must be systematically *false*. Reflective common sense recoils from this radical-looking conclusion, however—which generates strong pressure to back away from theses S3 and S4.

2.4.4 The Problem of the Many

In section 1.2 of chapter 1 we broached Unger's "problem of the many," and we pointed out that simple realism's response is to treat typical posits of everyday thought and discourse (and of science) as vague entities that conform to ordinary counting practices. For example, even if there are vastly many precise mereological sums of matter that all are equally good candidates for being Mt. Whitney, none of them is identical to Mt. Whitney, says simple realism; rather, Mt. Whitney is a vague object.

But once common sense reflectively comes to the conclusion that ontological vagueness is impossible, it becomes clear that the simple realist response to the problem of the many is not viable. So a theoretical branch point now looms, insofar as ontology is concerned: either (i) the right ontology includes vastly many more items falling under typical commonsensical kind-concepts (like the kind *mountain*), and all these items are perfectly precise, or else (ii) the right ontology does not include any items falling under typical commonsensical kind-concepts.

Austere realism embraces claim (ii), along with an account of truth that allows numerous commonsense and scientific statements to be true without being ontologically committed to their posits. Later in the book (chapter 5, section 5.5) we will consider a position that retreats from simple realism in a different way: it embraces an account of truth like the one we will presently set forth, but weds that semantics to the ontological claim (i). We will argue that this semantical-cum-metaphysical alternative to austere realism is not viable because it runs afoul of the weak logical incoherence endemic to vagueness.

2.5 Dialectical Interlude

At this point it should be acknowledged that neither the issue of meta-physically lightweight posits (section 2.2) nor the SCQ (section 2.3)—considered either separately or in tandem—*force* reflective common sense to abandon simple realism. Alternative approaches can be contemplated.

An alternative approach to lightweight posits, for instance, would be to claim (1) that ordinary thought and discourse really are ontologically committed to their posits, (2) that the correct ontology really includes items like corporations and nations, and (3) that such items are ontologically "lightweight" in the sense that their existence depends upon human thought and language (but not in the sense that they do not belong to the correct ontology at all). For a good articulation and defense of such a view, see Thomasson 2007.

Likewise, the Special Composition Question alone does not force reflective common sense to deny that posits like middle-sized dry goods, persons, and electrons do not belong to the correct ontology. An alternative approach, which prima facie looks less radical, would be to claim (1) that the correct ontology does include such items, (2) that the answer to the Special Composition Question is that any group of objects *always* jointly compose a complex object, (3) that statements like "There is an object comprising George Bush's nose, the Eiffel Tower, and the star Alpha Centauri" therefore are actually true, and (4) that the fact that such statements intuitively seem false is to be explained in terms of pragmatics, as a form of oddness or inappropriateness that is consistent with their truth. See, for instance, Richard 2006.

But of course there is a deeper challenge facing simple realism, which is no less a problem for the approach to ontology that retains ordinary posits but allows unrestricted composition—namely, the impossibility of ontological vagueness. This problem, we maintain, makes it *mandatory* for reflective common sense to repudiate simple realism because simple realism is ontologically committed to vague objects.

It bears emphasis that lightweight posits are typically at least as vague as are such posits as tables, chairs, and mountains. For, typically it is easy enough to construct sorites sequences for such posits, involving progressions of actual or possible arrangements of people, artifacts, buildings, contractual agreements, and so forth. Such a sequence will effect a stepwise, soritical, "morphing" of a lightweight posit, present early in the sorites sequence, into a lightweight posit late in the sequence that common sense regards as clearly nonidentical to the original one. Just as an image of Bill Clinton's face can be soritically morphed into an image of George Bush's face via a sorites sequence of images of possible faces, the U.S. Republican Party can be soritically morphed into the U.S. Democratic party via a sorites sequence of possible alterations of such matters as individual political affiliations, terminological practices, legal documents, and so forth. Similarly, mutatis mutandis, for virtually any lightweight posit you can name. So the impossibility of ontological vagueness, by itself, already mandates eschewing lightweight posits from ontology—no less than it mandates eschewing mountains and tables.

It also bears emphasis that posits belonging to the kind *living organism* are surely vague—for example, vague with respect to both synchronic composition and spatiotemporal boundaries. (Van Inwagen acknowledges this explicitly.) Thus, even if van Inwagen is right that the *otherwise* best answer to the Special Composition Question is that several things jointly compose a material being only when they jointly constitute a life, this answer nonetheless runs afoul of the impossibility of ontological vagueness—and hence yields a mistaken metaphysics. The impossibility of ontological vagueness mandates eschewing living organisms from ontology too, along with all other vague posits.

2.6 Summary

The main argumentative flow of this chapter has consisted in pointing out three challenges to simple realism. First, when common sense goes reflective about posits such as corporations and symphonies, it is disinclined to regard such posits as mind-independently real items that belong to the correct ontology. Second, the Special Composition Question puts pressure on simple realism by making reflective common sense realize both (1) that the question demands a systematic general answer, and (2) that evidently there can be no such general answer that comports with naive commonsensical beliefs about when a bunch of objects compose another object and when they do not. Third, when common sense goes reflective about the nature of vagueness, it realizes that ontological vagueness—which is embraced by simple realism—is impossible.

Notice that we have come to these conclusions by cleaving to the methodological maxim we announced in section 2.1: following commonsense reflection to where it leads. We did not back away from persistent inquiry when common sense began to fall into internal turmoil; rather, we sought to thematize the roots of this turmoil explicitly, in order to reveal why common sense itself has strong reasons to turn away from simple realism. At this stage in the dialectic of reflective common sense—the antithesis stage—reflective common sense is deeply in tension with itself. We turn next, in the following two chapters, to the synthesis stage.

Contextual Semantics: Truth as Indirect Correspondence

In this chapter and the next we press still further with reflective common-sensical reasoning. We argue that reflective common sense points the way forward toward a refined commonsense metaphysical realism (viz., austere realism), to be put in place of the naive version we have called simple realism. Austere realism rests centrally on the idea that, very often, truth is an indirect form of correspondence rather than being direct correspondence. In this chapter we develop this idea, and we situate it within a more general approach to thought-world and language-world relations that we call contextual semantics. In chapter 4 we will set forth the theses of austere realism in a way that draws directly upon what is said about truth in the present chapter, and we will explain how austere realism can successfully handle the problems, described in chapter 2, that undermine simple realism.

3.1 Methodological Remarks

We start with methodological remarks about how to pursue a suitable refinement of simple realism; these pertain both to the present chapter and to chapters 4–6. In the previous chapter we introduced several deep challenges to simple realism—challenges that common sense comes to appreciate when it begins to go reflective about matters of ontology and truth. In order to meet those challenges we will proceed to apply commonsensical modes of reasoning, seeking a new version of metaphysical realism that emerges from such reasoning—a yet further product of reflective common sense. Several methodological principles will guide this synthesis stage of the dialectic.

First, as already emphasized in section 2.1, it will be important to follow commonsense reflection where it leads. Commonsensical reasoning need not—and does not—lapse into paralysis upon confronting the internal tensions that came to light in chapter 2. On the contrary, it swings into high gear, seeking a way out of its predicament that will restore commonsensical reflective equilibrium. Common sense itself seeks to arrive at some replacement for simple realism that emerges fairly naturally and plausibly via commonsensical reflection on the deep problems that challenge the naive position.

Second, the view that emerges ought to retain the first ontological thesis of simple realism and the first and second semantic theses. Reflective common sense remains deeply committed to the core ontological claim that there is a mind-independent, discourse-independent world (thesis O1), to the semantic claim that truth is correspondence between thought/language and this world (thesis S1), and to the semantic claim that numerous statements and thought-contents involving the posits of both common sense and science are true (thesis S2). We see no plausible basis for seeking to overturn any of those assumptions in looking for a commonsensically motivated refinement of simple realism.

Third, the view that emerges ought to deal plausibly and satisfactorily with the antithesis problems. It needs not only to overcome those problems, but also to do so in ways that are independently credible and plausible from the perspective of reflective common sense. In particular, the *semantic* component of the sought-for position should be independently credible and plausible: insofar as it provides a refined conception of truth as correspondence to replace simple realism's naive construal of correspondence, this replacement should be natural and attractive from the perspective of reflective common sense rather than being unintuitive and ad hoc.

Fourth, although a radical error theory remains a possibility—that is, a view asserting that numerous beliefs of common sense (and of science) are simply false—this should be treated as a last-resort option. In principle, commonsense reasoning could get driven all the way to error theory. This could happen if sustained inquiry leads to the conclusion that there simply is no good way to resolve the antithesis problems without concluding that vastly many claims of nonscientific and scientific thought and discourse that are normally thought to be true are really just false. But the default presumption should be that the radical-error view is itself mistaken and that there is some plausible way to refine simple realism that avoids imputing systematic mistakes to common sense and to science. It is one thing for common sense to fall into error when it first goes naively reflective about ontology and truth; it is quite another thing for ordinary commonsensical and scientific beliefs to be false themselves. The default presumption is that the latter is not the case—even though the philosophical position we have labeled simple realism is clearly in trouble.

3.2 Correspondence: Generic, Direct, and Indirect

In this section we introduce the distinction between direct and indirect correspondence, and we argue that both kinds of correspondence are species of a form of correspondence that is generic enough to subsume them both.

3.2.1 Generic Correspondence

When a thought is true, and thus a natural-language sentence expressing it is true as well, what do the thought and the sentence correspond to? One item that serves generically as a correspondence-relatum is *the world itself*. This idea is familiar and is frequently invoked: truth is often described as *correspondence to the world*. On the approach we will describe, there are importantly different species of correspondence to the world. Nevertheless, there is real unity among these differing species: correspondence to the world is a unified genus.

The idea of truth as correspondence to the world fits nicely with a familiar conception of truth *conditions*: namely, the idea that a thought's or sentence's truth conditions are constituted by a range of *possible worlds*— or, better, by a range of "centered" possible worlds with a designated location as the location of the thinker/utterer of the thought/sentence. A centered possible world is a *potential* way the world is. It can be usefully thought of as a *maximal self-involving property*, instantiable by the entire cosmos.[1] Thus, a thought or sentence corresponds to the world just in case the world instantiates one of the maximal self-involving properties that collectively constitute the thought's/sentence's truth conditions.

The following point about this possible-worlds approach to truth conditions bears emphasis, in connection with themes to be developed below. The approach says nothing at all about whether or how the subpropositional constituents of a thought or sentence should be linked to specific *items* in the world, in order for the world to instantiate one of the truth-constituting maximal properties that constitute the thought's/sentence's truth conditions. That is, it says nothing at all about whether or how singular or quantificational constituents should be linked to *objects* in the world, or about whether or how predicative constituents should be linked to *properties* or *relations* that are instantiated by objects in the world.

3.2.2 Direct Correspondence: Truth via Truth-makers

One species of correspondence is very familiar: it is the form of correspondence that simple realism equates with the entire genus. We call it *direct* correspondence. To reiterate a portion of our characterization of such correspondence in section 1.1 of chapter 1, a logically atomic thought/statement directly corresponds to the world just in case (1) there are objects $o_1, \ldots, o_n$ in the correct ontology that are respectively denoted by the respective singular constituents of the thought/statement, (2) there is a monadic or polyadic relation R in the correct ontology that is expressed by the predicative constituent of the thought/statement,[2] and (3) R is jointly instantiated by $o_1, \ldots, o_n$ (in that order). When the logically atomic thought/statement directly corresponds to the world, the *truth-maker*—as we will here use this philosophical term of art—is the specific state of affairs in the world consisting of the objects $o_1, \ldots, o_n$ jointly instantiating (in that order) the relation R.[3]

Simple realism's semantic component flatly equates correspondence with what we are here calling direct correspondence. So for simple realism, the relation between truth and ontology is stark and direct. A thought/statement is ontologically committed to monadic and polyadic relations answering to its various predicative constituents, and to objects answering to its singular and quantificational constituents.[4] Truth, as direct correspondence, is a matter of (1) there being such objects and relations in the right ontology, and (2) the objects instantiating the relations in the ways required by the given thought/statement.

3.2.3 Indirect Correspondence: Truth without Truth-makers

Another species of correspondence between thought/language and the world is not a matter of singular, quantificational, and predicative constituents picking out objects, properties, or relations that are part of the correct ontology—and thus also is not a matter of the instantiation of such properties or relations by such objects. We call this species *indirect* correspondence. In the case of a logically atomic thought/statement, the idea is that correspondence between this thought/statement and the world does not consist in there being objects $o_1, \ldots, o_n$ respectively denoted by the thought/statement's constituents and a (monadic or polyadic) relation R expressed by the thought/statement's predicative constituent, such that $o_1, \ldots, o_n$ jointly instantiate (in that order) R. The correct ontology need not include any such objects or any such relation, and hence also need not include any such state of affairs. Instead, correspondence is a less direct relation between thought/language and the world.

Such indirect correspondence involves two factors, working in tandem. On one hand there are contextually operative standards for semantic correctness. On the other hand there is the actual distribution of genuine properties by genuine objects in the world, and thus the actual distribution of states of affairs. Indirect correspondence, for a given thought/statement, is *semantic correctness under contextually operative semantic standards*. Normally, whether or not a thought/statement has this status does indeed depend on how things are in the world.[5] That is, it depends on which centered possible world is actual—on which self-involving maximal property possibly instantiated by the world is actually instantiated by the world. Thus, the semantic correctness of a thought/statement depends on which objects in the world instantiate which properties and relations. So, being semantically correct under contextually operative semantic standards is indeed a form of correspondence to the world, under the generic rubric of correspondence described in section 1 above. But it is distinct from direct correspondence. The specific *kind* of indirect correspondence that counts as truth, in a given context of thought/discourse, is semantic correctness under the specific semantic-correctness standards at work in that context.

Is indirect correspondence, in the case of a logically atomic thought/statement, a relation between the thought/statement and some particular state of affairs that is the thought's/statement's "truth-maker"? No. Although normally there will be various states of affairs—in some cases, rather extensive ranges of states of affairs—that contribute fairly significantly to the semantic correctness of the thought/statement, none of these states of affairs will consist in the instantiation, by the object or objects posited in the atomic thought/statement, of the posited property/relation. In a sense, the thought/statement is made true by the world as a corporate body rather than by any specific state of affairs.

3.3 Contextual Semantics I: Coarse-grained Contextual Variation in Semantic Standards

The distinction between direct correspondence and indirect correspondence is a key feature of the broader approach to truth and meaning we call *contextual semantics*. The overall framework of contextual semantics includes theses not only about truth and falsity per se, but also about meaning, ontology, thought, and knowledge. Contextual semantics is intermediate between simple realism's conception of truth as direct correspondence to the world, and neopragmatist semantics (for short, neopragmatism), with its radically epistemic construal of truth.[6]

The point of the label "contextual semantics" is to emphasize the contextual variability of the semantic standards that combine with how the world is to yield truth or falsity. At a coarse-grained level, there is contextual variation between direct-correspondence semantic standards (DC standards) and indirect-correspondence semantic standards (IC standards). And there is finer-grained contextual variation too, at least within the coarse-grained IC rubric. Later we will be arguing that contextual semantics should be very attractive to reflective common sense—both because of its promise for dealing with the antithesis problems, and for other reasons too. We will be describing the semantic-cum-ontological position we call austere realism, and we will be arguing the virtues of the specific version of austere realism that incorporates contextual semantics. But our main purpose in the remainder of the present chapter is just to articulate contextual semantics itself (albeit in a way that will already make it sound plausible).

We will lay out the overall position in three installments. The first, in the present section, comprises various theses involving the coarse-grained distinction between DC semantic standards and IC semantic standards. These theses of contextual semantics are uncommitted about whether, and to what extent, thought and discourse are subject to more fine-grained forms of contextual variability in semantic standards.[7] But according to the overall position there is quite a lot of it, and coarse-grained variation between DC standards and IC standards fits hand-in-glove with various kinds of fine-grained variation. In the second installment (section 3.4) we will set forth various claims about fine-grained variation that are also part of contextual semantics. In the third installment (section 3.5) we will describe how contextual semantics deals with sameness–difference issues about meaning and about concepts—issues that inevitably arise given the claim that semantic standards exhibit contextual variation.

3.3.1 Core Theses

We will now present a reasonably compact articulation of the key claims of contextual semantics concerning the DC/IC distinction. In setting forth these claims, and for related expository purposes, we will employ the device of sometimes using boldface font for terms and phrases like 'object', 'property', and 'the world'; this makes it unambiguously clear when we mean to be talking about denizens of the mind-independent, discourse-independent world—the world whose existence is denied by metaphysical antirealists. (Antirealists typically regard as perfectly legitimate various everyday uses of the expressions and some of their philosophical uses as well. The boldface convention guarantees that claims that we intend to be incompatible with metaphysical antirealism will be construed as we intend them, rather than receiving a "compatibilist" reading.)

We will articulate the core framework of contextual semantics as a list of theses, interspersed with commentary:

(1)   Truth is semantic correctness, under contextually operative semantic standards.

Semantic correctness, as explained already, is a feature that depends jointly on what the operative semantic standards are and **the world**. Semantic correctness has nothing to do with matters of etiquette. A statement can be semantically correct even if it would be impolite, impolitic, or otherwise inappropriate to utter it.

(2)   Contrary to metaphysical antirealism, truth is normally a product of two factors: (i) the operative semantic standards, and (ii) how things are with **the world**.

This means that truth is normally a matter of *correspondence* to **the world**, although the nature of that correspondence depends on which semantic standards are operative.

(3)   At a coarse-grained level of differentiation, there are at least two kinds of semantic standards: *direct-correspondence* standards and *indirect-correspondence* standards (DC and IC standards).

DC standards require that a statement have a *truth-maker* in order to be semantically correct. (In the case of a logically atomic thought/statement, the truth-maker is an actual state of affairs consisting of **objects** $o_1, \ldots, o_n$ instantiating [in that order] a **relation** R, where $o_1, \ldots, o_n$ are respectively denoted by respective singular constituents of the thought/statement and R is denoted by the predicative constituent.) IC standards do not require a truth-maker; but they do nonetheless require, in order for a given thought/ statement to be semantically correct, **the world** to belong to a certain range of potential ways it might be (i.e., a certain range of **properties** instantiable by **the world**). This range constitutes the *truth conditions* of the thought/ statement.

(4)   Contrary to the semantic component of simple realism, in many contexts of language and thought, the contextually operative semantic standards are IC standards. In these contexts, the requisite form of correspondence between thought/language and the world is indirect, not direct.

Thesis (4) is the key departure from the naive conception of truth embodied in simple realism.

Under contextual semantics, there is a whole spectrum of ways that the semantic correctness of a thought can depend upon **the world**.[8] At one end of the spectrum are statements governed by semantic standards, in a given context of usage, that require direct correspondence (and thus coincide with those laid down by simple realism); under these standards a statement is true only if some unique constituent of **the world** answers to each of its singular terms and predicates, and at least one such entity answers to each of its assertoric existential-quantifier expressions. (Statements asserted in order to make serious ontological claims—like 'There exists a God', as asserted by a conventional theist—presumably are governed by DC semantic standards.)

At the other end of the spectrum are statements that are sanctioned as semantically correct by the contextually operative semantic standards alone, independently of how things are with **the world**. If there are such statements, then their truth is not a matter of correspondence to **the world** at all, either direct or indirect.[9] Rather, these statements are *analytic* under the contextually operative semantic standards. (Statements of pure mathematics are plausible candidates for this status. On this construal of mathematical truth, an existence claim like 'There exist even numbers' is true under IC standards, but is false under DC semantic standards because there are no **numbers**.)[10]

Both ends of the spectrum are limit cases, however: direct correspondence at one end and analytic truth (including analytic existence-claims, perhaps) at the other end. Various intermediate positions are occupied by statements whose semantic correctness, in a given context, does depend in part on how things are with **the world**, but where this dependence does not consist in direct correspondence between (i) the positing apparatus of the statements (its singular terms, quantifiers, and predicates), and (ii) **objects** or **properties** in **the world**.[11]

As a plausible example of a statement that normally would fall at an intermediate point in the spectrum just described, consider:

(B) Beethoven's Fifth Symphony has four movements.

The semantic correctness of (B) probably does not require that there be some **entity**, answering to the term 'Beethoven's Fifth Symphony', instantiating a **property** answering to the predicate 'has four movements'. Rather, (B) probably is semantically correct (i.e., true) by virtue of other, more indirect, connections between the sentence and the world. Especially germane is the behavior by Beethoven that we could call "composing his Fifth Symphony." But a considerably wider range of goings-on is relevant too: in particular, Beethoven's earlier behavior in virtue of which his later behavior counts as composing his Fifth Symphony, and also a broad range of human practices (including the use of handwritten or printed scores to guide orchestral performances) in virtue of which such behavior by Beethoven counts as "composing a symphony" in the first place.[12] Further plausible examples of statements governed by semantic standards that are not maximally strict include:

(a) The University of Ljubljana is a public institution.

(b) Mozart composed exactly twenty-seven piano concertos.

(c) There are more than twenty regulatory agencies in the U.S. Federal Government.

(d) Quine's *Word and Object* is an influential book.

DC standards might not often prevail in language and thought. Indeed, it is very likely that they do not, given the ubiquity of vagueness in language and thought, and given that ontological vagueness is impossible. Nonetheless,

(5)   In some contexts of language and thought, the contextually operative semantic standards are DC standards.

DC standards can be expected to be frequently operative, for instance, in
contexts of ontological inquiry. In these contexts, after all, one is asking
about what **objects** there are in **the world**, and what **properties** and **relations** are **instantiated** by these **objects**.

(6)   Contrary to neopragmatism, truth is not radically epistemic; for, semantic correctness is distinct from warranted assertibility, and even from
"ideal" warranted assertibility (Putnam 1981, 1983) and from "superassertibility" (Wright 1987, 1992).

This thesis says, in effect, that the kind of semantic normativity that makes
for truth and falsity is not reducible to epistemic normativity.[13] A thought/
statement may be semantically correct without being epistemically warranted. (Familiar examples include true claims about the distant past for
which no extant evidence exists either pro or con.) Likewise, a thought/
statement may be epistemically warranted—even ideally so—without
being semantically correct. (One familiar thought-experimental example,
good for prising truth apart even from "ideal" epistemic warrant, concerns
the systematically false external-world thoughts of an envatted brain that
was originally embodied and has only recently, unwittingly, become envatted. Stipulating *recent* envatment prevents any attempted challenge to the
thought experiment that invokes a strongly "externalist" account of mental content.)

Although contextual semantics asserts that the operative semantic standards governing truth (semantic correctness) can vary from one context to
another, it also asserts that contextually operative metasemantic standards
normally require truth ascriptions to obey Tarski's schema T:

(7)   Even in contexts of thought/discourse where the operative semantic
standards are IC standards, typically these standards sanction as true (i.e.,
as semantically correct) instances of Tarski's equivalence-schema:

(T)   "P" is true if and only if P.[14]

Thesis (7) says, in effect, that normally the contextually operative semantic
standards governing the truth predicate operate "in tandem" with those
governing first-order discourse; as we will put it, truth attributions are *affir-
matorily consistent* with first-order thought and talk.

If contextual semantics is right, so that truth is intimately bound up with contextually variable semantic standards, then meaning too is intimately bound up with these standards.[15] Intuitively and pretheoretically, meaning is what combines with how the world is to yield truth. Thus, if truth is correct affirmability under operative semantic standards, then the role of meaning is played by the semantic standards themselves. So matters of meaning are, at least in large part, matters of operative semantic standards. Contextual semantics makes the following nonreductionist claim about matters of meaning:

(8)   In general, if a statement S is semantically correct under IC semantic standards, but S is not semantically correct under DC standards, then S is not equivalent in meaning to—or approximately equivalent in meaning to—a statement that is correctly affirmable under DC semantic standards.

One is likely to be driven toward thesis (8) after pursuing for awhile the project of trying to systematically paraphrase ("regiment," in Quine's terminology) statements whose surface grammar posits ontologically dubious entities into a more austere idiom that eschews reference to such entities. Although the paraphrase strategy can sometimes be carried through piecemeal for certain local segments of discourse, very often it evidently will not work. (Trying to implement the strategy for statements like (B) and (a)–(d) tends to cause one to lose faith in it.)

Under contextual semantics the issue of ontological commitment becomes much more subtle than it is under the semantic component of simple realism, because whenever the contextually operative semantic standards are not DC standards, the positing apparatus of thought and discourse is not being employed in a way that connects thought/discourse directly to **objects** and **properties** in **the world**. Here then are several theses concerning ontology:

(9)   A distinction should be recognized between ontological commitment, which is incurred by thought/language when the contextually operative semantic standards are DC standards, and what may be called *ontic* commitment, which concerns the range of putative entities overtly posited by a given mode of thought/discourse.[16]

(10)   Quine's well-known criteria of ontological commitment are really only criteria of ontic commitment.

(11) Determining the genuine ontological commitments of scientific and nonscientific claims is a methodologically subtle matter, in which one inquires what **the world** is like **in itself** in order to be correctly describable, under various contextually operative semantic standards, by thoughts/statements that are true in everyday life and in science.

Whatever exactly the right story is about ontology, it seems quite plausible (given theses 9–11) that a complete and accurate accounting of what there really is in **the world** need not include entities like the University of Ljubljana, the U.S. Federal Government, Mozart's twenty-seventh piano concerto, or Quine's book *Word and Object*. In terms of metaphysics, such entities are plausibly viewed as artifacts of our conceptual scheme; they are not mind-independently, discourse-independently real. Although **the world** does normally contribute to the truth or falsity of thoughts/statements that are ontically committed to such entities, it does so quite indirectly.

Although contextual semantics rejects the epistemic reductionism of neopragmatism, it also acknowledges something importantly right that is reflected in that approach, namely:

(12) Contextually operative semantic standards are typically intimately linked to prototypical evidential standards for statements.

We all know quite well, for instance, what sorts of evidence are relevant to claims like (B) and (a)–(d); and the kind of evidence we would look for has rather little to do with the philosophical question whether the right ontology should include entities like symphonies, piano concertos, books individuated by title and content (so that there can be multiple distinct tokens of a single book), or a federal government. Under the semantic standards operative in ordinary thought/discourse contexts, it is quite appropriate (according to thesis 12) that the relevant epistemic standards should bypass the issue of ontology; for, the semantic standards themselves are not DC standards. There is a comparatively small "conceptual gap" between the epistemic standards for *warranted* affirmability and the semantic standards for *correct* affirmability (even though semantic standards are not reducible to epistemic ones).

There is a gap, though. For instance, Mozart might have engaged in behavior that would count as composing a twenty-eighth piano concerto, even though there is no extant evidence available; if so, then the statement that Mozart composed exactly twenty-seven piano concertos would be both warrantedly affirmable and yet false. In part, the gap between warranted affirmability and semantic correctness results from the holistic aspects of evidence:

(13) Attributions of truth and falsity usually are defeasible even under prototypical evidential conditions; for, the semantic correctness of any given statement normally depends, in part, on the semantic correctness of various other statements that are assumed, in a given evidential situation, to be semantically correct themselves.

As Quine and Duhem stressed long ago, one's claims really face the tribunal of empirical evidence jointly, not singly.

Contextual semantics also includes a psychologistic (or perhaps psychosocial) dimension:

(14) Which semantic standards are the operative ones, in any given context of thought/discourse, depends largely upon the contextually attuned, socially coordinated, truth-judging and falsity-judging dispositions of competent speakers.

The interconnections between the judgment dispositions of competent speakers and the contextually operative semantic standards are typically fairly subtle; surely no crudely reductive account will work. (For one thing, even competent speakers often exhibit linguistic performance errors. For another, normally a competent speaker's judgment dispositions are more directly indicative of what is *warrantedly* affirmable given available evidence; and sometimes this diverges from what is semantically correct under contextually operative semantic standards.) Nonetheless, such socially coordinated psychological dispositions do figure importantly in determining the contextually operative semantic standards. Those dispositions, and thus the standards themselves, typically will be heavily guided by agents' appreciation of the contextually specific purposes for which pertinent terms and concepts are being deployed—a theme that will recur below.

3.3.2 Degrees of Indirectness

The question naturally arises whether there are degrees of indirect correspondence—that is, whether some forms of indirect correspondence are "closer to direct" than others. Although we doubt that there are *quantitative* degrees of indirectness, it does seem that sense can be made of a comparative notion: some forms of indirect correspondence are more indirect than others. Three broad categories of indirect correspondence can be described, each of which is intuitively more indirect than the preceding one. The categories are somewhat vague and probably shade into one another.

First are posits—posited objects, properties, and relations—that are *immediately given* in perceptual experience and are immediately given independently of whether the experiencer is conceptually sophisticated or can deploy language. Various middle-sized objects plausibly are immediately perceptually given in this way, especially in visual experience. Likewise, various properties of such objects and relations among such objects plausibly are also immediately perceptually given—for example, shape, size, color, and experiencer-centered relative location. Dogs, cats, and young prelinguistic children very likely have experiences deploying such posits, even though they lack the conceptual repertoire and the intellectual sophistication that come with mastery of language.

Second are posits that are immediately given in perceptual experience, but whose givenness depends upon the experiencer's having mastered a certain range of concepts—often partly by linguistic means. For instance, seeing a rectangular object *as a table*, or seeing a transparent object with a certain shape *as a drinking glass*, or seeing a structure on which the sign-design B-A-N-K appears *as a bank* are all examples of such conceptually enriched experiential givenness. Although this is still a matter of what is immediately presented in experience—one *sees* these things *as* instances of such kinds, rather than consciously *inferring* that they fall under those kinds—nonetheless it is a kind of givenness that requires the experiencer to possess the pertinent concepts.

Third are posits that are not immediately given in experience at all. As one drives around in a certain part of Tucson, Arizona, for example, one is immediately presented in visual experience with various buildings, persons, athletic fields, and so forth—and also with various instances of the sign-design T-H-E--U-N-I-V-E-R-S-I-T-Y--O-F--A-R-I-Z-O-N-A. But one is not immediately experientially presented with some additional item, an item answering to the definite description 'The University of Arizona'. This is why it would be a "category mistake," as Ryle called it, to say, "I see all these buildings, athletic fields, students, and so on, but where is the University of Arizona?" The university is not some further item immediately presented in experience alongside those others. It is a posit of a different kind.

Why say that these three successive types of posit figure in forms of correspondence that are successively more indirect? A natural thought is as follows. A posit of the first kind fails to pick out a mind-independently real object or property mainly because *there are too many highly eligible candidates* for the role of mind-independently real referent-item. For instance, suppose that you are immediately experientially presented with an object that you experience in a manner not influenced by linguistically inculcated concepts—say, an unusually shaped object of a certain color and weight that you are looking at in an art museum. The principal reason that your perceptual-experiential posit does not pick out a genuine, mind-independently real object is that there are numerous perfectly precise homogeneous spatiotemporal regions, each only slightly different from the others, all of which are equally good—and *highly* good—candidates for being the region occupied by the putative object.[17] (The object cannot be *vague* with respect to the region it occupies, because ontological vagueness is impossible.)

Consider now the second of our three categories—posits that are immediately presented in perceptual experience, but only on the basis of having mastered a certain range of concepts that nonhuman animals and young nonlinguistic children do not yet possess. Suppose, for instance, that you see the object in the museum *as an ashtray*. There now arises another aspect of indirectness, over and above the aspect already mentioned regarding the first category—namely, that *being an ashtray* cannot be a mind-independently real property (since it is vague). By contrast, in the first category of posits, the experientially immediately presented properties of the experientially presented object were *precise*—precise apparent size, precise apparent shape, and so forth. Or at any rate, they were *more* precise than the category *being an ashtray*—which is enough to make the point.

Turn now to the third category—posits that are not immediately presented in perceptual experience at all. There now arises yet another aspect of indirectness, over and above the two aspects already mentioned regarding the former categories—namely, that now there are *not any* highly eligible candidates for the role of mind-independently real reference-item. Consider the University of Arizona, for example. No specific collection or mereological sum of items from the first two categories—for example, buildings, athletic fields, faculty members, students, computers, test tubes—counts as a *good* candidate for being the referent of the definite description 'The University of Arizona'—even though some such collections or mereological sums would certainly be better than others. None is a good candidate because any such proposed identification would commit a Rylean category mistake. A university is a socially constructed posit that has a certain irreducible abstractness: it is not a concrete particular, or a mereological sum of concrete particulars, or a collection of concrete particulars.

There may well be yet more factors that contribute to comparative indirectness, beyond those we have mentioned here. Also, comparative indirectness may well be a feature that can be assessed along different dimensions that are largely orthogonal to one another—without there necessarily being any natural way to combine these into some straightforward relation of comparative *overall* indirectness. But in any case, enough has been said to give some useful sense to the idea of comparative degrees of indirectness.

3.3.3   Indirect-Correspondence Uses of Semantic and General-Categorial Concepts

Contextual semantics provides an overall picture of how language and thought are related to **the world**—a picture according to which truth, in most contexts of thought/language, is indirect correspondence. It is important to stress that this picture also applies, reflexively, to the concepts that are employed in philosophical discourse about semantics and ontology. On the side of semantics, notions like *reference* are subject to contextually variable semantic standards of correct usage—and can be employed in IC ways as well as in DC ways. On the side of ontology, the same goes for general-categorial notions like *object*, *property*, and *relation*.

We have been articulating our recommended account of truth in a way that employs these notions in a largely DC manner.[18] This is appropriate, given the ontological dimension of the discussion: we are arguing that truth is generally a matter of correspondence to **the world**, and we are addressing, inter alia, the question of what the correct ontology needs to be like in order for a thought/sentence to correspond to **the world** in the requisite way. In the context of this kind of theorizing, the most natural and most contextually appropriate way to use notions like *reference*, *object*, *property*, and *relation* is a direct-correspondence way. Given this usage, it becomes correct to say that under IC semantic standards, the singular and quantificational constituents of a thought/sentence need not *refer* to *objects*, and that the predicational constituent need not *refer* to a *property* or *relation*. In terms of our boldface convention, what is being claimed is that the singular, quantificational, and predicative constituents need not **refer** to any **objects**, **properties**, or **relations**.

But the notions of reference, object, property, and relation are also usable in ways governed by IC semantic standards. Often such uses are the contextually appropriate ones—even though that has not been so in this context. Indeed, often it is appropriate to employ these notions at the metalevel in a way that runs so tightly in tandem with object-level usage that instances of the following schemas become platitudes:

The singular term 'r' refers to the object r.

The monadic predicate 'P' refers to the property P-ness.

The polyadic predicate 'R' refers to relation R.

Talk and thought employing the notions of reference, object, property, and relation serve a myriad of purposes both theoretical and practical, and normally the contextually operative semantic standards governing these notions will be those best suited to the purposes at hand. Philosophical inquiry directed at matters of ontology, ontological commitment, and the connections between truth and ontology creates a context in which DC uses are most apt. But, depending in part on what the right ontology is, such uses could well turn out to be much more the exception than the rule.

3.4 Contextual Semantics II: Fine-grained Contextual Variation

In this section we expand the account of contextual semantics. We introduce claims about fine-grained contextual variation in semantic standards and claims about the connections between coarse-grained DC/IC semantic variation on one hand and various kinds of fine-grained contextual variation on the other hand.

3.4.1 Scorekeeping in Language and Thought
In his landmark paper "Scorekeeping in a Language Game," David Lewis (1983b) argued very plausibly that a whole range of phenomena in

language and thought are most naturally understood as involving the operation of implicit, contextually variable, semantic parameters. These parameters are aspects of what he called the "score in the language game." Many such parameters seem uncontroversial once their operation is pointed out, although competent speakers/thinkers do not even notice them explicitly but instead comply with them fairly automatically.

One kind of example is a contextual *salience* parameter that helps determine the current referent of a definite description, 'the F', when there is more than one contextually eligible referent. Thus Lewis (1983b, 241–242):

> Imagine yourself with me as I write these words. In the room is a cat, Bruce, who has been making himself very salient by dashing madly about. He is the only cat in the room, or in sight, or in earshot. I start to speak to you:
>
> The cat is in the carton. The cat will never meet our other cat, because our other cat lives in New Zealand. Our New Zealand cat lives with the Cresswells. And there he'll stay, because Miriam would be sad if the cat went away.
>
> At first, "the cat" denotes Bruce, he being the most salient cat for reasons having nothing to do with the conversation. If I want to talk about Albert, our New Zealand cat, I have to say "our other cat" or "our New Zealand cat." But as I talk more and more about Albert, and not any more about Bruce, I raise Albert's salience by conversational means. Finally, in the last sentence of my monologue, I am in a position to say "the cat" and thereby denote not Bruce but rather the newly-more-salient Albert....
>
> One rule, among others, that governs the kinematics of salience is a rule of accommodation. Suppose my monologue has left Albert more salient than Bruce; but the next thing I say is "The cat is going to pounce on you!" ... What I have said requires for its acceptability that "the cat" denote Bruce, and hence that Bruce be once again more salient than Albert. If what I say requires that, then straightaway it is so.

A second kind of example involves contextually variable standards for the application of concepts that are both vague and "absolute," such as the concept *flatness*. Thus Lewis (ibid., 245–246):

> Peter Unger has argued that hardly anything is flat. Take something you claim is flat; he will find something else and get you to agree that it is even flatter. You think that the pavement is flat—but how can you deny that your desk is flatter? But flat is an *absolute* term: it is inconsistent to say that something is flatter than something that is flat. Having agreed that your desk is flatter than the pavement, you must concede that the pavement is not flat after all. Perhaps you now claim that your desk is flat; but doubtless Unger can think of something that you will agree is even flatter than your desk. And so it goes. Some might dispute Unger's premise that "flat" is an absolute term, but ... I think he is right.... The right re-

sponse to Unger, I suggest, is that he is changing the score on you. When he says that the desk is flatter than the pavement, what he says is acceptable only under raised standards of precision. Under the original standards the bumps on the pavement were too small to be relevant either to the question whether the pavement is flat or to the question whether the pavement is flatter than the desk.

Although 'flat' is indeed an absolute term, it is nonetheless governed by an implicit contextual parameter, involving the operative standards of precision.

A third sort of example involves implicit parameters delimiting the contextually operative domain of quantification, in a given context of conversation or thought. Suppose, for instance, that a group of first-year graduate students in the philosophy department are discussing the beginning-of-semester party that just occurred and the fact that they had been hoping to meet all the other philosophy graduate students and all the philosophy faculty. One first-year student might say to another, "We all went to the party, and it was disappointing that not everybody was there." In context, the implicit range-of-quantification parameter governing "We all" restricts its range to the first-year philosophy graduate students in the department, whereas the implicit parameter governing "everybody" fixes its range as the set of current students and faculty in the philosophy department.

Contextual semantics affirms, with Lewis, that much human discourse and thought involves the operation of implicit, contextually variable, semantic parameters. As we said, there are numerous examples that are fairly uncontroversial, once the contextual variability is pointed out explicitly. (See Lewis's paper for a variety of further examples.) From the perspective of contextual semantics, the various kinds of fine-grained variation in implicit contextual parameters that Lewis emphasizes are somewhat independent of the DC/IC distinction. We say *somewhat* independent because we will maintain in later chapters that much thought/discourse operates non-degenerately only on the IC side of the divide—so that the pertinent kind of fine-grained contextual variation occurs only under the IC rubric. (Much thought/discourse—indeed, *most* of it—employs vague concepts/terms. So, since ontological vagueness is impossible, affirmative claims employing vague concepts/terms will be systematically false under DC semantic standards—a theme we will stress in chapter 4.) But at least some aspects of fine-grained score-variation—for example, implicit contextual restriction of the range of quantification for a given use of a quantificational construction—might well occur under coarse-grained semantic standards of either the IC or the DC kind.

Once the frequency of implicit fine-grained semantic parameters comes to be recognized, this fact sheds important new light on the coarse-grained distinction between DC and IC semantic standards. If one attends just to the core theses of contextual semantics (as described in section 3.3.1) and not to all this fine-grained implicit contextual variation, then one might suspect that the DC/IC distinction is somewhat ad hoc and runs contrary to the alleged fact that ordinary discourse rarely involves contextually variable parameters. But once one appreciates how common is the phenomenon of fine-grained contextual variation, one comes to see the claim that there are both DC standards and IC standards in thought/language not as hypothesizing an anomalous kind of double-talk and double-think, but rather as yet another manifestation of the widespread operation of implicit contextual parameters whose variation is so readily accommodated by competent thinkers/speakers that these parameters are easy not to notice at all.

3.4.2 Fine-grained Contextual Variation in Some Philosophically Important Concepts

Contextual semantics claims that certain philosophically important concepts are themselves governed by semantic standards involving implicit, contextually variable parameters. In particular, certain semantic concepts work that way—for example, the concept of *meaning*, the concept of *concept*, and the concept of *truth*. Also, certain general categorial concepts that figure centrally in metaphysics work that way too—for example, concepts like *object*, *entity*, *property*, *relation*, and *fact*.

As an example of fine-grained contextual variation in semantically correct usage of the word 'meaning', consider a discussion between two audience members at a basketball game, Sam and Dave. As the first team comes out onto the floor, Sam says "Whooaa! Given what 'tall' means, those dudes really count as *tall!*" Dave replies, "Not really. Those guys are shorter than average at the guard position, and they don't have any inside players over six feet six inches. So, given what 'tall' means, they're not tall at all; in fact, they're rather short." Intuitively, each of these conversants seems right—not only in his own use of 'tall', but also (and this is our point) in his own use of 'means' as applied to 'tall'. Meaning-claims, as applied to concepts/terms governed by implicit contextual parameters, are *themselves* governed by implicit parameters—often the same ones that govern the concept/term about which the meaning-claim is being made. Such cases are readily multiplied.

On the side of general-categorial concepts, here is a case of fine-grained contextual variation in the semantically correct usage of the word 'entity'. Suppose a group of philosophers at a university begin meeting weekly to discuss topics and texts in metaphysics, and they label their group the Ontology Discussion Group. Over time the membership of the group gradually changes, as does the nature of the issues and texts discussed. After five years, none of the original members still participate, all the current members are psychologists rather than philosophers, these current members all use the word 'ontology' to refer to categories employed in human cognition and not to matters metaphysical, and all the discussion topics and readings are straight psychology. Is it right or wrong to say that the current group is the *same entity* as the original group? Well, surely this depends on context and on one's purposes in classifying the current group one way or the other. If you are the room-scheduling supervisor at the Student Union Building, where for each of the past five years the Faculty Lounge has been reserved from 4 to 6 pm on Thursday afternoons under the listing "The Ontology Discussion Group," then you will be speaking the truth if you say, "The same entity has been meeting in the Faculty Lounge from 4 to 6 pm on Thursdays for five straight years, a group of opinionated faculty members called the Ontology Discussion Group." If, on the other hand, you are a disgruntled metaphysician from the philosophy department, you too will be speaking truly if you say, "The group now calling itself the Ontology Discussion Group is a totally distinct entity from the group that bore that name five years ago, because the current group consists entirely of psychologists and it only discusses issues in psychology, not issues in metaphysics." As this example illustrates, implicit contextually variable parameters govern judgments of distinctness and identity in the use of the category *entity*, and the contextually appropriate settings of such parameters depend in part on the purposes lying behind one's specific judgment in a given context. Such cases are readily multiplied.

We remarked earlier that for many phenomena in thought and language, the claim that implicit, contextually variable, semantic parameters are at work is fairly uncontroversial, once the operation of these parameters is explicitly pointed out. (Numerous examples are provided in Lewis 1983b.) The same is true, we maintain, for semantically correct uses of notions like *meaning* and *object*: in light of examples like those just given, it is fairly uncontroversial that these notions too are governed by implicit contextual parameters that vary depending on context. But there is more to say about the contextualist aspects of these philosophically important notions, and we will pursue this theme further in section 3.5.

We can now take up a question broached in section 3.3.1 above (in endnote 11). Should one say that there is just a single body of coarse-grained IC semantic standards that apply to all forms of thought/discourse that are governed by IC standards, or should one say instead that IC standards themselves can vary somewhat from one context of thought/discourse to another? The most natural approach, we think, is to treat the distinction between sameness and difference of standards as *itself* subject to fine-grained contextual variation. On one way of making the distinction, any fine-grained contextual variation in parameter settings, within the coarse-grained rubric "IC standards," counts as a variation in the operative IC standards themselves. (Semantic standards are individuated in a narrow, contextually specific way, via an implicit "individuation parameter" governing the notion "IC semantic standards" itself.) But on another way of doing it, the coarse-grained IC standards remain the same across fine-grained variation in parameter settings. (IC semantic standards are individuated in a generic way, so that the same standards persist even when parameter settings change.) Either way of drawing the same–different distinction for IC standards can be appropriate in some contexts of thought/discourse about semantic standards, depending on one's purposes. Take the semantics of 'flat', for example. If one wishes to emphasize the *contextual variability* of correct usage, it is natural to say:

> The IC semantic standards governing 'flat' can change from one context to another.

This is the narrow, context-specific way of individuating IC semantic standards. But if one wishes instead to emphasize the *semantic commonality* among different uses of 'flat', it is natural to say instead:

> Common IC semantic standards govern the various contextually specific uses of 'flat', even though those standards include an implicit precision-parameter that takes on different specific values in different contexts.

This is the generic, context-transcendent way of individuating IC semantic standards. So the notion "IC semantic standards" is itself subject to fine-grained contextual semantic variation in usage, involving different settings of an implicit individuation-parameter.

3.4.3 Further Forms of Fine-grained Philosophical Contextualism

Contextual semantics maintains that numerous words and concepts— including certain philosophically important ones like 'meaning' and 'object'—are subject to contextually variable implicit parameters that partially determine semantically correct usage. This is fine-grained contextual variation in semantic standards. We have suggested that this idea meshes well with the core theses of contextual semantics set forth in section 3.3— theses that focus on coarse-grained semantic variation between DC and IC standards. But there is another way that contextualist ideas are often invoked in recent philosophy: namely, in seeking to resolve, or dissolve, certain specific philosophical problems by means of fine-grained contextualism about the pertinent concepts that figure in those problems.

Probably the best-known example of this strand of contextualist thinking pertains to the problem of radical Cartesian skepticism about external-world knowledge. Stewart Cohen, Keith DeRose, David Lewis, and others have maintained (1) that the concept of knowledge is governed by implicit contextual parameters, (2) that under normally operative parameter-settings numerous everyday knowledge-claims are true, (3) that under especially stringent parameter-settings those knowledge claims go false, and (4) that the very posing of a radical-deception scenario (e.g., a Cartesian evil deceiver, or an envatted brain) strongly tends to drive up the "score in the language game" to those stringent settings under which knowledge-claims go false.[19] Similar contextualist ideas sometimes have been invoked with respect to other well known philosophical problems too—for instance, the problem of freedom and determinism, the nature of causation, and the causal-exclusion problem concerning mental causation.[20]

We ourselves are sympathetic to the broad spirit of each of these specific versions of fine-grained contextualism about philosophically interesting concepts. We find fine-grained contextualism independently plausible in each case, and such versions of fine-grained contextualism mesh well with the overall framework of contextual semantics.[21]

Nevertheless, contextual semantics per se is not committed to any of them. In principle, one could accept everything we say in this book while yet rejecting any or all of these specific forms of philosophical contextualism. Contextual semantics does claim, as explained in section 3.4.2, that *some* important philosophical notions are subject to fine-grained implicit semantic parameters—namely, semantic notions like *meaning* and general-categorial notions like *object*. But contextual semantics is officially neutral about fine-grained contextualism concerning concepts like knowledge, freedom, and causation.

3.5 Contextual Semantics III: Semantic *Différance*

Do contextual variations in semantic standards—either fine-grained or coarse-grained—constitute the deployment (in thought) of different *concepts* and the deployment (in language) of different *meanings*? Here we explain how contextual semantics addresses this question. It should be borne in mind, as the discussion proceeds, that contextual semantics does claim that the notion of meaning is itself subject to fine-grained implicit contextual parameters; likewise for the notion of concept. But we will be recommending a particular way of deploying these notions that we take to be theoretically especially illuminating. One is allowed to use the notions under certain specific implicit parameter-settings in setting forth contextual semantics—even though the notions thus employed are, according to contextual semantics itself, subject to contextual fine-grained variation in the implicit parameters that govern them. The parameter-settings one relies upon are ones that the theoretical account itself takes to be *default* settings, at least for purposes of the semantic-cum-metaphysical inquiry at hand. Our treating them as default settings is something that will ultimately be justified by the overall explanatory virtues of the contextual semantics as thus elaborated.

3.5.1 Identity-preserving Differences in Concepts and Meanings
We contend that transcontextual variations in the settings of implicit semantic parameters do *not* constitute the use of nonidentical concepts or nonidentical word-meanings. It is more accurate to view matters of concept identity and meaning identity in the following way. (1) Generic semantic standards have certain contextually variable parameters (often implicit).[22] (2) Specific, contextually operative, semantic standards involve particular values of those parameters; these parameter values determine the "score in

the language game."[23] (3) The generic semantic standards hold transcon-
textually, whereas the specific parameter values differ from one context to
another. (4) Concept identity and meaning identity remain constant trans-
contextually because of the constancy of generic semantic standards. (5)
Contextual variability in parameter values constitutes a more subtle, more
fine-grained kind of semantic variation than does nonidentity of concepts
or meanings. As one might put it (adapting a term made famous by Derrida), changes in parameter values yield a *différance*—not a difference—in
meaning.[24]

Entities of various sorts certainly can change in some ways—can alter
through time—without thereby losing their identity. Persons, for instance,
change as they grow older, and yet they retain their self-identity all the
while. They undergo identity-preserving changes, and the differences between a person at one moment in time and that same person at another
moment of time are identity-preserving differences. Similarly, the idea of
différance can be put this way: whatever exactly concepts and meanings
are (and regardless of whether these posited items would be included
within the ultimately correct ontology), they are subject to certain kinds
of *identity-preserving differences* in correct usage. One and the same concept
can be used by two persons (or by one person, at different times) in ways
that are governed by somewhat different settings of implicit semantic
parameters, while still being the *same* concept. Likewise, one and the same
word can be used in two ways involving somewhat different implicit
parameters, while still possessing the *same* meaning under both uses. A
concept or word as used by one person can differ somewhat in its semantically proper employment from its proper employment as used by another
person (or by the same person at a different time), and yet it is the same
concept or word anyway: the differences are identity preserving. Such an
identity-preserving semantic difference is a *différance*.[25]

Let us consider some examples. Hilary Putnam has noted the diachronic
version of the phenomenon we are calling *différance* in concepts and
meaning—although he does not call it by this name. One of his examples
features the concept of momentum in physics:

> In Newtonian physics the term *momentum* was defined as "mass times velocity."
> (Imagine, if you like, that the term was originally equated with this *definiens* by
> the decision of a convention of Newtonian physicists.) It quickly became apparent
> that momentum was a conserved quantity.... But with the acceptance of Einstein's

Special Theory of Relativity a difficulty appeared. Einstein ... showed that the principle of Special Relativity would be violated if momentum were *exactly* equal to (rest) mass times velocity. What to do? ... Can there be a quantity with the properties that (1) it is conserved in elastic collisions, (2) it is closer and closer to "mass times velocity" as the speed becomes small, and (3) its direction is the direction of motion of the particle? Einstein showed that there *is* such a quantity, and he (and everyone else) concluded that that quantity *is what momentum is*. The statement that momentum is *exactly* equal to mass times velocity was revised. *But this is the statement that was originally a "definition"!* And it was reasonable to revise this statement; for why should the statement that momentum is conserved not have at least as great a right to be preserved as the statement "momentum is mass times velocity" when a conflict is discovered? ... When the statements in our network of belief have to be modified, we have "trade-offs" to make; and what the best trade-off is in a given context cannot be determined by consulting the traditional "definitions" of terms. (Putnam 1988, 9–10)

According to Putnam, then, the term 'momentum' and its associated concept has undergone, over time, an identity-preserving change. In this example and others like it, the meaning of at least some terms, and the nature of their associated concepts, depends to some extent upon a certain network of background beliefs; when those change sufficiently, the concept and meaning change in certain ways. (The network of background beliefs is thus functioning as an *implicit semantic parameter* constraining the correct usage of the concepts and terms: correct usage should *smoothly* fit that network.) But the difference between the concept and meaning at an earlier stage and the concept and meaning at a later stage, is an identity-preserving difference—a *différance*. As Putnam (ibid., 11) remarks about this phenomenon:

If this seems strange, it is because we are not used to thinking of meanings as being historic entities in the sense in which persons or nations are historic entities. ... There are practices which help us decide when there is enough continuity through change to justify saying that the same person still exists. In the same way, we treat "momentum" as referring to the same quantity that it always referred to, and there are practices which help us decide that there is enough continuity through change to justify doing this. Meanings have an identity through time but no essence.

Turn next to synchronic cases of *différance*. Here a given concept, and the meaning of a term expressing the concept, are both governed by implicit semantic parameters that can vary from one usage to another without the kind of diachronic/historical changes operative in cases like Putnam's example of momentum. Consider, for example, Lewis's above-quoted remarks (contra Unger) about competing uses of the term 'flat' with respect to whether or not a particular sidewalk is flat. We claim, with Lewis, that the semantically correct use of the notion of flatness depends upon certain implicit, contextually operative standards of precision—standards that can permissibly vary somewhat from one usage to another. The standards of precision that govern a particular use constitute the specific current setting of what may be called the *precision parameter* for flatness. As the passage from Lewis makes clear, this parameter is contextually variable: it can take on different specific settings in particular contexts. This contextual variability is semantically built into the *single* concept flatness and into the meaning of the term 'flat'. What you mean when you use 'flat' in such a way that the sidewalk counts as flat is somewhat different from what Unger means when he uses 'flat' in such a way that it does not; likewise, mutatis mutandis, for the nature of the concept of flatness as employed by you, as distinct from its nature as employed by Unger. But these differences in meaning and concept are *identity-preserving* differences. There is a *différance* in meaning and concept between yourself and Unger.

Two potential sources of *différance* in concepts and meanings have been mentioned in this section. One source, manifested in diachronic cases of *différance* like Putnam's example of momentum, is the fact that the synchronic nature of a concept or a word-meaning at a particular moment in history depends partly upon a network of background beliefs prevalent at that time; concepts and meanings can change through time, when the pertinent background beliefs change in certain ways. That belief-network functions as an implicit, diachronically variable, semantic parameter: correct usage should fit smoothly with the network of pertinent background beliefs (as did Newton's usage with the belief network prevalent in his day, and as does Einstein's usage with the new belief network ushered in by Einstein himself). A second source of *différance*, which can be manifested synchronically in cases like competing uses of the term 'flat', is the fact that such terms, and the concepts they express, are semantically governed by implicit, contextually variable, *synchronic* parameters—in the case of flatness, the precision parameter.

3.5.2 Case Study of *Différance*: Carnap and the Polish Logician

It will be useful to pursue a further case study of the applicability of the notion of *différance*—a case study with connections to van Inwagen's Special Composition Question.

Consider, for instance, Putnam's well-known example of Carnap and the Polish logician (Putnam 1987, 18–20; 2004, 32–47)—which Putnam uses to illustrate a phenomenon he calls "conceptual relativity."[26] In this scenario (slightly modified), Carnap and the Polish logician are presented with a number of objects (say, books lying on a table), and each of them is asked how many objects there are on the table. Carnap, employing the *concept* of object in a fairly ordinary way, reports that there are exactly three objects on the table: O1, O2, and O3. By contrast the Polish logician, who accepts a particular mereology of objects according to which for every two or more particulars there is an object that is their "mereological sum," counts the objects on the table and reports that there are exactly seven: O1, O2, O3, O1 + O2, O1 + O3, O2 + O3, and O1 + O2 + O3.

This scenario seems to be one in which the two parties have *conflicting* but *equally correct* judgments about the number of objects on the table. Such a combination of features, we take it, is the phenomenon that Putnam calls conceptual relativity. One might express this combination of ideas in terms of two principles:

Principle of affirmatory conflict: There is a genuine conflict in what Carnap and the Polish logician are respectively affirming about how many objects there are: Carnap's claim that there are exactly three objects on the table conflicts with the Polish logician's claim that there are exactly seven.

Principle of mutual correctness: Both Carnap and the Polish logician are correct in their respective claims about how many objects there are on the table, because each of them is making a claim which, relative to a specific way of using the concept of *object*, is true.[27]

It seems to us that Putnam is pointing to a genuine, and important, phenomenon. In a significant sense, Carnap's way of counting objects and the Polish logician's way are in conflict; they are not just talking past one another. And yet, given the principles for counting that they each are employing, they are both making claims that are correct.

How should one understand the phenomenon of conceptual relativity, in light of what was said above about implicit contextual parameters and *différance*? Consider first the principle of mutual correctness. Our suggestion is that the concept of *object* bears a structural similarity to concepts like *flat*; and likewise for the meanings of the respective terms expressing these concepts. That is, the concept of *object* is semantically governed by an implicit, contextually variable parameter—in this case a parameter that affects matters of counting and mereology. We will call it the *mereological parameter*. The idea is that on different occasions of use, the setting of this mereological parameter may vary. In the case at hand, Carnap employs the concept of *object* in a way that is semantically governed by one particular setting of the mereological parameter, whereas the Polish logician employs the *same* concept in a way that is semantically governed by another, somewhat different setting of the same mereological parameter. Given the mereological parameter-setting that governs the usage employed by Carnap, he correctly judges that there are exactly three objects on the table. Given the different mereological parameter-setting that governs the usage employed by the Polish logician, she correctly judges that there are exactly seven objects on the table. Each is right, as each respectively is employing the concept of *object*. Although the concept as employed by Carnap does *differ* from the concept as employed by the Polish logician (since the mereological parameter has different settings in the two cases), it is the *same* concept nonetheless; likewise, mutatis mutandis, for the meaning of the term 'object' as employed by Carnap and by the Polish logician respectively. We have here a *différance* in concept and in meaning—that is, an identity-preserving difference.

What about the principle of affirmatory conflict? To begin with, it is important that Carnap and the Polish logician are not rightly interpreted as making claims that are *implicitly relativistic in content*. That is, it is not the case that the full content of what Carnap aims at is expressible as

There are exactly three objects on the table, relative to such and such mereological principles for the concept *object*,

or that the full content of what the Polish logician is saying is expressible as

There are exactly seven objects on the table, relative to so and so mereological principles for the concept *object*.

The problem, of course, is this: relativizing content in this way is obviously at odds with the phenomenon of conceptual relativity because the statements being expressed, even if they are both correct, do not involve genuine affirmatory conflict at all. (Putnam's label "conceptual relativity" is potentially misleading because it might suggest that content is thus relativized.) Intuitively, this problem is something like a use/mention conflation. What is actually going on in the example of Carnap and the Polish logician is that each of these parties is *using* a certain conceptual scheme, a certain way of "carving" the world into objects. But according to the relativized-content view, in effect what each is doing is *mentioning* (implicitly) a certain way of carving, and then asserting that there are thus-and-such many objects relative to that way of carving. Both of these relativity claims are correct, all right, but they do not really conflict in any interesting way at all. Instead, their apparent conflict is merely a surface phenomenon, one that dissolves entirely when one makes explicit the full content of the two respective relativity claims. Indeed, once the content of the respective relativity claims is made explicit, both Carnap and the Polish logician could perfectly well affirm *both* statements.[28]

So Carnap and the Polish logician are not making relativity claims; implicit reference to a setting of the mereology parameter is not a component of the content of what either of them is saying. Rather, both Carnap and the Polish logician are speaking and judging *categorically*, from within respective semantic stances in which they are employing the notion of object in a way that is semantically governed by a specific parameter-setting. On our view, the content of what Carnap is saying is properly expressed this way: *There are exactly three objects on the table*, while the content of what the Polish logician is saying is properly expressed this way: *There are exactly seven objects on the table*. Both statements are categorical, and thus neither of them is an implicit relativity claim. Although the respective statements are semantically *governed* by different settings of the mereology parameter, and although each statement is correct under the particular parameter-setting that governs it in context, neither statement is implicitly *about* its own governing parameter-setting.

The failure of the relativized-content approach helps triangulate the kind of affirmatory conflict we seek to understand. A crucial feature of it should be this: there is no way to reformulate the respective claims of person P_1 at time t_1 and person P_2 at time t_2 such that *a single person at a single time* could correctly affirm both statements (as reformulated), and thus could correctly affirm their conjunction. As we will put it, the two statements are not *correctly co-affirmable*.

One way that two statements can fail to be correctly co-affirmable, of course, is for them to be directly inconsistent with one another. But, given our above account of synchronic *différance*, this is not the only way. Another way arises from the fact that the various permissible settings for contextually variable semantic parameters are *mutually exclusionary*; that is, for a single person P at a single time t, no more than one parameter-setting for a given concept or word can semantically govern correct usage, by P at t, of that concept or word.

So the affirmatory conflict at work in cases of conceptual relativity, we suggest, occurs when two claims made by two different persons (or by one person at two different times) exhibit semantic governance by respective, implicit, semantic parameter-values that are mutually exclusionary. The two statements fail to be correctly co-affirmable, and this failure stems from the fact that they are governed semantically by mutually exclusionary settings of some contextually variable semantic parameter. The claims of Carnap and the Polish logician fail to be correctly co-affirmable for just that reason; and this feature constitutes their affirmatory conflict with one another. The two parties are not just "talking past one another" by using two nonidentical concepts and employing the term 'object' with two non-identical meanings, but they are not directly contradicting one another either. They are doing something in between, something that emerges as a genuine possibility once one recognizes (i) that there can be synchronic *différance* in concepts and meanings, (ii) that the source of synchronic *différance* is contextually variable semantic parameters, and (iii) that such *différance* is the basis for what Putnam calls conceptual relativity. This in-between relation in their respective claims is one under which both claims are correct despite conflicting with one another in the sense of not being mutually co-affirmable.

3.5.3 *Différance* and the Two Forms of Semantic Variation
Let us now combine the three strands of contextual semantics, as set forth in our three installments above: coarse-grained contextual variation between DC and IC semantic standards, fine-grained contextual variation, and *différance* in meanings and concepts. When these elements are brought together, along with the account we have just proposed for the phenomenon of conceptual relativity, they prove mutually illuminating.

Although the kind of semantic conflict illustrated by the case of Carnap and the Polish logician is genuine, often it is apt to be viewed by the respective parties as also "no big deal." That is, each party can recognize and appreciate both (i) that the two parties are each speaking and judging correctly under the respective parameter-settings that govern their respective uses, and (ii) that the two mutually exclusionary parameter-settings are ones that can legitimately be allowed to contextually govern the relevant concept (in this case, the concept of *object*).[29]

Invoking the DC/IC distinction allows the following natural and plausible explanation of why a "no big deal" attitude is appropriate. Genuine ontological commitment is only incurred when one's language/thought is governed by DC standards. Thus, insofar as the entire discussion in a Carnap/logician scenario is being conducted under semantic standards that fall under the IC rubric, *it is not a debate about ontology*. Both parties to the discussion might very well appreciate this fact, at least instinctively (if not by way of explicit reflective acceptance of contextual semantics). Their intuitive judgment that their conflict is not a big deal reflects a correct—if perhaps not explicit or articulate—appreciation of the fact that issues of ontology are not really at stake at all.

One can, if one so chooses, deliberately undertake serious ontological inquiry—thereby employing discourse governed by DC semantic standards in order to make ontological claims. In this rarefied form of thought and discourse, conceptual relativity no longer holds sway. Thus, if Carnap and the Polish logician both were to deliberately shift into DC discourse, and also both were to persist in their respective claims about the number of objects, then their dispute would thereby become a "big deal" ontologically. For, although Carnap and the Polish logician can both be right about how many objects are on the table when at least one of them is speaking and judging under IC semantic standards, nevertheless if they intend their dispute to be a genuine *metaphysical* conflict about how many **objects** are on the table, then they cannot both be correct. (Our own view is that neither of them is, because the right ontology is blobjectivist. See chapter 7.)

But even if each party adopts the "no big deal" attitude, a sign that both are operating under IC semantic standards, each party might nonetheless persist in her or his own original usage—a usage governed by the same parameter-setting that she or he originally employed. Thus, Carnap and the Polish logician each can perfectly well stick to their own original claims, and each can stick to their original denials of one another's claims, even while regarding their dispute as "no big deal."

Insofar as the dispute being carried on is under IC semantic standards, and thus is not about serious metaphysics, why should either party prefer her or his own usage over the other's, given a "no big deal" attitude? This question underscores the importance of considerations of *point and purpose*, which typically play a central role in determining contextually appropriate settings of implicit parameters. What is the point in the given context, one wonders, of asking the question "How many objects are on the table," or of answering this question one way rather than another? Normally in a well-run conversation or a well-conducted course of thought, the participant(s) will understand what underlying purposes and goals are in play, and will allow thought and discourse to be governed by implicit parameter-settings that suitably serve the purposes at hand. If the point of the question "How many objects are on the table?" is to implement a lesson to first-graders in how to count, the contextually appropriate answer will be "Three." But if the point of the question is to implement for philosophy graduate students a lesson in the mereological principles of the calculus of individuals, then the contextually appropriate answer will be "Seven." (One reason that Putnam's scenario is somewhat fanciful and artificial is that it is hard to fill in the details of the case in such a way that Carnap's answer and the Polish logician's both seem sensible from a single point-and-purpose perspective.)

Emphasis on point and purpose in the deployment of words and concepts, and in the undertaking of ontic commitments in language and thought, is central to the spirit of contextual semantics. On some occasions one's ontic commitments, given the purposes for which they are undertaken, amount to full-fledged *ontological* commitments. (Sometimes people pursue serious metaphysical inquiry.) But on many occasions ontic commitments do not constitute genuine ontological commitments at all. (Indeed, on *most* occasions they do not. For, vagueness is almost ubiquitous in language and thought, and yet ontological vagueness is impossible.)

It is worth noting that Putnam's preferred way of describing the respective uses of 'object' by his two protagonists effectively construes them each as being well attuned, and similarly attuned, to *some* implicit parameters concerning the notion *object*. For, both Carnap and the Polish logician are treating the books on the table as what one might call *contextually basic objects*—that is, objects whose proper parts are not themselves to be included within the contextually operative scope of the notion *object*. Here we see another implicit contextual parameter in play, whose contextually appropriate setting (as with other parameters) is heavily driven by considerations of point and purpose. It might be called the *object-basicness* parameter—the idea being that this parameter determines what qualifies, in context, as an object that is not composed of any proper parts that qualify, in context, as objects themselves. 'Basicness' here does not mean that the contextually basic objects *do not have* proper parts; after all, both Carnap and the Polish logician know perfectly well that the books on the table each have proper parts of their own (e.g., pages). Rather, it means that *in the present context, for the purposes at hand,* such items shall not count as falling within the scope of 'object'. Plausibly, implicit contextual parameters like object-basicness operate ubiquitously in thought and language—although humans are so good at respecting them that normally such parameters and their contextual variability are not consciously noticed at all.[30]

Finally, it should be stressed that for many Rylean categories employed in thought and discourse, there are apt to be well-entrenched *default* IC semantic standards, and these standards are apt to operate in a way that is not highly dependent on people's local, contextually specific purposes. For example, thought/discourse about universities, corporations, and nations is apt to serve various practical and social-interactive purposes in a fairly stable manner—a manner that does not depend heavily on contextual parameters that are subject to significant fine-grained contextual variation.

Furthermore, the default standards for such categories are indeed IC standards, presumably—not DC standards. (This too is a theme we will revisit in chapter 4.) Suppose someone from the metaphysics wing of the philosophy department asks, with full metaphysical seriousness, "Are there *really* such entities as universities and philosophy departments, that is, does the right ontology include such putative items?" This person's family, friends, and university colleagues—including colleagues who are in philosophy but do not specialize in metaphysics—are likely to react to these questions with amusement. There is surely something deeply right about reacting this way—namely, doing so reflects a visceral appreciation of the fact that the default semantic standards governing such Rylean categories are IC standards, not the DC standards being so earnestly employed by the department metaphysician.

So the idea of fine-grained semantic variation, the idea of coarse-grained semantic variation between DC and IC semantic standards, and the idea of *différance* illuminate one another in a variety of mutually supporting ways. This theme will surface again in later chapters.

3.6 Summary

We have maintained that a thought or statement can perfectly well have truth conditions—understood generically as a range of centered ways the world might be (i.e., a range of maximal self-involving properties instantiable by the cosmos)—even if the right ontology does not contain objects, properties, or relations answering to the thought's or statement's posits. When that is the case, truth is still correspondence to the world—albeit indirect correspondence, rather than the direct kind. (Direct correspondence is the only form of correspondence acknowledged by the semantic component of simple realism.)

We also have maintained that the idea of truth as indirect correspondence fits smoothly and naturally within a wider semantic framework that is plausible and attractive in itself—contextual semantics. This framework features the idea that truth is semantic correctness, under operative semantic standards. It also features the idea that many concepts, and the terms in language that express them, are governed by implicit contextual parameters that figure in the contextually operative semantic standards determining semantic correctness. The concept of truth itself is such a concept, according to contextual semantics. For one thing, the metalevel contextual parameters governing its semantically correct use sometimes work in such a way that it expresses direct correspondence, but often work in such a way that it instead expresses indirect correspondence. Also, disquotational uses of 'true', which conform to schema (T), will inherit whatever fine-grained variation in contextual semantic parameter-settings is exhibited by first-order discourse itself. Such contextual differences in the use of 'true' are yet another instance of the phenomenon we have called *différance* in meaning.

Contextual semantics has various points of contact with the views of other philosophers on language–world and thought–world relations. It seems a natural and plausible extension, for instance, of the treatment of contextually variable discourse parameters in Lewis 1983b. Likewise, it seems to be a natural further step in a direction already taken by advocates of philosophical projects of "regimentation": namely, the direction of denying that the surface commitments of true statements—what we are calling *ontic* commitments—always constitute ontological commitments. We have already mentioned that it accommodates certain motivating ideas in neopragmatism (and in verificationism), but without the mistake of embracing epistemic reductionism. There are echoes of Carnap's famous contention (Carnap 1950) that a "linguistic framework" can automatically sanction existence claims concerning the entities posited by the framework, and that such existence claims are ontologically innocent. The approach is somewhat similar to the treatment of truth and ontology in Sellars 1963, 1968.[31] Finally, contextual semantics seems rather similar in spirit to the general approach to truth, and to philosophical debates about realism and antirealism concerning various forms of discourse, in Wright 1992.[32]

4 | Austere Realism: Overcoming Simple Realism's Problems

In this chapter we continue the synthesis stage in the dialectic of reflective common sense. We begin by offering a formulation of the theses of austere realism that draws upon the discussion in chapter 3; this is a further elaboration of the initial formulation we gave in the introduction. We then explain how austere realism generates natural and reflectively plausible solutions to the antithesis problems (discussed in chapter 2) that plague simple realism.

4.1 Austere Realism: The Ontological and Semantic Theses

In articulating the ontological and semantic theses of austere realism, the distinction between direct and indirect correspondence will figure centrally. The specific version of austere realism we advocate will also incorporate the wider framework of contextual semantics—although the defining theses of austere realism do not presuppose this entire framework, and in principle these theses could be embraced even without embracing all of contextual semantics. Here then are the austere ontological theses:

AO1. Metaphysical realism: There is a mind-independent, discourse-independent world.

AO2. Refined commonsense ontology: The right ontology excludes most of the posits of everyday belief and discourse, and also excludes many of the posits of mature scientific theories.

Thesis AO1 is identical to thesis O1 of simple realism. As we have stressed already, common sense is deeply committed to a mind-independent, discourse-independent world. Reflective common sense retains this commitment, even in the face of the antithesis problems that challenge simple realism.

Thesis AO2, on the other hand, is an ontological conclusion that one is driven to by persistent, reflective, commonsensical reasoning itself—reasoning that uncovers the deep challenges to simple realism, and then finds itself driven by those challenges to repudiate simple realism's claim that the right ontology includes many of the posits of everyday belief and discourse (and of mature scientific theories). In particular, reflective common sense realizes both (i) that most putative objects and properties posited by everyday thought/discourse, and also many that are posited by scientific thought/discourse too, would be *vague* in various respects—for example, putative individuals would be vague with respect to spatiotemporal boundaries and/or synchronic composition, and putative properties would be vague with respect to their range of potential instantiation—and also (ii) that ontological vagueness is impossible.

Thesis AO2 is negative: it is a claim about what the right ontology does *not* include. It leaves open a range of candidate ontologies, all of which would be austere in the sense that they exclude most posits of everyday thought/discourse and many posits of scientific thought/discourse. Blobjectivism is one such austere ontology, and in chapter 7 we will argue that it is theoretically preferable to various theoretically viable competitors. But austere realism itself is a more generic position, ontologically. It asserts that the right ontology is an austere one, without being more specific.

Austere realism also includes a semantic component, as does simple realism. The semantic theses are these:

AS1. Correspondence conception of truth: Truth is correspondence between language and thought on one hand, and the world on the other.

AS2. Abundance of truth: Numerous statements and thought-contents involving posits of common sense and science are true—including numerous counting-statements about such posits.

AS3. Refined construal of correspondence: Truth is semantic correctness under contextually variable semantic standards, and sometimes the contextually operative semantic standards require only indirect correspondence rather than direct correspondence.

AS4. Truth as indirect correspondence in most contexts: In most contexts of discourse and thought, including most contexts of scientific inquiry, truth (under the contextually operative semantic standards) is indirect correspondence rather than direct correspondence.

AS5. Refined construal of ontological commitment: When a thought/ statement is governed by contextually operative semantic standards under which truth is indirect correspondence, the thought/statement is not ontologically committed to its posits.

Theses AS1 and AS2 are identical to theses S1 and S2 of simple realism. As we have stressed already, common sense is deeply committed to the idea that truth is correspondence between thought/language and the world, and to the idea that numerous beliefs and statements that are normally held true are indeed true. What is being sought, in this synthesis stage of the dialectic of reflective common sense, is a way to retain these deeply held beliefs in the face of the antithesis problems for simple realism.

The way to do so is to replace simple realism's conception of correspondence with a refined conception that comprises not only direct correspondence (the only kind recognized by simple realism) but also indirect correspondence as well—thesis AS3. This refinement allows one to retain the abundance of truth (thesis AS2) despite the austerity of ontology (thesis AO2), by claiming that in *most* contexts of thought/language, the contextually operative semantic standards require only indirect correspondence rather than direct correspondence—thesis AO4. The posits involved in ordinary commonsense statements (and in many scientific statements) do not incur ontological commitment—thesis AO5; this is why such statements can be true despite the fact that the correct ontology will not include entities answering to these posits.

Austere realism does not reject truth as direct correspondence; it does not claim that truth is *always* an indirect kind of correspondence. Rather, the claim is that truth is *typically* indirect correspondence, and that contexts of thought or inquiry governed by direct-correspondence semantic standards are fairly rare and atypical. More on this theme presently.

Thesis AS5 can be reformulated using a terminological distinction we introduced in thesis (9) of contextual semantics in section 3.3.1 of chapter 3—the distinction between ontological commitment and *ontic* commitment. A thought or statement is ontically committed to certain putative items (individuals, properties, or relations) when it *posits* such items. Essentially this means that the thought/statement employs positing apparatus— singular terms, predicates, existential-quantificational expressions, and the analogues in thought of such statement-constituents—in a way that meets *Quinean* standards of ontological commitment. In terms of the ontological–

ontic distinction, thesis AS5 says this: when a thought or statement is governed by contextually operative semantic standards under which truth is indirect correspondence, the thought/statement is only ontically committed to its posits and is not ontologically committed to them. It is convenient to speak of the ontic commitments of a given thought or statement. The reader should well bear in mind that what we are calling ontic commitment is not a matter of ontological commitment to semireal entities, or to real but ontologically nonbasic entities. Rather, mere ontic commitment is not genuine ontological commitment at all, because it involves the use of the positing apparatus of thought and language under *indirect-correspondence* semantic standards.

Let us stress the very broad scope of semantic theses AS3–AS5. In order to address satisfactorily the antithesis problems (which will be discussed presently), austere realism needs to claim that very many posits of both nonscientific and scientific discourse are ones to which such thought/discourse is merely ontically, and not ontologically, committed. Austere realism should thus be understood as having this broad scope.

As remarked already, what we will be arguing for is a specific version of austere realism, a particular way of implementing it—namely, a version that also embraces the various claims of contextual semantics, as set forth in chapter 3. Contextual semantics is an independently plausible semantic framework, within which the theses of austere realism all fit very naturally. This framework can be motivated by a range of considerations, some of which go beyond its capacity for handling the antithesis problems—as shall be seen in chapter 5. Also, contextual semantics can help fend off certain initially plausible-looking objections to austere realism—as shall be seen in chapter 6. In short, we maintain that austere realism and contextual semantics can be combined into a very attractive package deal that should appeal strongly to reflective common sense.

4.2   Direct Correspondence and Serious Ontological Inquiry

Before proceeding to the principal business of this chapter, let us briefly comment on the role(s) that austere realism accords to direct correspondence. Although austere realism distinguishes between direct and indirect forms of correspondence and claims that in most contexts truth is indirect correspondence, it does not eschew direct correspondence altogether.

According to austere realism, language and thought that are governed by DC semantic standards are indeed possible, although they are quite rare.

One principal kind of context in which such standards can be operative is a context of serious ontological inquiry—a context in which one's avowed purpose is to theorize about what does and does not belong to the correct ontology, to the "furniture of the world." According to austere realism, however, *typical* contexts of thought/language are not ones in which serious ontology is at issue, and are not contexts governed by DC standards. Even scientific thought and discourse are not normally governed by DC standards—inter alia, because so many scientific theories posit vague entities and ontological vagueness is impossible.

Expressions of theism are another plausible candidate for being subject to DC semantic standards. Many theists, we take it, mean to make claims about the existence of God in a seriously ontological way.

Since austere realism does not claim that truth is *always* indirect correspondence, it does not reject ontology as being unintelligible. On the contrary: ontological questions about the nature of the mind-independent world are entirely meaningful from the perspective of austere realism— although one lesson of the antithesis problems is that the right ontology will have to be an austere one of some kind. We ourselves advocate the following ontological claim, which we maintain is true under direct-correspondence semantic standards: there is one and only one concrete particular, and it is the blobject. But that is for chapter 7. Meanwhile, we continue with the dialectic of commonsense realism.

4.3 Lightweight Posits Reconsidered

Let us return now to the three challenges to simple realism that arose in the antithesis stage of inquiry in chapter 2: lightweight posits, the special composition question, and vagueness. Our case for austere realism will rest heavily on its capacity to smoothly and naturally overcome the problems that these three challenges pose for simple realism.

The challenge posed by lightweight posits (as we called them) is that when common sense goes ontologically reflective, even in a preliminary way, it quickly finds itself strongly inclined to doubt that the right ontology includes such "socially constructed" items as universities, symphonies, or nations. In light of contextual semantics, with its distinction between direct and indirect correspondence, austere realism should say that the appropriate conclusion to draw about thought and discourse employing metaphysically lightweight posits is that the posits do not pick out **items in the world**—and that truth, for such thought/discourse, is indirect correspondence. In typical contexts where such posits are employed, the contextually operative semantic standards conspire with spatiotemporally local goings-on in **the world** to render various statements employing these posits semantically correct (i.e., true), even though **the world** does not contain **entities** answering to those posits.

Thus, austere realism accommodates and vindicates the thought, which common sense arrives at fairly quickly when it goes ontologically reflective, that even though ordinary statements employing lightweight posits are very often true, nevertheless the right ontology does not include items answering to these posits. Even naive common sense is fairly comfortable with this entering wedge for indirect correspondence, which so far is a relatively modest departure from full-fledged simple realism.

Of course, naive common sense finds itself initially much more strongly wedded to the thought that the right ontology must include such items as tables, trees, persons, and electrons. Yet the special composition question and the issue of ontological vagueness generate enormously strong challenges to these preliminary ontological conclusions too, as was seen in chapter 2. What is wanted from austere realism is a way to accommodate these further challenges as well, in a manner that reflective common sense will find intuitively satisfying.

4.4 The Special Composition Question Reconsidered

Recall that the Special Composition Question (SCQ) is this: When do several objects jointly compose an object? Commonsensical reflection on this question, with an eye toward serious ontological inquiry, forces one to appreciate (as we argued in section 2.3 of chapter 2) that an important constraint on an adequate ontology is that it needs to yield a systematic general answer to the SCQ. We called this principle *the nonarbitrariness of composition* (NAOC). Commonsensical reflection also makes it appear very likely that there is no such answer that fits well with ordinary object-positing practices; this is the upshot of van Inwagen's argumentation-by-counterexamples against various initially plausible potential answers to the SCQ.

Austere realism offers an appealing way out of this conundrum. First, at the level of serious ontology, accept that the right ontology (whatever it turns out to be) will posit either many more **objects** or many fewer than are posited in ordinary thought and discourse, and will eschew **objects** or **properties** answering to most of the posits of ordinary thought/discourse. In neither case will the positing-practices of ordinary thought/discourse be well respected by the ontology in question. Thus, in neither case will it turn out that under *DC* semantic standards, commonsense existence and nonexistence claims are largely true. For instance, if the right ontology is one according to which (i) there are numerous simple **objects**, and (ii) several **objects** *always* compose a composite **object**, then numerous existence claims that common sense considers blatantly false will turn out true—for example, "There is an object comprising George Bush's nose, the Eiffel Tower, and the star Alpha Centauri." Or, if the right ontology is van Inwagen's—according to which (i) there are numerous simple **objects**, and (ii) several **objects** compose an **object** only if they jointly constitute a life— then numerous existence claims that common sense considers blatantly true will turn out false—for example, "There are tables."

Second, embrace the claim that ordinary thought and discourse are typically governed by IC semantic standards rather than DC standards. When such standards are in play, thought/discourse is only ontically committed—not ontologically committed—to its posits. This means that positing practices that fail to conform to any systematic general answer to the SCQ *do not violate* the principle of the nonarbitrariness of composition; for, that principle is a constraint on the correct *ontology* rather than on ordinary object-positing practices, and the positing practices in question do not carry ontological commitment at all.

Third, embrace the claim that ordinary thought and discourse are typically governed by IC standards involving positing practices that do not, in fact, conform to any systematic general principles. Rather, the semantic standards governing the positing of complex wholes will be a relatively nonsystematic hodgepodge, and thus will be *particularistic* in nature—a theme to which we will return in chapter 6.

So, refined common sense accommodates both ordinary thought/talk as very often literally true and also the fact that the correct ontology involves some systematic, general principle(s) of composition. The apparent conflict between ordinary practices governing the positing of complex entities on one hand and the NAOC as an ontological constraint on the other hand is dissolved by claiming that ordinary thought and talk are typically governed by IC semantic standards. Such standards can be particularistic with respect to the semantically sanctioned positing of composites without thereby contravening the claim that the correct ontology must obey systematic, general principles of composition. This is because thought and discourse governed by IC standards simply are not ontologically committed to their posits.

4.5   The Boundarylessness of Vagueness Reconsidered

As we noted in section 2.5 of chapter 2, neither the problem of light-weight posits nor the SCQ—nor the two together—*force* reflective common sense to abandon simple realism. But we maintain that when common sense dwells reflectively and carefully on boundarylessness as an essential feature of vagueness, it will find itself driven to austere realism as the only viable way out of the deep conundrum posed by the impossibility of ontological vagueness. We will reiterate this conundrum, then explain how austere realism handles it, and then make some observations linking the discussion to a popular approach to the logic and semantics of vagueness—supervaluationism.

4.5.1   The Impossibility of Ontological Vagueness

We begin by briefly reiterating the problem. Vagueness essentially involves boundarylessness—namely, status transitions among successive items in a sorites sequence, but *no fact of the matter* about such transitions. Such boundarylessness essentially involves the governance of mutually unsatisfiable status-principles, which can be briefly summarized this way: (i) sufficiently small differences don't make a difference; (ii) sufficiently large differences do make a difference; and (iii) sufficiently many iterations of sufficiently small differences result in a sufficiently large difference.

Governance by such mutually unsatisfiable principles is intelligible in the case of vagueness in language and thought, because such governance can be understood in terms of mutually obeyable prohibitions on *affirmatory practice*—the Individualistic Status-Attribution Prohibition, which prohibits attributing a specific status (e.g., truth) to an item in a sorites sequence and a different, incompatible status (e.g., being neither true nor false) to its immediate neighbor, and the Collectivistic Status-Attribution

Prohibition, which prohibits affirming any determinate overall assignment of statuses to the items in a sorites sequence.

But with respect to the question whether there is, or can be, ontological vagueness, there is simply no intelligible analogue of the idea of practice standards. The only way that **the world** could conform to mutually unsatisfiable status-principles would be by *satisfying* them—which is impossible. It is impossible, for instance, for there to be a sequence of **objects** such that (i) initial items in the sequence are heaps, (ii) whenever an item in the sequence is a heap, then so is its successor, and (iii) eventually in the sequence there are nonheaps. Thus, heaphood cannot be a genuine **property**, one that belongs to the correct ontology. Similarly, it is impossible for there to be a sequence of closely spaced grains of sand such that (i) initial grains are on Mt. Whitney, (ii) whenever a grain in the sequence is on Mt. Whitney, then so is its immediate successor, and (iii) eventually in the sequence there are grains not on Mt. Whitney. Thus, Mt. Whitney cannot be a genuine **object**, one that belongs to the correct ontology. Likewise, mutatis mutandis, for putative ontological vagueness in general.

Under simple realism, affirmative thoughts/statements about heaps, mountains, and other vague posits cannot be true unless the correct ontology does contain such items. For, simple realism construes truth as direct correspondence between thought/language and the world, and it therefore construes vague thoughts/statements as ontologically committed to their posits. Yet simple realism embraces the abundance of truth: it claims that numerous affirmative statements employing vague terminology are indeed true. So reflective common sense, when it comes to appreciate that ontological vagueness is impossible, falls into deep internal tension. It seeks to vindicate its own commitment to the abundant truth of vague thoughts/statements, but it realizes that the right ontology *cannot* contain vague objects or properties.

4.5.2 Direct Correspondence, Sorites Arguments, and Ontology

How does austere realism handle this problem? To begin with, consider thought and discourse that is conducted under DC semantic standards. Such standards surely cannot tolerate logical incoherence. For, insofar as one is thinking or talking under DC standards, any logical incoherence in one's true thoughts or statements would have to be a direct mirror of logical incoherence in the world itself. But **reality** cannot be logically incoherent!

So, when one is employing DC semantic standards for the purpose of serious ontological inquiry, sorites arguments become sound reductio ad absurdum arguments against the existence of vague **objects** or **properties**.

4.5.3 Indirect Correspondence to the Rescue: The Transvaluationist Conception of Vagueness

Austere realism treats direct correspondence as just one species of truth, and it claims that in *most* contexts of thought and discourse, the contextually operative semantic standards are IC standards. This is the key to resolving common sense's antithesis dilemma concerning the boundarylessness of vagueness. Austere realism says that there are indeed numerous true statements involving vague terminology, and numerous true thought-contents involving vague thought-constituents. But truth, for all such thoughts/statements is (and must be) *indirect* correspondence. These thoughts/statements are (and must be) only *ontically* committed to their posits, rather than being ontologically committed to them.

Because vagueness is so hugely prevalent, both in ordinary thought/ discourse and in scientific thought/discourse, so too are IC semantic standards. This is not a defect, not even in contexts of serious scientific inquiry. Scientific theories positing vague objects and properties really do reveal important things about the world, even though they do so *under* IC semantic standards. Talk of electrons, cells, clouds, galaxies, and so forth does indeed track theoretically and explanatorily important aspects of **the world**, even though the right ontology does not contain such items. Theoretically illuminating scientific **reality**-tracking need not—and very typically does not—take the form of *direct* correspondence. Instead it can perfectly well—and very typically does—take the form of indirect correspondence, via vague terms and concepts. (We revisit this theme below, especially in section 7.4.1 of chapter 7.)

DC semantic standards cannot tolerate the weak logical incoherence endemic to the boundarylessness of vagueness; for (as we stressed in the preceding subsection) this would require **the world** to conform to mutually unsatisfiable satisfaction conditions, which is impossible. However, IC semantic standards evidently *can* incorporate the weak logical incoherence of boundarylessness, involving semantic governance of affirmatory practice by mutually unsatisfiable semantic-status principles that are respected in affirmatory practice (by obedience to certain mutually obeyable status-attribution prohibitions). Moreover, IC standards can, and do, operate in such a way that the incoherence gets kept in check rather than leading to malevolent consequences (e.g., strong logical incoherence, comprising commitments to contradictions). Indeed, the manner in which mutually unsatisfiable semantic-status principles exert their governance over correct affirmatory *practice*—namely, via the Individualistic Status-Attribution Prohibition and the Collectivistic Status-Attribution Prohibition—effectively quarantines the weak logical incoherence embodied in the semantic-status principles themselves. The semantically correct thing to do in practice, when confronted with the prospect of being backed into accepting a sorites argument, is to *refuse to accept such an argument*. The semantically correct thing to do, when confronted with the prospect of being force-marched through a sorites sequence and being asked at each step "What is the semantic status of this next statement, given what you have said about the semantic status of its predecessor?," is to stop answering these persistent queries at some point—but without assigning semantic significance to the point at which one stops. (It is best to stop well in advance of finding one-self in a penumbral portion of the sorites sequence, just as it is best to avoid the dangerous parts of town by keeping some comfortable distance away from them.) Obey the operative status-attribution prohibitions, thereby *respecting* in practice the mutually unsatisfiable status-principles that lie behind them—and you will avoid committing yourself to contradictions.

Since IC semantic standards do incorporate the governance of affirmatory practice by mutually unsatisfiable semantic-status principles, such standards cannot be expected to yield, in combination with how **the world** is, some full and determinate assignment of semantic statuses to all truth-evaluable thought-contents and sentences. For, any such total assignment, as long as it respects the principle *sufficiently large differences make a difference*, would end up positing sharp status-transitions of one sort or another, regardless of how many semantic statuses are in play. So the right way to think of IC standards is not as determinately fixing (together with how the world is) a complete assignment of semantic statuses, but rather as governing correct affirmatory practice.

Transvaluationism is our name for the general approach to vagueness we have been describing. Transvaluationism makes two fundamental claims. First, vagueness is weakly logically incoherent without being strongly logically incoherent. Second, vagueness is viable, legitimate, and indeed essential in human language and thought; its weak logical incoherence is benign rather than malevolent. Just as Nietzsche held that one can overcome nihilism by embracing what he called the transvaluation of all values, transvaluationism asserts that vagueness, although logically incoherent in a certain way, can and should be endorsed and embraced, not nihilistically repudiated.[1] Both claims emanate from reflective common sense—the second because vagueness seems uncontestably ubiquitous and unavoidable in human language and thought, and the first because of the considerations we have been emphasizing concerning boundarylessness.

Since vagueness essentially involves boundarylessness, and since boundarylessness essentially involves weak logical incoherence, an adequate treatment of vagueness will have to be some version of transvaluationism. Moreover, transvaluationism is a fairly generic position, potentially open to further development and articulation in a variety of different ways. Numerous details about the logic and semantics of vagueness remain open within the generic conception and might get handled differently in different versions.[2] But regardless of how the details go, any account of vagueness that seriously comes to grips with boundarylessness must be a version of transvaluationism—whether its proponents acknowledge this fact or not. Much of the recent literature on so-called *higher-order vagueness*—that is, vagueness of categories like truth, falsity, and the category "neither true nor false"—is best viewed as falling within the transvaluationist framework. In effect, specific proposals concerning higher-order vagueness amount to suggested strategies for theoretically quarantining the (ineliminable) weak logical incoherence of vagueness.

The weak generic logical incoherence that any such proposal must take on board, at least implicitly, will inevitably reveal itself when one considers what the advocate of the particular proposal will be forced to say when confronted with what we call a "forced march" through a sorites sequence. Consider, for instance, a sorites sequence for baldness: $B(0), B(1), \ldots, B(10^7)$, where '$B(n)$' abbreviates 'A man with n hairs on his head is bald'. A forced march through this sequence is a series of questions, with respect to each successive statement, "Is it true?" Each of the questions is perfectly meaningful. And for no two successive questions could it be correct to give different answers; for, that difference would mark a determinate semantic transition, contrary to the nature of vagueness. Suppose that one is being marched along through the members of the sequence and is being asked at each step to pronounce a judgment about the semantic status of the statement in question. Suppose too that one is in a maximally patient, maximally cooperative mood during this process. How should one respond to this stepwise querying? Well, at some point along the way one should say something like this:

> I realize that it would not be semantically correct for me to provide any determinate set of answers to all these questions, and that it would also be semantically incorrect for me to assign different statuses to any pair of adjacent items. So I am now going to stop providing answers, despite my cooperative mood. Furthermore, although I am stopping just here in the sorites sequence, I do not regard this choice of a stopping point as marking a sharp status-transition. On the contrary, vague categories are boundaryless.

Being patient and cooperative, one might then jump ahead to some point further in the sequence, and proceed to make polar-opposite status-assignments to that item and to all successive items. But if so, one should also say something like this when one resumes making judgments:

> Although I am resuming just here, I do not regard this choice of a resumption point as marking a sharp status-transition between the present item and the immediately preceding one. On the contrary, vague categories are boundaryless.

In short, the right way to deal with a forced march through a sorites sequence, even for someone who is maximally cooperative, is to refuse to answer all the queries (on the grounds that there is no semantically correct way to answer them all) and to claim (on the grounds that vagueness is boundaryless) that whatever stopping points or resumption points one happens to select do not mark status transitions. The only proper thing to do, when confronted with the prospect of forced-march querying, is to refuse steadfastly to play that question-and-answer game. Instead of announcing a judgment at each step in the forced march, adopt a Zen attitude: be tranquilly silent in the face of some of those persistent queries, in the knowledge that no complete set of answers is semantically correct. This is the *right* thing to do because it accords with the ISA and CSA Prohibitions, which themselves are grounded in the ISS and CSI Principles (see section 2.4.2 of chapter 2).

But although this refusal to take the forced march is entirely appropriate as a tactic for avoiding commitment to any logically contradictory statements, it would be self-deception to think that such an avoidance tactic somehow eliminates the weak logical incoherence of vagueness. On the contrary, the fact that semantically correct affirmatory practice requires "ducking the forced march" *cries out for explanation.* Given that the respective queries in the forced march are all perfectly meaningful, and given that each query semantically demands the same answer as its predecessor (on pain of there otherwise being a sharp transition in semantic statuses between the two statements), *why* is it correct affirmatory practice to refrain from addressing all those semantic-status demands? Why, in other words, is there no semantically correct way to provide a complete set of answers to the queries? The only remotely plausible explanation—and, therefore, the *best* explanation—is that vagueness essentially harbors weak logical incoherence. The ISS Principle and the CSI Principle both exert normative governance over semantically correct affirmatory practice, while yet being mutually unsatisfiable; their normative governance is the basis for the ISA Prohibition and the CSA Prohibition; and these prohibitions proscribe providing any complete set of answers to the queries (or any partial set of answers that affirms some precise status-transition). The forced march is essentially just the sorites paradox, with one's nose rubbed in it.[3] What it reveals is the weak logical incoherence of vagueness: normative governance of affirmatory practice by mutually unsatisfiable semantic-status standards.

4.5.4 A Nihlistic Objection and a Nietzschean Reply

We claim to be offering an account according to which (a) semantic vagueness is a genuine phenomenon despite harboring weak logical incoherence, and (b) its weak logical incoherence does not spawn strong logical incoherence. The following objection might be raised:

> Transvaluationism does not really provide an account of how semantic vagueness is both possible and logically benign. For, this approach employs theoretical categories that are themselves subject to sorites-paradoxical reasoning, such as the category expressed by the predicate 'would be rightly called bald in semantically correct judgmental/affirmatory practice'. Since transvaluationism employs categories that are logically incoherent according to transvaluationism itself, transvaluationism ends up being a logically incoherent theoretical position.

To this objection we would offer the following Nietzschean, nihilism-transcending reply. We readily admit that transvaluationism employs

vague theoretical categories in its account of the phenomenon of vagueness—and, specifically, that categories like *semantically correct judgment/
affirmation* are vague. But there is nothing inherently wrong with the use
of vague categories in one's theorizing, not even when one is theorizing
about vagueness itself. Theories that employ vague concepts are *weakly* logically incoherent, of course, since vague concepts are subject to semantic
normative governance by mutually unsatisfiable status-principles. But that
is not a problem, because such theories are not strongly logically incoherent. Very little serious theorizing about the world is ever done—or can
ever be done—in a strongly logically coherent way, because of the near-
ubiquity of vagueness across the range of human concepts (including
most scientific concepts).[4] If the objector wants to insist that an adequate
philosophical account of vagueness cannot employ vague concepts itself,
then the objector bears the burden of proof to show why this should be
so. If most scientific theories can deploy vague concepts to explain the
phenomena within their purview, then why cannot a philosophical theory
employ vague concepts to explain the phenomenon of vagueness? (We
do recognize, however, the need to secure the ontological foundations of
austere realism itself, and of whatever specific version of it one might seek
to defend. We address this matter in chapter 7, as regards the version of
austere realism that embraces blobjectivist ontology.)

4.5.5 Case Study: Supervaluationism as an Implementation

It will be instructive to briefly consider supervaluationism in relation to
what we have been saying about how austere realism handles the boundarylessness of vagueness. Supervaluationism is perhaps the most popular
approach in the philosophical literature to the logic and semantics of
vagueness (although there is certainly no consensus about the matter),
and one might initially think that it can provide an alternative to the
approach to vagueness we have been describing. We maintain, on the contrary, that although a suitable version of supervaluationism can provide
one potential *implementation* of transvaluationism, it does not provide a viable alternative to it.

As we pointed out in section 2.4.2 of chapter 2, supervaluationism construes truth simpliciter as truth under all "permissible interpretations"—
the idea being that there are multiple permissible interpretations of a
statement's vague vocabulary, each of which "precisifies" the statement's
vague vocabulary in a specific way. A vague statement is true simpliciter,

according to supervaluationism, if and only if it is true under all permissible interpretations, is false simpliciter if and only if it is false under all permissible interpretations, and otherwise is neither true nor false. *Classical* supervaluationism is formulated in a metalanguage governed by classical two-valued logic and semantics. *Iterated* supervaluationism (as we call it) holds that the metalanguage itself is vague, and thus it too is subject to a supervaluationist treatment in the meta-meta-language, and so on, all the way up the metalinguistic hierarchy. More specifically, the metalinguistic expression 'permissible interpretation' is itself vague, and thus has various permissible interpretations in a meta-meta-language, and so on up.

The first point we want to emphasize is that supervaluationism, in both the classical and the iterated varieties, provides one potential implementation of the idea of truth as indirect correspondence. Under supervaluationist semantics, truth is not a matter of direct correspondence; it is not undergirded by referential relations that vague singular terms and vague predicates hold to specific objects and properties in the correct ontology. Rather, truth is an indirect form of correspondence, involving multiple mappings from vague singular terms and predicates to the world—multiple ways of forging word–world relations each of which reflects an eligible precisification of a statement's vague vocabulary.

Fans of supervaluationism tend to be dubious about ontological vagueness, and they tend to regard vagueness as a purely linguistic/conceptual phenomenon. Insofar as they go this way—and this is our second point— they are effectively embracing a version of austere realism already: they are repudiating the vague posits of ordinary discourse and scientific discourse in favor of an austere ontology devoid of ontological vagueness, and they are embracing a semantic treatment of vague discourse under which truth is a form of indirect correspondence.[5]

Third, as already remarked in section 2.4.2 of chapter 2, *classical* supervaluationism utterly fails to come to terms with the boundarylessness of vagueness—and therefore is extremely implausible. Commonsense intuition balks very strongly at the idea that in a sorites sequence of statements there are always sharp transitions between sentences that are true, those that are neither true nor false, and those that are false. In order to accommodate boundarylessness within the supervaluationist framework, one needs to iterate supervaluationism up through the metalinguistic hierarchy.

Fourth, it might be thought that iterated supervaluationism is not a version of transvaluationism but is rather an alternative to it—a competitor view. After all, its proponents do not normally assert or acknowledge that boundarylessness involves mutually unsatisfiable semantic requirements for the successive statements in a sorites sequence.[6]

But fifth, a closer look reveals that this approach does not really eliminate the logical incoherence of boundarylessness, but instead offers one way of implementing the transvaluationist idea that vagueness harbors a weak form of logical incoherence that gets quarantined (so that commitment to rampant contradictions is avoided) but not eliminated. The best way to appreciate this is to note two facts. First, a fan of iterated supervaluationism will certainly agree with us that in the case of vagueness, semantically correct judgmental/affirmatory practice must conform to the ISA Prohibition and the CSA Prohibition—and will also agree that the normative grounding for these practice standards is semantic rather than epistemic. (The whole point of *iterating* the supervaluationist machinery, after all, is to avoid sharp semantic boundaries altogether.) But second, fans of iterated supervaluationism have no specific explanation on offer for *why* these practice-standards must be adhered to—rather than its being the case that the whole infinite supervaluationist hierarchy of metalanguages fixes a determinate overall assignment of semantic statuses (so that an agent could then engage in semantically correct practice by actually *assigning* those statuses to the successive statements). *Yet an explanation is needed!* Transvaluationism provides one—namely, that the two prohibitive practice-standards (the ISA and CSA Prohibitions) reflect the normative governance of mutually unsatisfiable status-principles (viz., the ISS and CSI Principles). In the absence of an alternative explanation—and advocates of iterated supervaluationism typically have not even acknowledged the need for an explanation, let alone tried to provide one—the only available explanation is the transvalutionist one. So, in the absence of an alternative explanation, iterated supervaluationism is really an implementation of transvaluationism rather than a competing position—whether its advocates realize this or not.

Sixth, iterated supervaluationism provides a way to quarantine this weak logical incoherence—basically, a specific way of *deferring*, on up through an infinite metalinguistic hierarchy, awkward questions about the semantic boundaries of vague categories. (Questions about the semantic boundaries of 'bald' get deferred to questions about the semantic boundaries of 'permissible precisification of "bald"', which in turn get deferred to questions about the semantic boundaries of 'permissible precisification of "permissible precisification of 'bald'"'—etc., ad infinitum.) Although such infinite vertical buck-passing does avoid strong logical incoherence, that is, commitment to contradictions, the underlying weak logical incoherence remains. It reveals itself in the need to go silent in the face of the forced march.

Seventh, the semantical apparatus of supervaluationism makes possible a distinction between conservative and nonconservative forms of indirect correspondence. A conservative form would require that there be **objects** and **properties** in the right ontology that serve as "eligible precisified referents" of vague singular terms and predicates—for example, perfectly precise physical **objects** (largely overlapping one another spatiotemporally), each of which is an eligible referent of 'Mt. Whitney', and perfectly precise **properties** (largely coinciding in extension), each of which is an eligible referent of 'baldness'. In contrast, a nonconservative form of indirect correspondence would impose no such requirement. So for instance, the truth of "General Motors Corporation is a U.S. company" would not require there to be **objects** in the correct ontology that count as "eligible precisifications" of the term 'General Motors Corporation'.

Eighth, various arguments we have given in this book underwrite the claim that an adequate version of austere realism will need to embrace the nonconservative version of indirect correspondence. For instance, what makes General Motors Corporation a *metaphysically lightweight* posit is the extreme implausibility—the aspect of being a Rylean "category mistake"—that attends any proposal to reductively identify General Motors Corporation with some mereological sum of (or some set of) objects like buildings, equipment, personnel, and so forth. Essentially the same problem will arise for any proposal to construe certain ontologically precise **objects** as "eligible precisified referents" of the name 'General Motors Corporation'.

Ninth, there are other potentially promising approaches to the logic and semantics of vagueness besides iterated supervaluationism. Arguably, however, any viable approach will need to iterate its own semantical approach through an infinite hierarchy, thereby adopting the infinite vertical buck-passing strategy as a way of quarantining weak logical incoherence. One such approach is described in Horgan 1994, sections 2 and 3. An advantage of Horgan's account is its treatment of statements like

$$(\exists n)[B(n) \ \& \ \sim B(n+1)],$$

where 'B(n)' abbreviates 'A man with n hairs on his head is bald'. Super-valuationism renders this statement true—which is very counterintuitive, since the statement *seems* to make the patently false claim that there is a sharp cutoff between being bald and being nonbald. (The statement is true simpliciter, under supervaluationist semantics, because it comes out true under every precisification of 'bald'.) Horgan's approach, on the other hand, treats the statement as neither true nor false—which seems significantly more intuitively satisfying.

4.6 Summary

Austere realism is a metaphysical-cum-semantic position that overcomes the antithesis problems confronting simple realism. Semantically, the key claim is that although truth is sometimes a direct form of correspondence (the only form recognized by the semantic component of simple realism), very often truth is indirect correspondence instead. This idea fits naturally within a broader semantic framework that we maintain has considerable plausibility—contextual semantics. Metaphysically, the key claim of austere realism is that the correct ontology is some *austere* one that repudiates numerous posits of commonsense thought/discourse and numerous posits of scientific discourse as well.

Austere realism handles the problem of metaphysically lightweight posits. Posits like corporations, nations, and symphonies are repudiated by an austere ontology, but numerous claims involving such posits turn out to be true nonetheless. Truth, for such claims, is indirect correspondence.

Austere realism handles the Special Composition Question. Any theoretically adequate version of austere realism must incorporate an ontological position that provides a systematic answer. Different candidate ontologies for concrete particulars will provide different answers. One candidate ontology, for instance, would comprise perfectly precise *spatiotemporal regions* and would recognize any mereological sum of such entities (however disjoint and gerrymandered) as another concrete particular. Another concrete ontology for concrete particulars would recognize just one of them—namely, the whole cosmos (the blobject). But regardless which specific austere ontology is adopted, austere realism renders numerous commonsense claims true while denying that these claims are ontologically committed to their posits. Truth for such claims is indirect correspondence.

Austere realism handles the problem of the impossibility of ontological vagueness (a consequence of the boundarylessness of vagueness). Vague objects and properties are repudiated by an austere ontology, but numerous claims involving vague posits turn out to be true nonetheless. Truth, for such claims, is indirect correspondence.

Austere realism meets the methodological desiderata we set forth in section 3.1 of chapter 3. First, the position emerges naturally from persistent commonsense reflection—specifically, persistent reflection about apparent morals of the antithesis problems that so deeply challenge simple realism. Second, the position leaves firmly in place simple realism's first ontological thesis and its first two semantic theses—the reality of a mind-independent world, truth as correspondence between thought/language and that world, and the genuine truth of numerous claims that common sense considers true. Third, the position is a commonsensically *plausible* way out of the antithesis problems, once one dwells upon them with sufficient care: construe truth (for much thought and discourse) as indirect correspondence, so that commonsense beliefs/statements typically are not really ontologically committed to their own posits. Moreover, the distinction between direct and indirect correspondence is a component of a more general semantic framework that *itself* is very plausible, once it gets explicitly articulated—namely, contextual semantics. Fourth, error theory is avoided: the position sanctions commonsense beliefs as *quite literally true* (rather than as systematically false), by treating indirect correspondence as a thoroughly respectable form of truth-constituting correspondence.

Austere realism, as we have articulated it, incorporates the various claims of contextual semantics. The distinction between direct and indirect correspondence fits especially well within this wider semantic framework—inter alia, because the framework treats numerous terms and concepts as governed by implicit contextual parameters, and it thereby becomes very natural to treat truth itself this way within the framework. From the perspective of contextual semantics, the distinction between direct and indirect correspondence is not a bifurcation of the notion of truth into two distinct senses or meanings, but rather reflects the fact that truth itself is one of the many concepts governed by implicit conceptual parameters. (We will return to this theme in chapter 6.) In principle, perhaps it would be possible to embrace the ontological and semantic theses of austere realism without also situating these theses within the wider framework of contextual semantics. But the version of austere realism that seems to us the most natural, most plausible, and most defensible is the one that incorporates contextual semantics.[7]

There is yet more to be said in support of austere realism, understood as including contextual semantics. There are additional positive arguments to be marshaled on its behalf, and there are potential objections that need to be addressed. These two tasks will be the business of chapters 5 and 6, respectively. Then, in chapter 7, we will turn to a defense of the specific form of austere realism we ourselves favor—blobjectivism.

5 | The Ascendance of the Austere: Further Arguments for Austere Realism

A range of theoretical considerations favor austere realism—specifically, the version that incorporates contextual semantics—over and above this position's capacity for overcoming the antithesis problems concerning simple realism. In this chapter we will set forth some of these considerations, thereby reinforcing and further strengthening the case for austere realism.

5.1 Methodological Remarks

A credible metaphysical-cum-semantic theory should meet various desiderata, beyond resolving internal tensions within naive philosophical thought. Theoretical parsimony is one such desideratum: not multiplying posits beyond necessity. In the case of metaphysics, this means not bloating one's ontology beyond necessity. Ceteris paribus, less is better in ontology.

Another desideratum pertains to epistemology. One's position on matters of ontology and truth should not make it a mystery how human beings can come to *know* the various kinds of truths they normally take themselves to know. This desideratum emerges in an especially stark way in the philosophy of mathematics: platonistic treatments of the ontology of mathematics and the semantics of mathematical discourse, for instance, encounter notorious difficulties accounting for the possibility of mathematical knowledge (cf. Benacerraf 1973). But the desideratum itself, and the epistemological challenges it generates, are much more general in scope (cf. Peacocke 1992).

Third, the overall strength of the case for a specific theory concerning ontology and truth depends, to a considerable extent, on the comparative advantages of the given theory over various extant alternative theories. In the case of austere realism, several alternative theories deserve consideration. One is simple realism—viewed now as a competitor to austere realism, with the antithesis problems temporarily set aside. Another is global irrealism, the view that there is just no such thing as a mind-independent, discourse-independent, world at all. And there are also several extant philosophical approaches to truth, other than contextual semantics, with its distinction between direct and indirect correspondence, that one might try wedding to an austere ontology.

On all three scores, we will maintain, austere realism does well. Such considerations reinforce its overall credibility.

5.2 Ontological Parsimony

In metaphysical theorizing, as in theory construction more generally, there is desirability in parsimony. Austere realism makes possible a substantial paring down of the ontological commitments of discourse. The desirable simplifications come not merely from minimizing the number of distinct kinds of entities one posits, but also from avoiding a baroque relational network involving entities at various ontological "levels": some in space-time (e.g., tables, electrons) and others not (e.g., numbers); some (e.g., corporations, nations) synchronically supervenient upon others (e.g., persons, buildings, land masses); some causally related to one another and others not; and so forth. Hence the attractiveness of austere realism over against a more bloated and more level-infested ontology (e.g., the ontology of simple realism).

5.3 Viable Epistemology

A second advantage of refined realism concerns knowledge. Contextual semantics holds out the promise of a tractable epistemology, particularly within the framework of a naturalistic conception of human beings as complex physicochemical systems. Consider, for instance, knowledge of the statement

(B) Beethoven's Fifth Symphony has four movements.

Philosophers who are concerned about ontological questions in aesthetics, and who approach these questions from within simple realism, have been much exercised by the ontological status of musical works of art. If one begins by assuming that a statement like (B) cannot be true unless some **object** answers to the term 'Beethoven's Fifth Symphony', then one is apt to suppose (as many have) that this term denotes a complex, internally structured **universal**—an abstract entity that exists eternally and is not part of the spatiotemporal causal nexus. But once one supposes this, it becomes very hard to see how mere humans could ever have knowledge about symphonies, such as the knowledge expressed by (B). For, humans cannot come into any sort of causal contact with these putative entities, but rather can causally interact only with those concrete things we call "performances of Beethoven's Fifth Symphony," "copies of the score of Beethoven's Fifth Symphony," and so on. One is tempted to say, of course, that one knows the symphony itself via knowledge of concreta that "token" it or "describe" it. But this only pushes the epistemological problem back a step. For, how could one know that a given event tokens a certain abstract **object**, or that a given manuscript describes it, unless one could somehow directly compare the event or the manuscript with the abstract **object** itself? Yet it is most implausible—especially given the naturalistic conception of human beings—to suppose that one can have some sort of quasi-perceptual cognitive communion with an **entity** that has no spatiotemporal location and does not causally interact with anything. And if someone replies by saying that performance-instances and score-copies are instances or copies of a particular abstract **universal** because people stipulate it so, rather than because they somehow directly compare those concrete things with the putative abstract entity, then again the epistemological puzzles are merely pushed back. For, now it becomes very hard to see either (i) how one can justifiably claim to know that there really exist such putative abstract **entities** as symphony-types at all, or (ii) how it could be the case that people's stipulative acts could link a term like 'Beethoven's Fifth Symphony' to one specific such complex **universal** rather than to some other one that is isomorphic to the first.

These highly vexing epistemological problems do not arise under contextual semantics, given that the semantic standards for symphony talk are standards under which a sentence like (B) can be semantically correct even though no actual denizen of **the world** answers to the term 'Beethoven's Fifth Symphony'. Similarly for a wide variety of other kinds of discourse. (Talk about numbers, sets, and other mathematical entities is another especially salient example. Under contextual semantics, it is plausible that the default semantic standards governing mathematical posits work in such a way that claims about these posits are rendered true or false *by the semantic standards alone*—and hence that mathematical claims make no demands at all on **the world**, let alone demands requiring that there be mathematical **objects**.) Thus, austere realism has a greater potential for rendering knowledge-claims justifiable than does simple realism. For, austere realism incorporates contextual semantics, whereas simple realism is constrained by its construal of truth as direct correspondence between thought/language and **the world**.

5.4 Austere Realism versus Austerity-based Layered Ontology

In the remainder of this chapter we will argue that austere realism, as situated within the wider semantic framework of contextual semantics, has important *comparative* theoretical advantages over various alternative philosophical positions. (In some cases these advantages include comparative ontological parsimony, as described in section 5.2. But other comparative advantages will figure in too.) In this and the next two sections, we compare the view to several philosophical positions that differ from it metaphysically. Then, in section 5.7, we compare the view to a range of philosophical positions that also embrace austere ontology but wed it to some semantic framework different from contextual semantics.

By "austerity-based layered ontology" we mean a metaphysical position with the following features. First, it distinguishes sharply between fundamental and nonfundamental items in the correct ontology. Second, it asserts that fundamental-level ontology is austere: its **objects** and **properties** are perfectly precise in all respects, and its **objects** obey some systematic, general, principle(s) of composition. Third, it asserts that there are also *nonfundamental* **items** in the correct ontology—including many of the items posited by common sense and science.

On one version of such a view, the nonfundamental items are "mind-dependent" and "socially constructed": their existence depends essentially on human positing-practices. Because they are thus dependent, they do not obey any systematic, general, principle(s) of composition—since ordinary positing-practices evidently do not conform well to any such principles (as van Inwagen so persuasively argues). But they are nonetheless **real**: they do belong to the correct ontology, even though their ontological status is derivative.

Our own position—austere realism—scores better than this alternative metaphysical position on grounds of parsimony: ours gets by without introducing any of the putative derivative entities into ontology at all—and without needing to. This theoretical advantage of austere realism was already stressed, in section 5.2 above.

But, quite apart from considerations of comparative parsimony, this proffered position is decisively precluded by the impossibility of ontological vagueness. As we have pointed out repeatedly, virtually all the objects and properties posited by common sense, and many of those posited by science, are vague: the posited objects are vague with respect to matters like spatiotemporal boundaries and synchronic composition, and the posited properties are vague with respect to matters like the extent of their instantiation vis-à-vis sorites sequences of actual and possible objects. So, if the correct ontology really did include **objects** and **properties** answering to these posits—albeit ontologically derivative ones—then **the world** would exhibit ontological vagueness. But ontological vagueness is impossible—because vagueness essentially involves boundarylessness, and boundarylessness essentially involves weak logical incoherence. Therefore, there *cannot* be vague items in the correct ontology—not at the fundamental ontological level, and not at any nonfundamental, derivative level(s) either.

5.5 Austere Realism versus Fence-straddling Realism

By "fence-straddling realism" we mean a metaphysical-cum-semantic position with the following features. First, there is no ontological vagueness: all **objects** and **properties** are perfectly precise in all respects. Second, there really are **objects** that fall under commonsense kind-categories like 'cat', 'table', 'person', and so forth. Third, there are vastly many more such **objects** than would be in conformity with ordinary counting practices. Fourth, thoughts and statements employing vague terms or concepts should normally receive a supervaluationist semantic treatment; hence truth, for vague thought/discourse, is supervaluationist supertruth—that is, truth in all permissible interpretations of the vague concepts and terms. (Likewise, falsity is supervaluationist superfalsity—i.e., falsity under all permissible interepretations.) Fifth, in the context of serious ontological inquiry, truth is direct correspondence rather than supervaluationist supertruth. Sixth, in the context of serious ontological inquiry, familiar counting-claims about ordinary objects become false; instead, the far greater multiplicity of such objects gets explicitly acknowledged.

Semantically, this position embraces a version of the distinction between direct correspondence and indirect correspondence. Indirect correspondence is the norm and is construed supervaluationally; but direct correspondence kicks in when one is doing serious metaphysics. Ontologically, this position straddles the fence in its approach to commonsense kind-categories. On one hand it claims that there really are **objects** that fall under these categories; but on the other hand it claims that these **objects** are perfectly precise, and thus are vastly more numerous than common-sensical counting practices recognize. In response to Unger's "problem of the many," this approach *embraces* the many. Whereas common sense thinks there is one cat on the mat, fence-straddling realism says that there are very many **cats** there (perhaps nondenumerably many)—and very many **mats** there too.

Although it is hard to find a fully explicit articulation and defense of fence-straddling realism, one text that can be interpreted this way is Lewis 1999—a paper about the problem of the many. Lewis writes (1999, 167):

> Cat Tibbles is alone on the mat. Tibbles has hairs $h_1, h_2, \ldots, h_{1000}$. Let c be Tibbles including all these hairs, let c_1 be Tibbles except for h_1; and similarly for $c_2, \ldots, c_{1000}$. Each of these c's is a cat. So instead of one cat on the mat, Tibbles, we have at least 1001 cats—which is absurd.... To deny that there are many cats on the mat, we must either deny that the many are cats, or else deny that the cats are many.... I think both alternatives lead to successful solutions.

The first solution is to embrace a supervaluationist semantic treatment of everyday statements about cats (including statements about how many of them there are at specific locations):

> Super-truth, with respect to a language interpreted in an imperfectly decisive way, replaces truth *simpliciter* as the goal of a cooperative speaker attempting to impart information. We can put it another way: Whatever it is that we do to determine the 'intended' interpretation of our language determines not one interpretation but a range of interpretations.... Each intended interpretation of our language puts one of the cat-candidates on the mat into the extension of the word 'cat', and excludes all the rest. Likewise each intended interpretation picks out one cat-candidate, the same one, as the referent of 'Tibbles'. Therefore it is super-true that

there is just one cat, Tibbles, on the mat. Because it is super-true, you are entitled to affirm it. (Ibid., 172–173)

The second solution is to acknowledge that all those cat-candidates are really cats, and to repudiate everyday counting-claims:

Any two of our cat-candidates overlap almost completely.... Assume our cat-candidates are genuine cats. (Set aside, for now, the supervaluationist solution.) Then, strictly speaking, the cats are many.... We have many cats, each one almost identical to all the rest.... [W]hat's true is that for some x, x is a cat on the mat, and every cat on the mat is almost identical to x. (Ibid., 177–178)

Lewis goes contextualist, suggesting that sometimes the first solution is better and sometimes the second one is, depending on context:

Sometimes, especially in our offhand and unphilosophical moments, ... the super-valuation rule ... will entitle us to say that there is only one cat. But sometimes, for instance when we have been explicitly attending to the many candidates and noting that they are equally cat-like, context will favor the ... many-cat sort of interpretation.... [W]e explicitly choose to say that the many are all cats, and we thereby make the supervaluation go away. (Ibid., 179–180)

As we say, these remarks can be interpreted as propounding a version of fence-straddling realism. So interpreted, Lewis is effectively treating the concept of truth as governed by an implicit contextual parameter. He is effectively saying that in some contexts this parameter is set for supertruth (a form of indirect correspondence), whereas in other contexts it is set for direct correspondence. He is saying that ordinary counting-statements about cats qualify as true under the supervaluationist IC standards, but are false under the DC standards that prevail in serious ontological inquiry. In the context of philosophical discussion of ontology, the statement 'There is exactly one cat on the mat' is false. Ontologically speaking, the right thing to say is that there are numerous **cats** located there (perhaps nondenumerably infinitely many), but that each is "almost identical" to all the rest.

But fence-straddling realism is not tenable, as we will now explain. (Nor need Lewis be interpreted as advocating it—a matter to which we will return presently.) To begin with, ordinary kind-categories like the kind *cat* are vague. Since ontological vagueness is impossible, there is no such **property** as **cathood**. Since there is no such **property**, no **object** can instantiate such a property. Therefore, there are not—and cannot be—any **cats**.

One might try to evade this line of thought, by arguing in the following way. Even though the kind-term 'cat' is vague (as is the concept this word expresses), nevertheless **cathood** is a real **kind**, and an ontologically *precise* one. For, an **object** falls under the category **cathood** just in case it falls under every permissible interpretation of the kind-term 'cat'. And some **objects** really do meet this condition, even though ontological vagueness is impossible.

But the trouble with this line of argument is that the boundarylessness of vagueness precludes any precise transition between items that belong to every precise interpretation of 'cat' and items that do not. Rather, the expression *belongs to every permissible interpretation of 'cat'* is vague itself. Hence, because of the impossibility of ontological vagueness, this expression does not express a **property**. Since there is no such **property**, no **object** can instantiate such a property. Therefore, there are not—and cannot be—any **cats**.

Might one perhaps hope to get a precise category of **cathood** by means of some complicated construction that somehow invokes the whole infinite metalinguistic hierarchy in which each metalanguage receives a supervaluationist semantic treatment in the next-higher metalanguage? No, for two reasons. First, as we stressed in sections 4.5.3 and 4.5.5 of chapter 4, there is a pressing need to explain why the only semantically correct way to deal with a "forced march" through a sorites sequence is to refuse to answer all the questions about the statuses of successive items in the sequence. All of those questions are perfectly meaningful, and each demands to be answered (if it gets answered at all) in the same way as was its predecessor—on pain of there being a sharp semantic transition at the given point in the sorites sequence. As we argued, the only available credible explanation for this need to "duck the forced march" is that vagueness harbors weak logical incoherence, in the form of mutually unsatisfiable semantic standards. Given such logical incoherence as an essential aspect of vagueness, no construction over the whole hierarchy of supervaluationist metalanguages can deliver any genuine, precise property of **cathood**.

Second, if there were such a precise **property**, then its very precision would effect sharp transitions in the first-order metalanguage between permissible and impermissible interpretations of 'cat', in the second-order metalanguage between permissible and impermissible interpretations of 'permissible interpretation of "permissible interpretation of 'cat'"', and so on up. Thus, the upshot would be that the word 'cat' and the concept it expresses are not really vague after all. But of course they are.[1]

So fence-straddling realism is precluded by the impossibility of onto-logical vagueness. There cannot be any such **property** as **cathood**, and hence there cannot be any such **objects** as **cats**.

Let us return to Lewis's recommended treatment of the problem of the many. Since fence-straddling realism is an untenable position, so is his ac-count *insofar as it is interpreted as an implementation of fence-straddling real-ism*. But Lewis does not explicitly put it forth that way, and it need not be so interpreted. It will be useful to see how his proposal can be situated within the framework of austere realism and contextual semantics.

Lewis is addressing a philosophical problem that arises within a mode of thought/discourse with these two features: (i) it posits a range of objects each of which is only slightly different from the others (in this case, a range of almost-identical catlike objects), and (ii) it operates in such a way that the term 'cat' is correctly applicable to some of these posited objects. Now, from the perspective of austere realism, the contextually operative seman-tic standards governing this mode of thought/discourse clearly fall under the broad rubric of IC standards—not under the rubric of DC standards. One reason why this is so is that the posited catlike objects are all still somewhat *vague*, even though they are individuated in such a way that each of them has a determinate number of hairs. (Each is still vague with respect to its synchronic composition, for instance, and with respect to its precise spatiotemporal boundaries.) Another reason is that the category *cat* is vague, which means that under DC semantic standards there would be no semantically correct, affirmatively predicative, applications of this cate-gory at all.

Philosophical problems can and do arise within modes of thought/ discourse governed by IC semantic standards. The problem of the many, in the version set forth by Lewis, is a case in point. Once those various almost-identical cat-candidates are posited, the question arises whether or not they are all cats; and other questions arise too, such as whether it is true or false that there is exactly *one* cat on the mat. Lewis proposes answers to such questions. In a nutshell, what he offers is a fine-grained contextual-ist treatment of thought/talk about cats, *all within the coarse-grained rubric of IC semantic standards*. On one hand (according to his account), everyday counting-statements about cats operate under fine-grained IC standards that are amenable to a supervaluationist semantic treatment; under these specific IC standards, such counting statements are true. On the other hand, in the mode of IC thought/discourse in which the various almost-identical catlike objects are all explicitly posited and the question of their cathood-status is explicitly posed, the contextually operative semantic standards are fine-grained IC standards under which ordinary counting-statements about cats are *false*. Under these specific IC standards, the statement "There is exactly one cat on the mat" is false; what is true is this: "For some x, x is a cat on the mat, and every cat on the mat is almost identical to x."

So, although the philosophical problem that Lewis is addressing is still genuine, given austere realism, it is not an issue of *ontology*. (As far as ontology is concerned, the right thing to say—i.e., the semantically correct thing to say under DC semantic standards, the standards that are contextually appropriate for serious ontological inquiry—is that there are no **cats** at all, and no **mats** either.) His own proposed solution is viable looking, and, as far as we can see, is entirely compatible with austere realism. It amounts to a fine-grained contextualist account of two legitimate ways of using the word 'cat' and the concept it expresses, each of which is appropriate in some contexts but not others. The two pertinent modes of usage involve fine-grained contextual variation, all taking place within the coarse-grained rubric of IC semantic standards; neither mode of usage involves DC semantic standards. Thus interpreted, his account is not an implementation of fence-straddling realism at all. And, as explained above, fence-straddling realism is ruled out by the impossibility of ontological vagueness.

5.6 Austere Realism versus Global Irrealism

Some philosophers—including Goodman (1978), Dummett (1976), Putnam (1987, 1988), and Rorty (1979, 1982)—have argued that metaphysical realism is itself a philosophical mistake. They maintain that there is no mind-independently real world at all (i.e., no **world**), and hence that truth cannot be correspondence to such a **world**.

How is austere realism, in a form that incorporates contextual semantics, preferable to such global metaphysical irrealism? We will argue that the fundamental and all-important difference between the two positions is that austere realism is intelligible, whereas global irrealism is not.

Simple realism, including the conception of truth as direct correspondence between thought/language and the world, is in many ways the naively natural view, the view seemingly embodied in everyday thought and discourse. We humans believe that many objects in our environment exist quite independently of us, our mental activity, or our discourse: trees exist unperceived; stars and galaxies existed before humans ever came on the scene; many of the subatomic particles out of which our own bodies are composed have existed since the Big Bang; and so forth. We believe, likewise, that many of our singular terms determinately denote these objects and many of our predicates determinately apply to them: expressions like 'the cactus in Terry Horgan's front yard', 'the duck swimming in the stream in front of the house owned by Matjaž Potrč', 'the Andromeda galaxy', 'is a star', and 'is a neutrino' stand in quite definite reference relations to these entities.

No plausible philosophical position can simply deny outright that there is a mind-independent, discourse-independent world, or that words stand in determinate reference relations to objects in this world and to properties instantiated by those objects. For, at the level of ordinary discourse, these claims are virtual platitudes. Rather, any philosophical position that backs away from simple realism must accommodate the statements qua platitudes—even though the position maintains that they are seriously mistaken when invoked, outside of ordinary contexts, as answers to certain philosophical and/or theoretical questions, such as philosophers' questions about ontology.

This methodological constraint creates a dilemma for the philosopher who seeks to reject simple realism. One needs to employ ordinary language to convey one's position, even though one might spice it up with specialized jargon or other related linguistic devices (such as our use of boldface words); and yet one also needs to use language in a somewhat nonstandard way, in order to explain why one repudiates the platitudes as guides to philosophers' questions. We call this conundrum *the Kantian dilemma*, because Kant faced it so vividly and explicitly in trying to articulate his own philosophical position. He acknowledged the platitudes, by allowing that cacti, ducks, stars, and the rest are "empirically real." And yet he also maintained that these objects are, in a somewhat special and philosophical sense, mind dependent: they are "transcendentally ideal." The Kantian dilemma poses a serious prima facie problem of intelligibility: since language inevitably must be strained in articulating a philosophical position distinct from simple realism, there is a constant danger of lapsing into incoherence.

So if one wants to claim that many or all of the entities people normally talk about are, in some philosophically special sense, "mind dependent" and "discourse dependent," then one takes on a heavy burden of making one's position intelligible. This burden includes (i) explaining cogently what the philosophical notion of mind-dependence and discourse-dependence comes to, (ii) motivating the claim that the objects of ordinary and scientific discourse have this status, and (iii) reconciling this claim with the platitudinous fact that in the everyday sense, many of those objects do not depend upon mind or language. Global irrealists and supporters of austere realism both face this task. The defenders of global irrealism tend not to acknowledge the burden, however. Instead they often write as though the metaphysical realists are the only philosophers who take language on holiday—a curious stance, given how initially peculiar looking is the claim that things like cacti, ducks, stars, and electrons are mind dependent and discourse dependent!

Since advocates of global irrealism repudiate **the world** entirely, they face an especially virulent form of the Kantian dilemma. Not only must they explain the special philosophical sense of mind/language dependence; they must also explain how there could possibly be entities that depend—in the relevant sense of 'depend'—upon mind and discourse, even though there allegedly does not exist anything independent of them (in that special sense). Yet prima facie, this task looks impossible. To see the problem, consider Putnam's own succinct summary of his own irrealist view:

> In short, I shall advance a view in which the mind does not simply 'copy' a world which admits of description by One True Theory. But my view is not a view in which the mind makes up the world, either (or makes it up subject to constraints imposed by 'methodological canons' and mind-independent 'sense-data'). If one must use metaphorical language, then let the metaphor be this: the mind and the world jointly make up the mind and the world. (Or, to make the metaphor even more Hegelian, the Universe makes up the Universe—with minds—collectively—playing a special role in the making up.) (Putnam 1981, xi)

We do not object in principle to the use of metaphorical language in explaining a position that repudiates metaphysical realism; metaphor may be hard to avoid, given the internal logic of such a position. But Putnam's description of his position seems unintelligible even at the metaphorical level, because the metaphors only pose again the question of how anything mind dependent could ever exist unless something mind independent also exists. How could mind and the world create themselves, if both are genuinely mind dependent? Wouldn't a mind-dependent universe require for its existence an already existing, metaphysically real **mind**, such as a Berkeleyan **mind** or a divine **mind**?

These questions indicate how far Putnam is from providing a viable solution to the Kantian dilemma, and how heavy is the burden of proof that the dilemma has any solution within the framework of global irrealism. And other current versions of global irrealism seem no better off in this respect. So unless and until that burden is discharged by Putnam or some other champion of the view, we think the reasonable course is to conclude—at least provisionally—that global irrealism is incoherent.

Of course, austere realism must address the Kantian dilemma too. But the prospects for successfully doing so, within the framework of contextual semantics, look fairly promising. Since **the world** plays an integral role within contextual semantics, austere realism's form of the Kantian dilemma does not include the impossible-looking task of explaining how absolutely everything could be mind dependent.

Platitudes about the mind-independence and discourse-independence of the objects in one's environment, for instance, are accommodated this way: these statements are indeed literally true, under the semantic standards that actually prevail in contexts of discourse where such statements usually occur. (The same goes for semantic platitudes like "The predicate 'is a cat' applies to cats"; for, metalinguistic discourse is subject to context-dependent semantic standards too; cf. section 3.3.3 of chapter 3 above, and Horgan 1986b.) The special, philosophical sense in which many objects and properties are mind dependent and discourse dependent, on the other hand, comes essentially to this: (i) numerous posit-involving claims fail to be true under DC semantic standards, and (ii) although the truth or falsity of such claims, under various contextually operative semantic standards, is normally determined by how things are with **the world** itself, the standards do not actually require that **the world** contain **entities** corresponding to the positing-apparatus employed in these claims.

To what extent do the posits of ordinary and scientific discourse turn out to be mind dependent and discourse dependent, in this philosophically special way? To a very great extent indeed, according to austere realism. For, austere realism maintains that the correct ontology must be an austere one—an ontology devoid of innumerable posits of both ordinary and scientific thought/discourse (including all vague posits).

5.7 Austere Ontology and Alternative Semantic Frameworks

There are various potential ways of wedding an austere ontology to a semantic framework other than contextual semantics. Some ways might count as alternative versions of austere realism itself: they would retain austere realism's official semantic theses (in addition to its ontological theses), but would situate austere realism within a wider semantic framework different from contextual semantics. Other ways might repudiate not only contextual semantics but also some of the official semantic theses of austere realism—while still cleaving to an austere ontology.

There might also be approaches to the concept of truth that on one hand are consistent with both the official semantic theses of austere realism and the wider framework of contextual semantics (and perhaps even fit smoothly with them), but on the other hand make additional claims about truth too. Such an approach would effectively amount to a proposed way of *implementing* austere realism and contextual semantics, rather than a competing view.

In this section we consider a range of recently influential philosophical treatments of the concept of truth, each of which could be combined with an austere ontology. We compare and contrast each of these with the package-deal position we ourselves seek to defend—a position comprising both austere realism (including both its ontological and its semantic theses) and the wider framework of contextual semantics. Our principal goal in doing so is to further bolster the case for our own view by underscoring its theoretical advantages over various other approaches. But the discussion will also further triangulate our position, by highlighting its differences from (and similarities to) others that also embrace an austere ontology.

5.7.1 Realist Neopragmatism

Epistemic reductionist theories of truth seem to exert a perennial attraction for some philosophers. Recently influential versions include Putnam's some-time contention that truth is "ideal warranted assertibility" (Putnam 1981, 1983) and Wright's some-time suggestion that truth is identical to a form of idealized warranted assertibility that he calls "superassertibility" (Wright 1987, 1992).

Fans of neopragmatism, like Putnam and Dummett, tend to wed this semantic framework to a globally irrealist metaphysical picture. But one can also envision a version of austere realism that incorporates neopragmatist ideas. Such a view, which we will call neopragmatist realism, would have the following features. First, it would retain not only all the definitive onto-logical theses of austere realism, but all its definitive semantic theses too. (Thus, it would embrace **the world**, unlike global irrealism.) Second, it would offer a construal of the distinction between direct and indirect correspondence that does not situate this distinction within the wider framework of contextual semantics. (Contextual semantics insists on an ineliminable conceptual gap, in the cases of both direct correspondence and indirect correspondence, between truth and any form of epistemic warrant.) Third, it would offer a neopragmatist, epistemically reductive ac-count of indirect correspondence. (Contextual semantics repudiates any such account.) Fourth, it would explicitly deny that direct correspondence can be given any neopragmatist account.

But neopragmatism about truth, and/or about indirect correspondence only, faces at least two very serious objections, not faced by contextual se-mantics. First, unless one idealizes all the way up to something like a "God's-eye epistemic vantage point," there will be persistent cases where truth and idealized warranted assertibility evidently diverge—for instance, (i) statements about the distant past for which no extant evidence exists one way or the other, (ii) statements about certain goings-on in distant por-tions of spacetime outside the light-cone of the human race, and so forth. Second, even if one idealizes so much that idealized warranted affirmability coincides—or necessarily coincides—with truth (given the extent of ideal-ization), it will nevertheless be the case that when a statement is ideally warrantedly affirmable, this will be *because* it is true—rather than its being true *because* it is ideally warrantedly affirmable. (This is what Wright calls "the Euthyphro contrast.") Contextual semantics does not face these problems—which constitutes a very considerable advantage of contextual semantics over epistemically reductionist accounts of truth.

Nonetheless, according to contextual semantics there is indeed an impor-tant element of truth in neopragmatism, namely this: in the case of indi-rect correspondence, often there is a comparatively small gap between what is warrantably affirmable (given available evidence) and what is true. Thus, ordinary evidential standards regulating various forms of thought/discourse often are a very instructive guide to the workings of the contextu-ally operative *IC semantic standards* governing such thought/discourse. The leading idea is that operative semantic standards are ones relative to which the evidential standards people actually employ for the pertinent form of thought/discourse are *epistemically appropriate*. These evidential standards are not, for instance, ones that are far too lax relative to the operative semantic standards. Thus, one reason why everybody is amused when the philosophy department's metaphysican asks, "Do there really exist such entities as universities and philosophy departments?," is that everybody knows well enough what counts as adequate evidence for existence-claims about such entities, and the available evidence is legion.

So it is an attractive feature of contextual semantics that IC semantic standards typically are closely intertwined with epistemic standards of warranted affirmability, even though the former are not reducible to the latter. Such intertwining is entirely to be expected: since systematic true belief is an evaluative ideal with respect to normative epistemological notions like justification and warrant, semantic standards and epistemic standards ought to "fit" one another. Warranted thoughts and statements will be ones that are *likely to be true given the available evidence*—that is, likely to be semantically correct given the available evidence. Small wonder, then, that contextually operative epistemic standards of warranted belief will be closely intertwined with contextually operative semantic standards of semantic correctness—notwithstanding the fact that one cannot reduce semantic correctness to epistemically warranted affirmability (or to some idealization of the latter).

Another, related, point to stress is that facts about contextually operative standards of epistemic warrant can be expected to be a *good guide* to contextually operative semantic standards (given the fit between them). Consider, for instance, what would need doing in order to obtain good epistemic warrant for the claim that Warner Brothers Films is owned by the Miramax Entertainment Corporation. The relevant evidential standards just do not require obtaining good evidence that there are entities, in particular, **Warner Brothers Films** or **Miramax Entertainment Corporation**, included in the furniture of the universe.

So although the conceptual gap between semantic correctness and epistemic warrant is often relatively small in the case of indirect correspondence—especially when the operative notion of epistemic warrant is idealized or "beefed up" in certain ways (as in Putnam or Wright)—the conceptual gap persists nonetheless. Our own recommended position can accommodate this fact, whereas neopragmatist realism cannot.[2]

5.7.2 Paraphrase Strategies

It has been common in philosophy to try paraphrasing claims containing posits that may be thought ontologically dubious into claims whose apparent ontological commitments look less dubious. There are various ways of trying to "paraphrase away" discourse that posits offending entities—for example, (i) offering paraphrases that just drop out the putative reference altogether (as in paraphrasing 'She has a charming smile' as 'She smiles charmingly'), or (ii) offering paraphrases that effectively identify the erstwhile offending entities with entities one considers ontologically more respectable (as in identifications of numbers with *sets* of one sort or another).

If and when plausible paraphrase strategies are available, contextual semantics certainly can take them on board. When available, they are one way of implementing the idea of indirect correspondence. The original, unparaphrased claim can be viewed as a convenient way of saying what can also be said—albeit perhaps more awkwardly and more laboriously—using discourse that avoids the problematic posits. (Whether or not the paraphrase-claim is governed by DC semantic standards, at least it eschews the offending posits. And if the paraphrase-claim is itself still governed by IC standards, perhaps it too can be given a yet further paraphrase, and so on yet again—until one reaches an ultimate paraphrase-claim that is governed by DC standards.)

But (to reiterate some themes from section 2.2 of chapter 2), there is little reason for faith in the paraphrase approach as a general strategy for avoiding dubious-looking ontological commitments. One problem is that often there are no terribly plausible candidates for paraphrasing. How, for instance, might one plausibly paraphrase the statement 'The University of Ljubljana is in Slovenia' into some statement that eschews university-talk and nation-talk? A further problem is that often, among the *marginally* eligible candidate paraphrases, there will be far too many that look *equally* (albeit marginally) eligible. For instance, there will be too many equally eligible ways to paraphrase talk about the University of Ljubljana into talk about things—or sets or mereological sums of things—like people and buildings and computers and vehicles and such.

An obvious advantage of contextual semantics, in comparison to the paraphrase approach, is that the former eliminates the *need* for systematic "paraphrasing away" of discourse involving posits that one has reason to think are not really ontological commitments of the discourse. Instead of reformulating the relevant claims in ontologically austere language, one "goes soft on truth" for the relevant discourse: one claims that the discourse operates under *indirect-correspondence* semantic standards—and that *truth*, for a discourse governed by such standards, is just semantic correctness *under* those standards. The upshot is truth without ontological commitment, and without the need for systematic paraphrasing.

5.7.3 Alethic Functionalism

In a series of recent papers, Michael Lynch has put forth and defended a functionalist treatment of truth—both the property of truth and the concept of truth.[3] He calls this view "alethic functionalism." The approach is motivated by two initial considerations. First is the prima facie appeal of what he calls alethic *pluralism*—the idea that "there is more than one way for a proposition to be true" (Lynch 2004, 384). Second is the implausibility of, and the theoretical problems encountered by, the claim that there is more than one concept and property of truth.

We will briefly summarize the main ideas of his alethic functionalism (mainly by selected quotations from Lynch 2005), and we will then make some comparative remarks about his approach vis-à-vis ours. He begins with a proposed functionalist account of what he calls the "truth-role":

> According to [alethic] functionalism, our intuitive beliefs about truth form a folk theory of truth. Some of these beliefs illustrate the connections between truth and related semantic properties, including e.g., "true propositions correspond to facts", and "the proposition that p is true if and only if p" and "a proposition is true just when its negation is false". While others relate truth to other sorts of properties, such as: "Other things being equal, it is good to believe that which is true"; and "if a proposition is justified it may not be true", and so on. Taken collectively they tell us about the truth-role, as we might put it. As it turns out, the familiar Ramsey-Lewis method can be used to specify that role, and to identify the lower-order properties that realize it. Let A be a conjunction of our intuitive beliefs about truth. Replacing all occurrences of "true" with a variable, and quantifying over this variable, we arrive at the so-called modified Ramsey sentence for A. We can then use this sentence to say what it is for a property to realize the truth-role, in the familiar way. That is,
>
> F: x has the property that plays the truth-role if and only if $\exists t_1[A(t_1 \ldots O_1 \ldots O_n) \ \& \ x \text{ has } t_1]$.
>
> This then allows us to succinctly state the conditions under which a proposition is true:
>
> FT: A proposition p is true if and only if p has a property that plays the truth-role.

Naturally enough, a proposition will be false when it is not the case that it has a property that plays the truth-role. (Lynch 2005, 30)

He points out that FT does not yet tell us what truth is. One option is to identify truth with the property that plays the truth-role:

We might, for example, follow the route paved by Lewis (1972, 1980) and others and take FT and F as actually defining the property of truth. In other words, we identify truth with the "realizer property"—with whatever property plays the truth-role. We might then take "true" as a non-rigid designator for the property that plays that role. Of course, which property does play that role may vary from domain to domain. (Ibid., 30)

But he rejects this approach, on the grounds that it threatens to end up committed to a multiplicity of different truth-properties for different domains of thought/discourse. Instead he goes this way:

The better alternative is to take truth to be the "role" property. We still take FT as telling us the conditions under which a proposition is true. But we take "true" to rigidly designate a single property, and define that property as follows:

FTP: the property of truth = the property of having a property that plays the truth-role.

That is, truth is a higher-order property of propositions. (Ibid., 31)

He proceeds to put forward this functionalist approach, not only as an account of the nature of truth itself, but also as an account of the *concept* of truth. He says, "As we might put it, our concept of truth is the concept of the property a proposition has when it *is such that it has a property that plays the truth-role*" (ibid., 32). Also, in order to address the possibility of multiple realizing properties, he modifies FT in a way intended to make the relevant realizing property depend on the specific "domain" to which a proposition p belongs:

A better way of thinking about realization ... is to see it as many psychological functionalists do: as domain or context-sensitive. That is, we hold that

FT_2: The proposition p in domain D is true IFF p has the property that plays the truth-role in D.

Here we keep the truth-role fixed across domains, but relativize realizers of that role to domains. In short, a proposition is true when it has the property that plays the truth-role for the specific domain of which it is a part, while its being false implies that it lacks that property. (Ibid., 34)

We turn now to commentary. First, Lynch's alethic functionalism is prima facie consistent with contextual semantics, and furthermore can be viewed prima facie as one potential *implemention* of contextual semantics. For, the functional definition of truth could be seen as a proposed explication of semantic correctness; and different realizations of truth could be seen as different forms of correspondence (direct, indirect, and various different fine-grained types of indirect correspondence).

Second, contextual semantics is also prima facie consistent with the *denial* of alethic functionalism. Even if alethic function is indeed one potential implementation of contextual semantics, Lynch's position does not appear to be mandated by ours.

Third, we heartily applaud the two initial desiderata that motivate Lynch's approach: (1) accommodating the idea that "there is more than one way for a proposition to be true," while also (2) repudiating the idea that there is more than one concept and property of truth. But contextual semantics *already* honors both of these desiderata without embracing alethic functionalism. Desideratum (1)—alethic pluralism—is honored, because the form of correspondence that constitutes truth, for a given thought/statement as employed in a given context, can vary considerably from one case to another. IC semantic standards, in particular, can make very different kinds of demands on the world, depending, for instance, upon whether the thought/statement is about middle-sized dry goods like tables and toasters, or about social-institutional entities like nations or corporations, or about numbers, and so forth. Desideratum (2)—avoiding a multiplicity of truth-concepts or truth-properties—is also honored: according to contextual semantics, truth is semantic correctness under contextually operative semantic standards, always and everywhere. Likewise, the concept of truth is the concept of such a property. So, one need not embrace alethic functionalism in order to meet the desiderata that Lynch puts forward as the principal motivations for the view.

Fourth, in light of the above three points of commentary, we could rest content in this book by remaining neutral about alethic functionalism. We could say that it appears to be one potential implemention of contextual semantics, and we could refrain from either embracing or repudiating this way of implementing our position.

But fifth, in fact we think there are reasons to be dubious about Lynch's position, to which we now turn. To begin with, his account is committed to the claim that for any statement S that belongs to a discourse-domain D, there is a *unique* property P that occupies the truth-role for statements in D. The account is also committed to the claim that this property P is distinct from truth itself; for, truth itself is the higher-order property of instantiating the property that fills the truth-role (for statements in D), whereas P is the lower-order property that *fills* that role. But these claims entail a very awkward conclusion: namely, that the various folk-theoretical platitudes about the property truth are not actually *satisfied* by that property! Truth fails to play the truth-role, even though the truth-role is specified by means of platitudes all of which make claims *about the role of truth*. This consequence of Lynch's alethic functionalism seems to be a very large bullet to bite, and there is no clear reason to bite it. On the contrary, contextual semantics already accommodates the very desiderata that motivate Lynch's view, as explained above. Moreover, as long as alethic functionalism is repudiated, contextual semantics can avoid the need for such bullet biting; it is entirely consistent with—and indeed fits smoothly with—the contention that folk-theoretical platitudes about truth are satisfied by the truth itself.

One might try to rescue alethic functionalism from this awkward consequence by weakening the view. Drop the requirement that there be a *unique* property that occupies the truth rule (for domain D) and replace it with the requirement that there be a unique such property *that is not higher order with respect to the truth-role*. Define truth thus:

FT$_3$: The proposition p in domain D is true iff p has the property that (1) is not higher order with respect to the truth-role, and (2) plays the truth-role in D.

Now add the claim that truth *itself* always plays the truth-role, alongside whatever non-higher-order property plays the truth-role in a given domain.

But this modified version of alethic functionalism still lacks plausibility. Why exactly should one think that the very essence of a statement's being true is that the statement has *another* property, apart from truth itself, that plays the truth-role? Even if playing the truth-role is essential to the property truth, why exactly need this same role be played by some other property too? Consider: contextual semantics identifies truth with semantic correctness; and normally, when the contextually operative semantic standards impose requirements on **the world** in order for a statement to qualify as semantically correct, semantic correctness thereby is a species of *correspondence*. According to contextual semantics, correspondence to the world is *identical* to semantic correctness, provided that the contextually operative semantic standards do constrain the ways **the world** might be in such a way that such semantic correctness is a matter of **the world** belonging to one range of ways it might be (viz., the range of truth-constituting ways) rather than another (viz., the range of falsity-constituting ways). Now, it is a folk-theoretical platitude that a statement S about the world is true just in case S corresponds to how the world is. This platitude certainly holds for truth itself, according to contextual semantics—and holds essentially. (Truth, after all, *is* correspondence, insofar as cooperation by **the world** is required for semantic correctness.) But why should it be part of the essence of truth that the platitude holds for some other property distinct from truth itself, that is, distinct from semantic correctness? (And even if the platitude does hold for some other property, why exactly should it be part of the essence of truth that the platitude only holds, relative to a discourse domain D to which the statement S belongs, for a *unique* property distinct from truth itself?)

In any case, there is yet another reason to be dubious about alethic functionalism, either as Lynch formulates it or as modified along the lines of FT_3. The guiding spirit of functionalism about truth, we take it, is that the folk-theoretical platitudes about truth fully capture its essence. Anything else about truth, beyond what these platitudes say about it, is not a matter of truth's essence, but rather is a matter of realization.[4] But we ourselves doubt that the full essence of truth—that is, semantic correctness under contextually operative semantic standards—is fully capturable by general principles *at all*, let alone by general principles all of which are folk-theoretical platitudes about truth.[5] We return to this theme in chapter 6, when we advocate semantic particularism.

5.7.4 Semantic Pretense and Error Theories

Lately there has been enthusiasm for "semantic pretense" theories of ontologically questionable thought and discourse—theories that treat such thought/discourse as being effectively a form of fiction (e.g., Walton 1990; Crimmins 1998; Woodbridge 2005). We take it that according to these views, numerous beliefs that are commonsensically held true are not really true at all—just as it is not really true that there is a person named Santa Claus who lives at the North Pole and dispenses presents at Christmas, or that there was a person named Sherlock Holmes who lived on Baker Street in London and was a brilliant sleuth. An obvious theoretical advantage of contextual semantics, in comparison to semantic pretense theories, is that the former allows us to respect the persistent belief that numerous ordinary beliefs are *literally true*, whereas semantic pretense theories do not. Contextual semantics has the same advantage over a more generic class of theories of commonsense thought and talk: *error* theories. (Semantic pretense theories, we take it, are naturally construed as a species of this wider genus.) So, given contextual semantics as an option on the menu of potential theoretical positions, fans of error theories bear a very strong burden of proof. Given that there is no apparent reason why one needs to embrace the hypothesis of radical error in order to explain how and why many commonsense beliefs are not really ontologically committed to their posits, the error theorists owe a convincing argument that one *should* embrace this hypothesis even so. We wish them well, but we would bet against them.

Why might one be attracted to an error theory in the first place? It could happen in the following way, for example. On one hand, one comes to appreciate some of the reasons for repudiating from ontology various posits of commonsense thought and talk (e.g., lightweight posits). On the other hand, one remains in the grip of simple realism's conception of truth—namely, the idea that the only kind of truth-constituting correspondence is *direct* correspondence. Combining these ideas, one concludes that much of common-sense belief and talk is radically false—even though it nonetheless remains semantically *appropriate* in some non-truth-constituting sense. Indeed, one perhaps also concludes that applying the label 'true' to such semantically appropriate falsehoods is *itself* semantically appropriate in this same way—even though such truth ascriptions are actually false too.[6]

But such a way of thinking faces serious internal tensions (over and above the fact that its radical-falsity claim is undermotivated, given contextual semantics). For, the view must acknowledge the importance and centrality of *semantic correctness*, even while denying that semantic correctness constitutes truth. (It should even acknowledge the semantic appropriateness of using the label 'true' for semantic correctness, even while continuing to deny that semantic correctness constitutes truth.) And it must also acknowledge that semantic correctness is a feature that typically is a joint product of contextually operative semantic standards plus how things are with **the world**—which means that there is a distinction between ways **the world** might be that *accord* with semantic correctness and ways **the world** might be that *do not accord* with it. Well, given that error theory must acknowledge a form of semantic correctness that exhibits all these

truth-like properties, the error theorist's own theory now raises the following question in a pressing way: *Why isn't such semantic correctness a form of
truth?* In short, the error theorist's own need for a truth-like notion of semantic correctness generates strong internal pressure toward the view that
such semantic correctness is itself a form of truth, even though it does not
involve direct referential linkages from the positing apparatus of thought/
language to **objects** and **properties** in the correct ontology. That is, there
is strong internal pressure toward giving up the dogma that truth can only
be direct correspondence. Contextual semantics, of course, does just that.

One final point. Although we would argue that these considerations
show the very considerable theoretical preferability of contextual semantics
over error theories about truth (including semantic pretense theories), nevertheless the recalcitrant fans of such theories probably could adapt much
of what we say in this book for their own purposes. They could embrace *almost* everything that contextual semantics says about semantic correctness
(including what it says about indirect correspondence as a form of semantic
correctness) *except* the contention that indirect correspondence is a form of
truth. And they could embrace a variant of austere realism that replaces
'truth' by 'semantic correctness', but is otherwise much like canonical austere realism as described in section 4.1 of chapter 4. But of course they
would do better to shake free from the grip of the direct-correspondence
conception of truth, thereby avoiding the need to embrace a hypothesis of
radical error.

5.7.5　Minimalism

Lately there has been considerable enthusiasm for one or another version
of "minimalism" or "deflationism" about truth—roughly and generically,
the view that the various instances of the Tarskian schemas T and F pretty
much exhaust all there is to the concepts of truth and falsity. (See, e.g.,
Field 1986; Horwich 1990, 1998; Soames 1999.)

One major disadvantage of minimalism/deflationism is this: although
there certainly are schema-T uses of the truth predicate, there are important
correspondence uses too. For instance, for someone who holds that the
overall content of moral judgments or statements is nondescriptive, *one*
importantly right thing to say about them with respect to truth—under
one legitimate usage of 'true'—is that *they are neither true nor false*. A significant advantage of contextual semantics over minimalism/deflationism is

that contextual semantics can smoothly accommodate *both* schema-T uses of the truth predicate and correspondence uses, for modes of discourse for which (according to nondescriptivist treatments of these modes of discourse) these uses diverge.

Here are a few aspects of how this accommodation works. (For more details, see Timmons 1999; Horgan 2001b; Horgan and Timmons 2000, 2006.) First, one may distinguish between *tight* and *nontight* contextual semantic standards. A judgment or statement is governed by *tight* semantic standards if those standards conspire with how **the world** is to render the judgment or statement semantically correct or semantically incorrect; otherwise, the semantic standards are *nontight*. Second, contextually variable semantic standards govern the truth predicate itself. Third, under one usage of 'true' that is sometimes contextually appropriate—a *correspondence* usage—a judgment or statement whose governing semantic standards are nontight counts as neither true nor false. (Horgan and Timmons claim that under this usage, *moral* judgments/statements are neither true nor false in their standard usage since normally they are governed by nontight semantic standards.) Fourth, on *another* usage of the truth predicate that is sometimes contextually appropriate, the truth predicate conforms to schema T. (Horgan and Timmons claim that on this usage, truth ascriptions to moral judgments/statements are *morally engaged* metalevel judgments/statements; they inherit the morally engaged expressivist aspects of the first-order judgments/statements to which they ascribe truth. Such a truth predication is a fusion of semantic and moral evaluation.)

Vagueness also makes trouble for standard versions of minimalism/deflationism about truth. It is extremely plausible that thought-contents and statements applying a vague category to a "borderline case" are neither true nor false. Suppose, for instance, that Jones is borderline-bald (and thus is also borderline nonbald). Then the natural thing to say about truth and falsity is that the statement 'Jones is bald' is *not true*, and also is *not false*. But the minimalist/deflationist is hard pressed to avoid reasoning in the following way:

> Suppose that 'Jones is bald' is not true. By schema T, 'Jones is bald' is true iff Jones is bald. Hence Jones is not bald. By schema F, 'Jones is bald' is false iff Jones is not bald. Hence, 'Jones is bald' is false.

But the conclusion of this reasoning seems wrong. Since Jones is a borderline case of baldness, the statement 'Jones is bald' is neither true *nor* false.

Suppose that minimalists could somehow deflect such problems. Could austere ontology perhaps be wedded to minimalism about truth, rather than being wedded to the semantic claims of austere realism and to the wider semantic framework of contextual semantics? Perhaps, but the problem is to find a theoretically satisfying way of getting the austere ontology to fit smoothly with the truth of everyday statements about the very posits that are repudiated by austere ontology. On one hand, doesn't austere ontology claim that there are no corporations or nations or tables or people? On the other hand, don't people commonly assert statements entailing that *there are* such entities, and then (via schema T) also assert of such statements that they are true? How can one have it both ways? That is, how can one have both the austere ontology and the ordinary truths? Contextual semantics addresses this question head-on and provides an answer. But it is very far from clear, to say the least, whether minimalists have the resources to answer it in a theorically satisfying way.

In this section we have briefly set forth some significant prima facie advantages of contextual semantics in comparison to a range of other approaches to truth and realism now on offer. We have stressed that under contextual semantics, semantic and epistemic normative standards are apt to be closely intertwined, even though semantic standards are not reducible to epistemic ones (or to some idealization thereof). We have also stressed the tight–nontight distinction and the way it allows for contextually variable semantic standards to govern the truth predicate itself. In particular, given a nondescriptivist treatment of moral discourse, it allows for both correspondence uses of the truth predicate and schema-T uses.

5.8 Summary

Even apart from its capacity to handle the antithesis problems confronting simple realism, austere realism has considerable theoretical motivation. It dramatically enhances the parsimony of ontology in comparison to simple realism. It lends itself much better to a tractable epistemology than does simple realism. By eschewing vague **objects** and **properties** altogether, it avoids the fatal problem encountered by layered ontologies that countenance vague **entities** at derivative ontological levels—namely, the impossibility of ontological vagueness. By repudiating any nonvague **entities** that supposedly fall under the vague categories of common sense and science, it

avoids the internal conceptual instability that plagues fence-straddling realism. It avoids the seemingly unavoidable threat of unintelligibility that
plagues global irrealism. And its semantic component—comprising theses
AS1–AS5 of chapter 4, situated within the framework of contextual
semantics—has substantial comparative advantages over various alternative approaches to truth that also call simple realism into question: realist
neopragmatism, the paraphrase program, alethic functionalism, semantic
pretense theory and error theories more generally, and minimalism/
deflationism. So, by the methodological criteria described in section 3.1 of
chapter 3, austere realism has lots going for it. Not only is it a position that
reflective common sense gets pushed toward as a result of confronting the
antithesis problems, but it also has substantial independent theoretical
appeal.

There may well be further strong arguments favoring austere ontology,
beyond those we have set forth in this book. If so, then such arguments
would also enhance the ontological-cum-semantic package deal of austere
realism. The theoretically most attractive way to reconcile austere ontology
with commonsense thought and talk is to wed it to the semantic theses
of austere realism and to the wider semantic framework of contextual
semantics.

6 | Objections to Austere Realism

In this chapter we further develop our articulation and defense of austere realism, by addressing three challenges that are likely to be raised against it. Thereby we elaborate austere realism's treatment of the antithesis problems. Briefly, the three challenges are these. First, austere realism, because it advocates austere ontology, threatens to be *grossly* contrary to common-sense beliefs about the world and/or grossly contrary to what the best science seems to tell us about the world. Austere realism, after all, denies the existence of vastly many of the entities posited in ordinary thought or talk and in scientific thought or talk. Second, our appeal to contextual variability of semantic standards faces an unhappy dilemma: the need to make a choice between (i) claiming (implausibly) that thoughts and statements that seem categorical (e.g., 'The University of Ljubljana is in Slovenia') are really implicitly relativistic and noncategorical in content, or instead (ii) claiming (again implausibly) that thought and discourse harbor extensive unnoticed semantic ambiguity (since the specific meaning of one's thoughts and statements depends so heavily, according to contextual semantics, upon implicit contextual factors). Third, skeptical doubts are apt to arise about whether an adequate general account—in terms of general, systematic, normative principles—can be given of matters like (i) indirect-correspondence semantic standards of various sorts, and (ii) the dynamics of contextual variation in semantic standards.

6.1 Methodological Remarks

Replies to natural-looking objections should be well motivated theoretically and should be independently plausible. They should not be ad hoc and should not be blatantly question-begging.

Sometimes a reply involves charging the objector with making a mistake; in giving the reply one seeks to "explain away" the presuppositions of the objection, rather than accommodating them theoretically. Such debunking replies often take the form of proffered psychological explanations, especially when directed at an objection that appeals to an intuitive judgment. The debunking account purports to explain why and how the intuitions behind the objection are apt to be generated psychologically in the course of ordinary or typical cognitive processing, even though those intuitions are mistaken.

Several methodological points should be stressed about such debunking replies. First, normally such a reply will be credible only if the alleged mistake is fairly subtle and is a natural one to make, rather than being a crude blunder. Second, the proffered explanation should be independently plausible, rather than invoking otherwise unlikely looking psychological processes merely to fend off the recalcitrant intuitive judgment underlying the objection. Third, the intuitive judgment or judgment-tendency being "explained away" need not necessarily *dissolve* intuitively if and when one accepts the proffered explanation as correct. For, in some cases the debunking account might very well explain the judgment-tendency as resulting from psychological mechanisms that are difficult or even impossible to subdue in oneself—even when one believes them to be generating mistaken judgments. Judgment-tendencies based on visual illusions like the Müller-Lyer illusion (the Brentano illusion) provide a model to bear in mind—a point that will recur below.

6.2 Commonsense Balking Reactions

Common sense balks, and balks strongly, when the claims of some austere ontology are put forward. If we say to you, "There aren't really such things as tables, chairs, or people," you are apt to react by finding such a claim preposterous—not just false, but screamingly false. That this reaction is apt to occur, and to occur with this kind of strength and intensity, is a datum—one that needs to be dealt with by an advocate of austere realism.

Austere realism does not directly accommodate the datum in a straightforward manner; that is, the position is not one that treats the balking reaction as correct and that vindicates it. Rather, on our view you are making a mistake if you reject our claim that there are no such things as tables, chairs, or people. For, as we intend our claim—namely, as one that is being made under DC semantic standards—what we are saying is *true* if indeed some austere ontology is the correct one.

As already indicated in section 6.1, we take it that one serious obligation of a philosophical theory is to give a suitably respectful treatment of intuitively plausible judgments or statements that the theory rejects—all the more so if the judgments are as intuitively plausible as are judgments like "*Of course* there really are tables, chairs, and people" (thought or said in response to our own claim that there are not really such things). Respectfulness means, inter alia, that although the judgments or statements in question get treated as embodying some kind of error, it is not a silly or stupid or merely careless error. Rather, the account will be better if the error is treated as particularly subtle, and one that people are particularly apt to make given the normal workings of their cognitive apparatus.

6.2.1 Competence-based Performance Errors

In this and the next subsection we will develop two complementary lines of thought that jointly constitute our overall proposed treatment of common sense balking reactions to the ontological claims of austere realism. Let us introduce the notion of a *competence-based performance error*. The idea is that although the cognitive system falls short of its own competence in generating the given judgment or intuition or belief, nonetheless it is producing this performance error in a way that in some sense emanates from competence. (For further discussion of this idea, with applications of it to philosophical puzzlement about the freedom/determinism issue and about the issue of mental causation, see Graham and Horgan 1994 and Horgan 2001a.)

Think, for instance, of the Müller-Lyer illusion, shown in figure 6.1. The cognitive system is working the way it is designed to, in producing a perceptual presentation of the one horizontal line as longer than the other. If

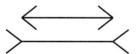

Figure 6.1
The Müller-Lyer illusion.

you form the perceptual belief that the horizontal lines are not the same length, you are committing a competence-based performance error. Your visual system is working the way it has been designed to work (although it happens here to be yielding up a visual illusion), and you are forming a mistaken perceptual belief by reliance on the presentational content of your visual experience.

There is something right and something wrong in what you are doing. The something right is that the lines really do *look* to be not the same length. Someone not knowing better would justifiably form the *belief* that they are not the same length. Something has gone wrong, though. They are in fact the same length, as can be determined by ordinary measurement techniques. You are competent to tell whether they are the same length or not; they are the same length; and yet here you are, judging them to be different in length.

It is important, too, that they are apt still to look different lengths even after the measurement has been carried out. They will still look that way even when you realize that they are actually the same length. The appearance will persist (or at least there will be a strong tendency for it to do so) even after you come to believe that it is nonveridical.

Return now to the fact that common sense balks, seriously balks, at the claims of austere ontologies. We propose to treat this as also a competence-based performance error, of a certain sort. Although it is *mistaken* to repudiate austere ontologies on commonsense grounds, in a very important sense this is a mistake that is rooted in semantic/conceptual competence itself.[1]

We now describe the basic picture in eight steps. First: As competent users of concepts and terms that are governed by various implicit contextual parameters (aspects of what Lewis called the score in the language game), people typically deal with these parameters so smoothly and competently that they do not even notice them. Witness, for example, Lewis's charming little spiel about Bruce the cat and Albert the cat (quoted in section 3.4.1 of chapter 3), in the section of Lewis 1983b in which he is illustrating how well people accommodate to the current contextually relevant score that determines which contextually eligible referent of a definite description 'the F' (e.g., 'the cat') counts as the most *salient* F (and hence as the referent of 'the F'). One accommodates to score-changes without necessarily realizing that one is doing so, and without necessarily noticing that contextual parameters are in play at all. Witness, for other examples, the other kinds of phenomena Lewis canvasses in that landmark paper, all of which he persuasively argues are ones in which implicit, contextually variable parameters of "score in the language game" are in play. Humans appear to be hugely good at scorekeeping in most ordinary contexts—so good that they do it without noticing that implicit semantic parameters are in play and that they vary.

Second: Normally when one employs certain categories, and certain terms expressing them, there is a very strong default presumption in play that the contextually operative semantic standards are ones under which certain affirmative, ontically committing thoughts and statements employing those categories will be true (i.e., semantically correct).

Third: On the view we advocate, contexts in which DC semantic standards are being employed are *extremely* rare and rareified: they are contexts of serious ontological inquiry.

Fourth: When we say to you "There are no tables, chairs, or people," there is a strong tendency for you to react to this statement as though it were being made under relatively typical contextually operative standards for categories like 'table', 'chair', and 'person'. This is partly because of the default presumption just mentioned (the second point), and partly because of the extremely rareified nature of thought/discourse that is conducted under direct-correspondence semantic standards (the third point). There is a strong tendency, that is, for you *not* to accommodate properly to the contextually operative score in the language game that governs our own remark (even though normally people accommodate to one another's remarks smoothly and naturally), and for you instead to respond to us with a remark that itself is governed by more ordinary semantic standards (IC standards) for categories like 'table', 'chair', and 'person'.

Fifth: So there is something importantly right in your balking reaction. Your claim "Of course there are tables, chairs, and people!" is certainly true, *under the contextually operative standards governing your own usage*. And your claim is also in line with the strong default presumption that a discourse in which familiar, commonly used categories are in play is governed by semantic standards in which certain affirmative claims employing those categories can turn out to be true (i.e., semantically correct).

Sixth: But even though your balking reaction is in these ways competence based, there is something importantly wrong in it nonetheless. To wit: you have failed to accommodate to the semantic standards that are contextually appropriate, given that serious ontological inquiry is the game we mean to be playing.

Seventh: Also, you fail to appreciate that implicit contextually variable semantic parameters are in play at all, and that our remark was made under a different language-game score than your own. Here, the fact that you normally accommodate to score-changes so smoothly and naturally that you do not even notice score-parameters and their variation is contributing to the mistake you are making.

Eighth: The sense of oddness and screaming falsity of claims like "There are no people" is apt to persist, even for someone who accepts (as we do) an ontology that does not include **people**. The various factors cited above explain why this should be so.

This kind of mistake is what we will call a *scorekeeping confusion*. Given the overall picture we are presenting, such scorekeeping confusions are entirely to be expected. This is because of the ways they emanate so naturally from one's own semantic/conceptual competence, including one's competence at normally handling implicit contextual parameters so smoothly and naturally that one typically does not even notice that they are there.

So the upshot is that your balking reaction is being respectfully explained away as a certain kind of competence-based performance error—a scorekeeping confusion on your part. Although this aspect of commonsense belief gets repudiated by our account rather than being vindicated, our account has the significant virtue of explaining nonetheless why such mistaken commonsense thinking occurs—and also why it will likely continue to exert a strong intuitive pull, even upon those who come to accept that the right ontology is some kind of austere ontology.

The larger upshot so far, concerning common sense, is (1) that common sense is *mostly* accommodated within austere realism (because the many posit-involving claims that common sense considers true really are true under the contextually operative IC standards in which such claims are made), and (2) that common sense's mistaken tendency to balk at austere ontological claims can be plausibly explained as a subtle kind of competence-based performance error—namely, a scorekeeping error.

6.2.2 The Psychological Persistence of Experientially Presented Posits

Although the preceding discussion goes a long way toward providing an adequate, and respectful, debunking explanation of balking reactions to the ontological claims of austere realism, there is yet more explanatory work to be done. For, common sense balking reactions seem to arise much more strongly vis-à-vis some kinds of posits of ordinary thought and discourse than vis-à-vis others. For example, the remark "There are not really such entities as corporations" seems intuitively much less odd, much less outrageous, and much less blatantly false than the remark "There are not really such entities as tables, chairs, or persons." This difference is a phenomenon that needs explaining too. But the appeal to scorekeeping confusions does not by itself appear to do the job (although this appeal might yet figure as *part* of an adequate explanation).

How then can one explain why common sense balks so much more strongly at ontological nonexistence claims about tables and chairs than at ontological nonexistence claims about socially constructed items like corporations? The account we will offer does still appeal to scorekeeping confusions; but it claims that humans are just much more prone to these very confusions concerning tables and chairs than concerning corporations. What is needed, then, is an explanation of *why* humans are differentially susceptible in this way to scorekeeping confusions.

Here it is appropriate to recall our discussion of degrees of indirect correspondence, in section 3.3.2 of chapter 3. There we emphasized that certain posits are immediately presented in perceptual experience. Some posits presumably are immediately presented perceptually even if the experiencing subject does not possess language or the kinds of concepts that typically are linguistically inculcated—for example, experience of various discrete objects in one's ambient environment as instantiating various specific shape properties, size properties, color properties, self-oriented relative position properties, and the like. Other posits presumably are immediately presented in perceptual experience only if the experiencing subject possesses a richer repertoire of concepts—for example, the concept of a table, the concept of a bank building, the concept of a basketball, and so forth.

It is a very plausible psychological hypothesis that humans will be especially prone to think of experientially presented posits as items that are mind-independently, discourse-independently real—much more prone to do so than to think of socially constructed items like corporations or nations as having this status. After all, experience immediately *presents* such items to the experiencer, and presents them as existing "out there" independently of oneself. Common sense takes the world to be as it appears to be—except for those comparatively rare circumstances in which one's perceptual system is being somehow tricked (colored glasses, optical illusions, and the like). But of course, the world appears to be composed of tables, chairs, persons, and so on—the posits that are immediately presented in experience.

Is it a *mistake* to think of experientially presented posits as mind-independently real, while allowing that socially constructed items are not? Well, no—and understanding why not will help reveal where mistakes actually arise. Since truth, for thought/talk about experientially presented posits, is a less indirect form of correspondence than is truth for thought/talk about corporations (cf. section 3.3.2 of chapter 3), there can be natural and appropriate score-settings of implicit parameters under which the contextually operative semantic standards work this way: (i) they allow a moderate degree of indirectness under which affirmative claims about experientially presented posits are semantically correct (i.e., true), but (ii) they do not allow the higher degree of indirectness that would be needed in order for affirmative claims about corporations to be semantically correct. According to austere realism, these are just the kinds of contextually operative semantic standards that prevail when someone says or thinks, "Although corporations and philosophy conferences are not mind-independently real, tables and chairs and persons certainly are." The claim being made is perfectly correct, under the contextually operative semantic standards that actually govern it. Tables, chairs, and persons are experientially *encountered*, after all, and in that sense are mind independent and discourse independent—whereas corporations and philosophy conferences are not thus encountered.

So we come now to the explanatory question at hand: Why are one's intuitive balking reactions so much stronger for claims like "There are no tables, chairs, or persons" than for claims like "There are no corporations or philosophy conferences"? Well, the very naturalness of a statement like

Although corporations and philosophy conferences are not mind-independently real, tables and chairs and persons certainly are,

together with the naturalness of the *somewhat*-ratcheted-up contextual standards under which this claim is semantically correct, tends to enhance substantially one's susceptibility to scorekeeping confusions concerning claims that are intended to be understood under DC semantic standards. It is *much* harder psychologically to back away from semantic standards under which affirmative claims about experientially presented posits are true than it is to back away from standards under which corporation-talk is true. Experientially presented posits are what one encounters most immediately in everyday experience, and what one experiences as most saliently and palpably "out there" independently of oneself. Small wonder, then, that humans are so strongly inclined to balk at ontological claims like "There are no tables or cats," thereby reacting to such claims in a way that manifests a scorekeeping confusion.

A final point deserves emphasis. Is austere realism committed to the claim that perceptual experiences are systematically nonveridical and that the world is not as it perceptually appears to be? Not at all. Rather, austere realism claims that the content of perceptual experience itself is governed by IC semantic standards. A perceptual experience is veridical just in case the contextually operative semantic standards that govern its content conspire with **the world** in such a way that the experience's intentional content is semantically correct. Perceptual experiences normally meet this requirement, and hence are normally veridical rather than illusory. As we have emphasized repeatedly, DC semantic standards operate only *very* rarely—for instance, when serious ontological inquiry is being conducted. Just as DC standards normally do not govern language and thought, likewise they do not govern the content of perceptual experience.

6.3 Contextual Variation of Semantic Standards: *Différance* in Meaning

We turn next to an objection to the idea—central to contextual semantics—that numerous terms and concepts (including the concept of truth itself) are governed by implicit, contextually variable, semantic standards. The objection is that this position confronts an untenable dilemma: implausible content-relativism on one hand, or implausible semantic ambiguity on the other. In brief, our reply will involve going between the horns of this putative dilemma.

One idea that sometimes gets invoked in connection with context dependence is that contextual factors are an implicit aspect of the very content of a thought or sentence involving such factors—so that the actual content is really relativistic content. For example, when one says that the table is flat, one really means that it is flat relative to such-and-such standards. When one says that Miramax Entertainment Corporation owns Warner Brothers Films, one is saying that *relative to such-and-such semantic standards*, Miramax Entertainment Corporation owns Warner Brothers Films.

This approach seems just wrong. The trouble is that even when contextually variable semantic parameters are in play, typically the discourse or thought governed by such parameters operates categorically: one is speaking or judging from within a semantically committed stance in which one accepts the semantic standards as operative. When one says that something holds relative to such-and-such standards, on the other hand (even if the "relative to such-and-such standards" part is implicit), one need not be accepting those standards at all. (Carnap might say to the Polish logician, for instance, "There are only three objects on the table, even though the claim that there are seven is true under the semantic standards you yourself are using.") People do sometimes talk and think in a relativistic way, but when they do so they typically employ *explicit* relativization.[2]

But if indeed discourse and thought governed by contextual parameters are normally categorical in content rather than implicitly relativistic, then the following question naturally arises: What is the semantic relation between a statement/thought that is affirmed under such-and-such contextually operative semantic standards, and one (expressed the same way) that instead is affirmed under so-and-so alternative semantic standards? A looming worry is that this contextualist approach is effectively positing massive equivocation in the use of concepts and terms that are governed by contextual parameters. Commonality of content across different uses is threatened.

Our position on this matter is as follows. According to contextual semantics (as we stressed already in chapter 3, especially section 3.5), intercontext variation in operative semantic parameters (variation in aspects of what Lewis called the "score in the language game") constitutes identity preserving change and difference in meaning and concepts. This is what we are calling *différance* in meanings and concepts (adapting Derrida's terminology), rather than what is ordinarily called "difference in meaning/concept." The idea is to think of meanings and concepts (whatever exactly they are) as items that can exhibit, from one context of usage to another, certain identity-preserving differences—much as other kinds of entities (e.g., persons) can differ in certain ways over time (e.g., in hair color).

Examples of such *différance* were given in chapter 3, including our recommended treatment of Putnam's fanciful case of Carnap and the Polish logician. For another pertinent example, consider the following two-part remark that might be made by a philosopher while discussing ontology and commonsense belief: "Are there corporations? *Of course!* Are there *really* corporations? No!"[3] One can assert both parts of this remark in close succession to one another, but not in the same breath. There is a subtle semantic variation at work across the respective uses of 'corporation' and of quantification, but not a semantic difference that constitutes anything nearly as great as ordinary semantic ambiguity (as with 'bank' as financial institution or edge of a river). The word 'corporation' has the *same* meaning when employed under different semantic standards governing the first part of the remark and the second part, even though this contextual variation is indeed a difference—it is an identity-preserving difference in meaning. Likewise for the quantificational idiom 'there are'.

Another way one might put the point is this. Certain terms, as used in two different token statements made under somewhat different settings of implicit semantic parameters, are *weakly synonymous* but not *strongly synonymous*. One can also use this terminology about the respective thought-contents expressed by the statements. Statements or thoughts that are weakly but not strongly synonymous do exhibit certain meaning or content differences, but these (again) are much less stark than ordinary semantic ambiguity—and the differing uses exhibit much more semantic commonality despite these differences.

Suppose, then, that you say "There is a table in front of me," and we reply "There are no tables." Although the respective uses of 'table', and of 'there is/are' are weakly synonymous, there does remain a semantic *différance* between these uses. Because of the variation in the contextually operative semantic standards governing the respective uses, your claim and ours do not actually contradict one another—despite the fact that you and we respectively do "mean the same thing" by 'table' and by idioms of existential quantification; that is, our usages are *weakly* synonymous. For, you make your claim under IC standards, while we make ours under DC standards. This is a *différance* in meaning, not a matter of ordinary ambiguity. Again: *différance* is a much more subtle and fine-grained form of semantic variation than are equivocation or ambiguity.

To summarize: The first horn of the putative dilemma is avoided because claims governed by specific settings of contextually variable parameters are categorical in content rather than being implicitly relativized to the parameter-settings that govern them. Although content-relativism is indeed implausible, this is not our view. The second horn of the putative dilemma is also avoided because the fine-grained semantic differences involved in different settings of contextually variable parameter-settings are identity-preserving differences in meaning and in concept rather than being instances of ordinary semantic ambiguity. Although the hypothesis of massive ambiguity is indeed implausible, we do not embrace this claim. *Différance* in meaning/concepts—that is, weak synonymy—is a much more subtle form of semantic variation than ordinary ambiguity.

6.4 Put Up or Shut Up: The Challenge to Give General Principles of Semantic Correctness

Various questions and demands are apt to be posed to us about IC semantic standards, and also about the dynamics of intracontextual determination of—and transcontextual variation in—such standards. We might get challenged to articulate *general principles* that govern semantic normativity. Unless and until we do so, a skeptic might think, we will not yet have articulated a determinate and internally coherent ontological-cum-semantical position. Arguments in favor of "the position" will be entirely premature (this skeptic will say) since no real position has even been put forward yet.

6.4.1 Vertical Systematizability, Horizontal Systematizability, and the Learnability Argument

Two kinds of challenges are apt to be posed for contextual semantics, perhaps in an attitude of skepticism about whether these challenges can be met. The first demand is for *vertical systematizability*.[4] It starts by granting (at least for the sake of the argument) the claim that truth is often indirect correspondence. But then it claims that this approach to truth will only have a chance if it complies with the following requirement:

> Give a general, systematic, exceptionless truth theory for statements that are governed by IC semantic standards—a theory that entails, for each such statement S, a cognitively surveyable formulation of S's truth condi-

tions, formulated in a way that quantifies over only ontologically "kosher" entities.

The vertical systematizability demand allows for the distinction between truth as direct correspondence and truth as indirect correspondence. But it requires there to be a truth theory, itself governed by DC standards, and thus ontologically committed to its posits, that provides for each statement S a cognitively surveyable formulation of S's truth conditions—where the only posits cited in the truth conditions are items to which the truth theory is ontologically committed. For the case of metaphysically lightweight posits, in effect this amounts to the requirement of systematic *analyses* (via the truth theory) that will provide a paraphrase of each statement S employing ontologically dubious posits in terms of an associated statement S* (viz., the statement of S's truth conditions) employing only ontologically kosher posits. Take the statement:

(C) The 1968 Arab–Israeli war lasted six days.

Assuming that the correct ontology does not include items that fall under the rubric "war" or the rubric "day," the vertical systematizability demand requires of contextual semantics that it deliver a tractable, cognitively surveyable formulation of (C)'s truth conditions that does not posit such items as wars or days. More generally, the demand is for a truth theory that systematically generates cognitively surveyable, ontologically perspicuous truth conditions for *every* statement that is governed by IC semantic standards.

A second challenge that might get posed to contextual semantics is the *horizontal systematizability* demand. If indeed there are contextually variable semantic standards, as is claimed by contextual semantics, then the task is to formulate general, exceptionless, cognitively surveyable rules governing the dynamics of such contextual variation. Such rules need not necessarily be formulated in an ontologically austere vocabulary whose only posits are items in the correct ontology. Rather, the rules might well be governed by IC standards themselves, and thus might well employ posits that are not items in the correct ontology. In the final analysis, though, the vertical systematizability demand is apt to be applied to such horizontal rules too: there should be a truth theory (perhaps in a second-order metalanguage) that systematically generates truth conditions for *these rules*—truth conditions that are cognitively surveyable and employ only ontologically kosher posits.

Those who pose such questions and demands might claim that unless and until we provide the answers being asked for, our position will not really be a full-fledged position so much as a mere skeleton of a position. They might think that the skeleton needs some meat on its bones before it will be worthy of serious consideration, and before it can even be assessed for intelligibility. Also, those who pose these questions and demands might be skeptical that principles of the kind being asked for even exist; and on that basis, they might doubt that there really is any conceptually stable, viable position about truth and ontology of the kind we have been seeking to delineate here.

Why suppose that in order for austere realism and contextual semantics to be right, there need to be general principles that horizontally systematize intracontext semantic normativity of any given kind, and yet more general horizontal principles by which specific normativity is determined within any given context and is altered across any given change in context? Likewise, why suppose that there also need to be general principles that vertically systematize all IC semantic normativity in a way that would systematically generate cognitively surveyable, ontologically austere truth conditions? Why think that there *must* be fully exceptionless general principles at work, horizontally and vertically?

One line of reasoning that is apt to come to mind appeals to the thought that without such principles, semantic normativity would be too complex and unsystematic and idiosyncratic to be learnable and masterable by humans. We will call this the *learnability argument*. The reasoning is that semantic standards for indirect correspondence must be vertically and horizontally systematizable, because otherwise they could not be internalized and mastered by humans.

Our own view (cf. Horgan 2002, Horgan and Potrč 2006a, Potrč and Strahovnik 2004b) is that (i) the kinds of demands we have mentioned probably cannot be met, but (ii) they very probably do not need to be met. We doubt very much that semantic normativity conforms to fully general principles at all—let alone to fully general principles that could be stated in an ontologically austere vocabulary. We therefore doubt very much that semantic normativity needs to conform to such principles in order to be learnable and masterable by humans. We think there is strong reason to believe that the learnability argument is seriously mistaken. Its premise is false: learnable/masterable semantic normativity need not conform to exceptionless general principles. And its conclusion is false too: the kinds of semantic normativity normally at work in human thought and discourse just do not conform to such principles; rather, the operative normativity is more subtle, more complex, and more nuanced than that.

We will use the expression 'particularist semantic normativity' for semantic normativity that cannot be fully systematized by exceptionless general principles. The use of the term 'particularist' allows for the possibility that to some extent the relevant kind of normativity can be *partially* systematized by *nonexceptionless* general principles—principles that are vague enough to allow for exceptions (whether or not these principles have explicit ceteris paribus clauses in them).[5] Such partially systematizing general principles might be at work within contextually specific forms of semantic normativity, and/or they might partially systematize the dynamics of trans-contextual variation in semantic normativity.

6.4.2   Dialectical Interlude

Before we mount a case for particularism about semantic normativity, it will be useful to pause and take stock of the dialectical state of play, between ourselves and those who would press upon us the vertical systematizability demand and/or the horizontal systematizability demand. Several points deserve emphasis.

First, suppose for the moment that any form of semantic normativity that is learnable and masterable by humans does need to conform to exceptionless general principles. (We deny this, but we are momentarily granting it for argument's sake.) This hardly means that in order to make a good philosophical case for the claim that semantic correctness is sometimes indirect correspondence, one must actually *articulate* the general principles that constitute IC semantic standards. On the contrary: we maintain that we have already provided strong evidence for the nearly ubiquitous operation of IC semantic standards in human language and thought. If indeed such standards must conform to exceptionless general principles in order to be learnable and masterable by humans, then it is a *further* philosophical task—albeit an important one—to articulate these principles. They need not be set out in advance, in order for one to possess strong grounds for the claim that IC semantic standards are prevalent.

Second, some may think that we have made no adequate sense of the idea of indirect correspondence unless and until we set forth some of

the exceptionless general principles that supposedly *constitute* such normativity. The thought seems to be something like this: "I just don't know
what you are talking about when you invoke the notion of IC semantic
standards, unless you tell me what some of those standards *are*; but standards are exceptionless principles." But of course the thought that semantic
standards are a matter of exceptionless general principles is entirely
question-begging against particularism about semantic normativity. And
in any event, you surely have *some* idea what we are talking about if you
find amusing the department metaphysician's worried queries about
whether there are really such entities as universities and philosophy
departments—and if you find intelligible (and perhaps even plausible) the
claim that because the *evidential standards* for a statement like "Mozart
wrote exactly twenty-seven piano concertos" swing free of philosophical
theories about the ontological character of musical works of art, the default
contextual *truth conditions* for this statement do not require the right ontology to contain entities falling under the category 'piano concerto'.

Third, it is important to appreciate that the preceding two points together undercut the contention that we must "put up or shut up." We
have *already* made a case in this book for the claim that in very many contexts of thought and discourse, truth is indirect correspondence rather than
direct correspondence. The intelligibility of this claim, and the strength of
the case we have made for it, are not put in jeopardy by the fact that we
have not here articulated exceptionless general principles that systematize,
vertically and/or horizontally, the workings of IC semantic normativity. If
indeed there are such principles, then articulating them is indeed an important theoretical task. But it is not a task that must already have been accomplished in order for contextual semantics to be intelligible or in order
for there to be strong evidence supporting it. On the contrary.

Fourth, the demand for vertical systematizability is certainly one we will
repudiate, since it effectively requires cognitively surveyable paraphrases of
statements governed by IC semantic standards via paraphrasing statements,
in a metalanguage, that are governed by DC semantic standards. We have
already made it clear that we think such paraphrases are not in general
available; indeed, this is one of the motivations for contextual semantics.

Fifth, lying behind the demand for vertical systematizability might be
the supposition that in order for austere realism and contextual semantics
to be viable, this package-deal philosophical position needs to be formu-

lable in its entirety within a mode of theoretical discourse that is governed by DC standards. The thought behind the demand seems to be something like this: "In order to make good on your theoretical claim that certain first-order forms of discourse are not ontologically committed to their posits, you need to tell us—in ontologically committal language—what the conditions are under which such a first-order statement is semantically correct." But we repudiate that thought. We have already pointed out, in section 4.5.4 of chapter 4, that our theoretical treatment of vagueness employs vague terms itself—and hence is an account that is given within a form of theoretical discourse that is governed by IC semantic standards. The same point applies here: our theoretical treatment of semantic normativity is given within a form of theoretical discourse that itself is governed by IC semantic standards. Contextual semantics does *not* seek to say, in direct-correspondence terms, what are the conditions under which a first-order statement governed by IC standards is semantically correct. On the contrary, contextual semantics maintains that in general this cannot be done.

The conception of philosophical theorizing that goes with austere realism and contextual semantics is this. One inquires about the nature of language–**world** and thought–**world** relations from within a theoretical framework that largely employs words and concepts that are vague. (Notions like *semantic correctness*, for example, are surely vague.) The overall philosophical theoretical account no more needs to be formulated under DC semantic standards than do scientific theories. The philosophical account can, and does, provide the sought-for theoretical illumination without having to meet such an exacting standard. To be sure, one can and does occasionally shift into DC discourse when making overtly ontological claims—for example, when one claims that there are no vague **objects** or **properties**. But this hardly means that one's *total* ontological-cum-semantic philosophical theory needs to be couched in purely DC discourse. (We do recognize the need to secure the ontological foundations of the total theory, however—a matter we take up in chapter 7.)

Sixth, we acknowledge that the learnability argument has considerable prima facie plausibility. We will shortly argue, however, in support of particularism concerning the semantic normativity that is operative in actual human thought and discourse. The considerations favoring particularism will also tell *against* the learnability argument, even though they will not themselves explain why and how humans could be capable of mastering forms of normativity that fail to be systematizable by exceptionless general principles.

Seventh, one does not need to have such an explanation in hand in order to have good evidence that humans are *somehow* capable of mastering particularistic kinds of normativity. Thus, addressing that explanatory question is not an inherent part of our dialectical burden in this book. But we will do so anyway—because we have something to say about the matter, and because we think that our remarks will further bolster the case for semantic particularism.

The remainder of section 6.4 will proceed as follows. We will set forth two complementary lines of argument in favor of semantic particularism (sections 6.4.3 and 6.4.4). We will then describe the conception of semantic competence that fits particularism, with an emphasis on the ways this competence operates in the absence of general normative principles answering either to the vertical systematizability demand or to the horizontal systematizability demand (sections 6.4.5 and 6.4.6). Then, invoking ideas from Horgan and Tienson 1996, in section 6.5 we will discuss how cognitive science potentially might explain particularistic semantic competence.

6.4.3   An Argument for Semantic Particularism: Commonsense Compositional Judgments

One powerful-looking line of argument for the claim that semantic normativity does not in fact conform to exceptionless general principles can be extracted from van Inwagen's investigation of the Special Composition Question (the SCQ). If there are exceptionless general semantic principles conformed to by the semantic normativity normally at work in commonsense thought and discourse, then these principles presumably ought to generate some kind of exceptionless general answer to the SCQ—an answer that also nicely systematizes people's various commonsense judgments about whether or not, in various specific cases, a bunch of things jointly compose a whole thing. But the apparent lesson of van Inwagen's careful investigation of the SCQ is that *commonsense judgments about composition do not conform to any such general principle.* (That is why one gets driven to an austere ontology, insofar as one seeks a systematic general answer to the SCQ.) Rather, commonsense judgments about object composition are something of an unsystematic hodgepodge—which presumably means

that the semantic-normative standards these commonsense judgments reflect are also an unsystematic hodgepodge—which presumably means, in
turn, that as far as object-composition judgments and statements in ordinary contexts are concerned, *semantic normativity does not conform to exceptionless general principles.*

The point can perhaps be generalized. If the semantic standards governing ordinary thought and talk about object composition do not conform to
exceptionless general principles, then there is no clear reason why other
aspects of semantic normativity should do so either. If humans can learn
and master semantic standards for object-composition claims that outstrip
the kind of principle-based systematizability invoked by fans of the learnability argument, then there is no clear reason why humans couldn't also
learn and master numerous other aspects of semantic normativity that
also defy principle-based systematizability.

The point *should* be generalized, we maintain. We turn next to another
argument for semantic particularism, which reveals why.

6.4.4   A Second Argument for Semantic Particularism: The Relevance Problem in Computational Cognitive Science

There are reasons to believe that the conception of human cognition advocated by the classical theoretical framework in cognitive science—briefly,
cognition as *computation*—is seriously mistaken. These reasons involve
what is known as the *relevance* problem in cognitive science, also sometimes called the "frame problem" (in a broad sense of this expression).
Here we will briefly summarize the case against the computational theory
of mind, which is articulated at greater length elsewhere.[6] We will then
argue that considerations very similar to those that tell against the computational theory of mind also tell against vertical and/or horizontal systematizability of semantic normativity in terms of exceptionless general
normative principles.

There has been a persistent pattern of failure in computational cognitive
science to generate plausible models of what Jerry Fodor (1983) calls "central" cognitive processes—processes like (i) the rational generation of new
beliefs on the basis of prior background information plus newly acquired
sensory information, and (ii) rational planning. As Fodor has persuasively
argued for quite a long time—for example, in the late parts of Fodor 1983
and more recently in Fodor 2001—and as was argued at some length (in

elaboration of Fodor's argument) by Horgan and Tienson (1996), there is good reason to believe that the problems with attempts to computationally model such central cognitive processes are *in-principle* problems. These problems involve the fact that the pertinent kind of information processing normally needs to be highly holistic in nature, potentially drawing upon virtually any item of information the cognitive system might possess, and sometimes (e.g., in making comparative-simplicity assessments of particular hypotheses) drawing upon highly holistic features of large bodies of information (e.g., large bodies of information relative to which the given hypotheses are effectively being assessed for relative simplicity). These two aspects of the holism of central cognitive processes are what Fodor (1983) calls the *isotropic* and *Quinean* features, respectively. It bears emphasis that they are also aspects of the holism of reasons—specifically, nondemonstrative reasons in support of specific beliefs and/or specific plans of action.

Fodor (2001) continues to press these points. Here is his bleak assessment of the current situation of artificial intelligence and the computational theory of mind. (He here uses the phrase "context sensitivity" to refer to the holistic relevance of information internal to the cognitive system, rather than to features of the cognitive agent's environmental–social context.)

> The failure of artificial intelligence to produce successful simulations of routine commonsense cognitive competence is notorious, not to say scandalous. We still don't have the fabled machine that can make breakfast without burning down the house; or the one that can translate everyday English into everyday Italian; or the one that can summarize texts; or even the one that can learn anything much except statistical generalizations.... It does seem to me that there's a pattern to the failures. Because of the context sensitivity of many parameters of quotidian abductive inferences, there is typically no way to delimit a priori the considerations that may be relevant to assessing them. In fact, there's a familiar dilemma: Reliable abduction may require, in the limit, that the whole background of epistemic commitments be somehow brought to bear in planning and belief fixation. But feasible abduction requires, in practice, that not more than a small subset of even the relevant background beliefs is actually consulted. How to make abductive inferences that are both reliable and feasible is what they call in AI the frame problem.... In the general case, it appears that the properties of a representation that determine its causal-cum-inferential role, though they may be exhaustively syntactic, needn't be either local or insensitive to context. As things now stand, Classical architectures know of no reliable way to recognize such properties short of exhaustive searches of the background of epistemic commitments. I think *that's* why our robots don't work. (Fodor 2001, 37–38)

What Fodor calls the "frame problem," using this expression broadly, is what we are calling the relevance problem—namely, the problem of accommodating the holistic relevance of background information possessed by the cognitive agent. Briefly, it is the problem of understanding how human cognition manages to quickly and efficiently accomplish cognitive-state transitions that are suitably sensitive to enormous amounts of relevant background information—and to do so without first searching for all that information and then explicitly representing it all in one's "central processing unit" during cognitive processing. This appears to be an in-principle problem for the computational theory of mind. Fodor's considered conclusion is this:

> Computational nativism is clearly the best theory of the cognitive mind that anyone has thought of so far (vastly better than, for example, the associationistic empiricism that is the main alternative); and there may indeed be aspects of cognition about which computational nativism has got the story more or less right. But it's nonetheless quite plausible that computational nativism is, in large part, not true. (Ibid., 3)

What seems needed is a fundamentally different theory of the cognitive mind, in place of the computational theory of mind. Fodor evidently thinks so, and we think so too. (We discuss what such a replacement might look like in section 6.5 below.)

Horgan and Tienson (1996) argue that the problem plaguing attempts to produce computational models of central cognitive processes lies with the assumption that the relevant sort of holistically information-sensitive processing is *computation* over representations—that is, the assumption that such processing conforms to *exceptionless rules* of symbol manipulation, rules expressible as a computer program. The moral of the relevance problem, Horgan and Tienson argue, is competent and content-appropriate cognitive-state transitions too subtle and too complex to conform to exceptionless general rules—especially insofar as cognition accommodates holistic aspects of background information. Central cognitive processes are too holistically complex to be a matter of computation (i.e., rule-governed symbol manipulation) over mental representations. This means that cognitively competent cognitive-state transitions will be, at best, only partially systematizable, via certain inherently exception-ridden generalizations with built-in ceteris paribus clauses—the kind of generalizations that Horgan and Tienson call *soft laws*. Such soft laws are not—and cannot be refined into—exceptionless algorithmic rules. Nor can they be refined into general rules that are exceptionless apart from cognition-external factors (e.g., having a stroke or being hit by a bus).

But if indeed relevance-accommodating human cognition (e.g., belief updating) is too complex to conform to exceptionless general rules, then presumably so too are the normative standards for appropriateness of cognitive-state transitions. In particular, epistemic normativity will fail to conform to exceptionless general rules—since such rules, if they did exist, could presumably generate exceptionless, programmable rules for forming and updating beliefs. Likewise, semantic normativity governing indirect correspondence presumably will fail to conform to exceptionless general rules too—since contextually appropriate settings of contextually variable semantic parameters will often depend heavily on isotropic and Quinean aspects of holistic background information. To a very great extent, the same kinds of holistically information-sensitive cognitive processing that are needed for intelligent belief formation and intelligent planning are also needed in the intelligent deployment of concepts and terms under contextually appropriate semantic standards, and in the intelligent (if implicit) appreciation of which semantic standards are themselves appropriate in various contexts of thought/language one might find oneself in. For, to a very great extent, semantic appropriateness *itself* is apt to be particularistically dependent on holistic elements of the cognitive agent's total situation. More on this theme presently.

So, because contextually appropriate settings of contextually variable semantic parameters typically are sensitive to relevant holistic background information, the semantic normativity governing indirect correspondence very likely just does not conform to exceptionless general principles. It is more subtle, more complex, and more nuanced than that. The semantic normativity that governs indirect correspondence is normally particularistic in nature, rather than conforming to exceptionless general rules (either vertical or horizontal).

6.4.5 Semantic Normativity and Semantic Competence without Vertical Systematizability

We turn now to further articulation of both the particularist conception of semantic normativity and the accompanying picture of human cognitive competence vis-à-vis such normativity. We will focus in the present section on how the vertical systematicity demand gets transcended by semantic normativity and semantic competence, and in section 6.4.6 on how the horizontal systematicity demand gets transcended.

Statements governed by IC standards, we claim, just need not—and very probably *do* not—have short, sweet, cognitively surveyable truth conditions formulable in an ontologically austere vocabulary that quantifies over only "kosher" entities. (In effect, such formulations of truth conditions would constitute reductive paraphrases of just the kind that are unlikely to be forthcoming.) Still less do statements governed by IC standards conform to highly general, exceptionless, semantic principles that constitute a truth theory of the kind called for by the vertical-systematizability demand—a truth theory that entails, as instantiations, a reductive formulation of truth conditions for each object-language statement governed by IC semantic standards. The contextually operative semantic standards governing indirect correspondence simply need not—and very probably do not—conform to a reductive truth-theory of the kind demanded. Humans can, and do, master the semantic standards despite the nonexistence of such a truth theory.

Well then, what is actually required by way of cognitive competence in order for humans to learn and master indirect-correspondence semantic standards? Basically, this: humans should be reasonably good at tracking and judging context-specific semantic correctness, modulo available evidence. And humans are indeed quite good at doing so, modulo available evidence. In the first instance, they are good at forming judgments about when various claims are epistemically *warranted* (under contextually operative semantic standards), given the available evidence. And thus, to the extent that the available evidence is not misleading, they thereby are quite good at forming judgments about when various claims are *true* (i.e., semantically correct, under contextually operative standards).

This is a subtle cognitive *skill*—too subtle to conform to programmable general rules of the kind envisioned in computational cognitive science, because the underlying semantic normativity is itself too subtle to conform to the kind of truth theory envisioned by the vertical-systematizability demand. We will call this skill *particularistic projection*—the idea being that someone who has mastered the relevant semantic normativity is able to project appropriately from previous contextually appropriate indirect-correspondence uses of concepts and terms to new such uses, even though there are no exceptionless general principles guiding such projection. (In section 6.5 we will briefly characterize a nonclassical framework for cognitive science, described at some length in Horgan and Tienson 1996, that provides the general outlines of a positive, noncomputational, scientific approach to human cognition that has promise for explaining how such a particularistic skill might be within the capacity of humans.)

Holistic aspects of relevance figure importantly in the semantic normativity that governs context-specific semantic correctness. For example, point-and-purpose factors that lie behind specific uses of concepts and language, in specific circumstances, figure importantly in determining the contextually appropriate settings of semantic parameters. Furthermore, the determination of such settings normally will depend on how such factors link up, in holistic Quinean–isotropic ways, to a ramified body of relevant background information. In order to illustrate this point, it is useful to envision someone who is somewhat deficient in the capacity for particularist projection, who we will call a *category klutz*—someone who is susceptible to what Gilbert Ryle famously called "category mistakes."[7] Such a person, unlike normal humans, does not fully master the typical contextual parameters governing semantically correct use of various concepts.

Take, for example, the concept of a *philosophy conference*. The category klutz might say, for instance: "Where is this philosophy conference you were telling me about? All I see is people talking and interacting in meeting rooms and restaurants, discussing philosophy. I don't see, over and above these people, rooms, restaurants, etc., some further thing—some item that is the thing you are referring to with the expression 'the 2005 Bled Philosophy Conference'. There is no conference here."

Variations on the category-klutz construct can be used to illustrate a whole range of linguistic/conceptual practices that normal humans skillfully master over a variety of cases, in the course of exercising their holistically relevance-sensitive capacity for particularistic projection. We will return to this theme below.

Taking into account lessons to be learned from the relevance problem in computational cognitive science, and what we said about practices of skillfully mastering discursive/conceptual engagements that are holistically dependent on the rich, structured, cognitive background in ways so puzzling for the category klutz, it is very unlikely that semantic normative standards would conform to the vertical systematizability demand. They seem rather to be particularistic. Human judgment-forming processes manage to track this holistic normativity reasonably well (modulo available evidence), via exercise of the skill we are calling particularistic projection.

6.4.6 Semantic Normativity and Semantic Competence without Horizontal Systematizability

Various point-and-purpose factors are normally behind contextually appropriate semantic standards, and behind contextually appropriate variation of such standards. Such factors are often linked to a highly ramified structure of relevant background information—for instance, information about an extensive body of interconnected social practices and social institutional structures. Because of the richness of this background, and because of its Quinean–isotropic holistic relevance to context-specific uses of language and concepts, it is most unlikely that the dynamics of contextual determination and transcontextual variation in semantic parameters conforms to any set of exceptionless general normative principles. That is, it is most unlikely that the demand for horizontal systematizability can be met—or needs to be met—in order for humans to master the normativity that governs such contextual dynamics.

It is also plausible, however, that there are certain *soft* general principles that govern contextual dynamics—the synchronic score in the language game and diachronic changes of score. Such generalizations would contain ineliminable ceteris paribus clauses, and hence would partially—but not completely—systematize normative appropriateness of scores and score-changes. They would have normative authority, rather than being mere statistical summaries of bodies of particular normative fact—and hence would provide some degree of generalist rationale for specific score-settings and score-changes. Nonetheless, they would leave lots of "slack" to be taken up by cognitively competent semantic judgment that does not conform to algorithmic rules—for instance, judgment about whether or not *cetera* are *pariba* in a specific circumstance, vis-à-vis a given soft general principle (so that the principle applies, in the circumstance), and judgment about whether or not a specific circumstance falls under a category that figures in a given soft principle.

A position claiming that a given form of normativity conforms to such soft generalizations, but not to exceptionless ones, can be called *softly generalist particularism*. Although particularistic judgment plays a critical and ineliminable role, so too do (soft) general principles that carry normative authority. *Extreme* particularism about some form of normativity, by contrast, would claim that it conforms to no normatively authoritative generalizations at all, not even soft ones. Softly generalist particularism about normativity is well worthy of the label "particularism," we maintain, because of both (1) its emphasis on the failure of such normativity to be fully systematizable by exceptionless, authoritative generalizations (such systematizability being the hallmark of traditional generalist aspirations in theorizing about normativity), and (2) its emphasis on the ineliminable need for particularist moral judgment, for instance in determining whether or not a soft generalization applies in a given circumstance and (if so) in determining how best to apply it.[8]

As an example of a normatively authoritative soft horizontal generalization about the dynamics of score, consider Lewis's *rule of accommodation for presupposition*, which he formulates as follows:

> If at time *t* something is said that requires presupposition *P* to be acceptable, and if *P* is not presupposed just before *t*, then—*ceteris paribus* and within certain limits—presupposition *P* comes into existence at *t*. (Lewis 1983b, 234)

This rule is overtly soft, by virtue of its ceteris paribus clause. It is normatively authoritative since it provides a rationale for the kind of accommodation it prescribes. Yet, accommodation in accordance with the rule clearly requires particularistic skill—even though humans are so good at exercising such skill that often they do not even notice the implicit contextual parameters (in this case, presuppositions) at work, or the dynamic changes in such parameters that occur in the course of a well-run conversation, or their own accommodations to such changes. In the case of the rule of accommodation for presupposition, for instance, particularistic skill is needed to ascertain whether or not a given proposition *P* really is a required presupposition in order for what was just said to be acceptable; in light of the Quinean and isotropic aspects of the holism of relevance, there is no reason to expect there to be rules for how to do *that*. In addition, particularistic skill is also required to ascertain whether or not allowing *P* to become hereafter a presupposition in the conversation would fall *within appropriate limits* for accommodation—again, something that often will involve Quinean and isotropic aspects of the holism of relevance.

To thematize such particularistic skill in action, it is useful to resort again to our hypothetical friend the category klutz—who we will call Karl. Suppose, for instance, that Karl and his friend have just checked into the conference hotel in Bled, and as they were checking in they overheard the clerk inform a guest that the hotel does not allow children. A few minutes later Karl's conversation partner says this, as the conversation partner peers from the hotel window out onto Lake Bled and the surrounding mountains: "It is so beautiful and peaceful here. Another thing I like about it is that there are no children here." To this Karl replies: "What do you mean? Of course there are children here. I saw some children playing in the park just a block away from our hotel." Karl has failed to accommodate properly, vis-à-vis a contextual presupposition-parameter governing the operative scope of the term 'here'; he has failed to realize that this parameter shifted, midway through his conversation partner's remarks, from referring to Bled and surroundings to referring to the interior of the hotel. Klutzy, yes—but this mistake helps one see how subtle and complex are the cognitive aspects of accommodation, even though humans are so good at it that typically they do not even notice they are doing it.

The skill of particularist projection, already at work in fairly mundane cases like ascertaining the contextually appropriate presuppositions governing the use of indexicals like 'here', also is operative with respect to the myriad of ways that various kinds of thought and discourse can correspond indirectly to the world. On this matter, the following remarks of Jonathan Dancy (2004, 196) seem eminently applicable:

> To know the meaning of the term, then, is to be a competent judge of how to project it.... To know the meaning of the term is to know the *sorts* of semantic contribution that the term can make to a larger context, and to have a general understanding of what *sorts* of context are those in which it will make this or that *sort* of contribution.... But if the meaning of the term consists in an open-ended *range* of available *sorts* of contribution in this way, it is essentially inarticulable. Competence with it will therefore have to consist in a kind of *skill*....

Projection consists in applying to the current situation a competence that stems from mastering a wider holistic net of possible contributions. Just consider what is required to comprehend the meaning of the following statement:

(N) NATO conducted a massive bombing campaign against Serbia.

In order to grasp the meaning of (N), one first has to possess an implicit mastery of the typical semantical workings of metaphysically lightweight posits such as NATO. This is a complex accommodation skill in itself, involving as it does the Quinean and isotropic holistic relevance of an enormous and highly ramified background of interconnected concepts and the various purposes for which they are typically employed—war, nation, international organization, form of government, oppression, and so on, and so forth. The accommodation usually happens effortlessly. But suppose that Karl the category klutz, hearing (N), says: "I understand that soldiers dropped bombs. And there were military personnel around, together with their leaders, following orders from still higher leaders in distant locations. But where the heck is this NATO? I did not see NATO dropping bombs. People, not NATO, fly airplanes. What is the 'Organization'?" The case of (N) offers an interacting range of concepts, such as government, nation, and political conflict. You do not master one without mastering many of these social constructs, and you do not correctly apply one without deploying particularistic projection in a way that suitably reflects the Quinean and isotropic relevance of others within the whole interconnected network.

Plausibly, such particularistic projection operates in human cognition via psychological processes that are too subtle and complex to conform to exceptionless, general, programmable rules. And plausibly, the need for such noncomputational, nonalgorithmic, *psychological* processes reflects the fact that *normative* semantic standards governing indirect correspondence are themselves too subtle and complex—largely because of the Quinean and isotropic aspects of the holism of reasons—to conform to exceptionless general normative principles (either vertical or horizontal). It does seem likely, though, that IC standards nonetheless do conform to certain soft horizontal generalizations with normative authority, such as Lewis's rule of accommodation for presupposition. Softly generalist particularism is still full-fledged particularism, both because of its repudiation of exceptionless normative generalizations and because of its emphasis on the skill of particularistic projection.

According to softly generalist particularism about semantic normativity, there do not exist general and exceptionless horizontal semantic rules dictating the intracontext import of the contextually operative settings of contextually variable implicit semantic parameters, and there do not also exist general and exceptionless horizontal semantic rules governing how such parameters get set in a context and how they change across contexts. And human semantic mastery does not require that there be such principles. What is needed, rather, is that a cognitively competent agent possesses a level of skill in particularistic projection that tracks reasonably well both

(i) contextually appropriate settings of implicit semantic parameters, and (ii) the effects of such parameter settings on semantic correctness of whole statements and thought-contents. Softly general principles may well be operative, but they are ineliminably soft, and hence do not obviate the need for particularistic projection.

6.5 Dynamical Cognition and Semantic Particularism

In defending particularism about semantic normativity, we have claimed that human cognition is too subtle and too complex to conform to exceptionless programmable rules. But if the mind doesn't work that way—namely, via the computational manipulation of mental representations—then how *does* it work? More generally, how is it even *possible* for physical systems like human brains to appropriately accommodate, and appropriately bring to bear, vast amounts of contextually relevant background information in the course of cognitive processing? If indeed the task is not—and cannot be—accomplished via computation over mental representations, this means that the relevant cognitive-state transitions are not tractably computable. So we have the following "How Possibly?" question:

> HP: How is it possible for physical-state transitions in a human brain, or in a brain-like neural network, both (1) to systematically subserve cognitive-state transitions that do not conform to a tractably computable transition function, and (2) to do so in a way that automatically accommodates vast amounts of relevant background information that does not get explicitly represented during processing?

In this section we briefly explain the answer to this question that is proposed by Horgan and Tienson (1996), which appeals to what they call the *dynamical cognition framework* for cognitive science (for short, the DCF).[9] (See also Potrč 1993, 1999b, 2004a.) Our aim in doing so is to fend off the worry that no intelligible positive picture of noncomputational cognitive processing is even possible—and thereby to bolster our case for semantic particularism. (This section can be skipped without loss of continuity.)

6.5.1 Connectionism and Dynamical Systems: The Nickel Tour

Can connectionism perhaps illuminate this question? Fodor, as is well known, is a philosophical arch-enemy of connectionism. In essence, this is because he sees connectionism as a return to associationistic empiricism, and because he construes connectionist networks as essentially mere devices for computing statistical inferences. Associative/statistical processing, he maintains, just cannot capture the systematic semantic coherence of rational thought.

We agree with Fodor's pessimistic assessments of both "computational nativism" and "associationistic empiricism." We also agree with Fodor that many extant connectionist models do indeed appear to engage in associative-statistical information processing, and hence are not likely to scale up from "toy" cognitive tasks to tasks like real-life belief-formation or real-life action-planning. In our view, what is evidently needed is a fundamentally *new* foundational approach to cognitive architecture.

Unlike Fodor, however, we believe that there are ideas to be found in connectionism that potentially point the way forward, toward an approach to cognition that is indeed fundamentally new and different. This nonclassical framework for cognitive science, the dynamical cognition framework (DCF), repudiates the idea that cognition is always computation over mental representations. (It does not repudiate the idea that mental representations are language-like, although its approach to representational compositionality is very different from the classicist approach.)

The DCF is inspired partially by connectionism and partially by the persistence of the problem of relevance within classical computational cognitive science. The DCF treats cognition in terms of the mathematics of dynamical systems: total occurrent cognitive states are mathematically–structurally realized as points in a high-dimensional dynamical system, and these mathematical points are physically realized by total-activation states of a neural network with specific connection weights. The framework repudiates the classicist assumption that cognitive-state transitions conform to a tractably computable transition function over cognitive states.

We will explain how the DCF makes conceptual space for the possibility of systematically content-sensitive cognitive-state transitions that (i) automatically accommodate lots of relevant information without explicitly representing it during cognitive processing, and (ii) are too subtle to conform to any tractably computable cognitive transition function. First we provide a brief sketch of some key salient features of the DCF. Then we describe an overall answer to the HP question that arises within the DCF—an answer that we think should be taken very seriously within cognitive science.

To characterize a physical device mathematically as a *dynamical system* is to describe mathematically its full behavioral *potentiality profile*—its full profile of potential temporal evolutions from one total physical state to another. Each separate magnitude that is a component of the physical device's total physical state, at any time, is assigned a separate mathematical dimension in the dynamical system's state space. Each potential total physical state of the physical device is thus mathematically represented as a point in the state space. Think now of an n-dimensional state-space as an n-dimensional surface, topologically "molded" in $n+1$ dimensional space in such a way that the steepest descent "downhill" on the surface corresponds to the way the physical device would evolve through time from any initial total physical state (as represented by a point on the landscape) to successive subsequent states (as represented by successive points on the steepest-descent downhill trajectory). This high dimensional "temporal landscape" is the dynamical system describing all the potential temporal evolutions of the physical device, from any initial physical state it might be in to subsequent physical states.

For an n-node neural network with fixed weights on its connections, the network's physical potentiality-profile is naturally describable mathematically via a dynamical system that is an "activation-landscape": an n-dimensional surface oriented horizontally in $n+1$ dimensional space (with a separate dimension in this surface corresponding to each node of the network), with "downhill" being the direction of time.

For a *self-modifying* physical device that contains a neural network with n nodes and m internode connections, and that also contains internal mechanisms that somehow alter connection strengths diachronically—that is, a physical device that automatically and internally modifies the weights of its own weighted connections—a dynamical system describing the device's physical potentiality profile would be an $n+m$ dimensional "weight/ activation landscape" oriented horizontally in $(n+m)+1$ dimensional space, with "downhill" on the landscape again being the direction of time.

A fact that needs stressing is that high-dimensional dynamical systems can have enormously complex, and exquisitely subtle, mathematical structure—especially if elements of *nonlinearity* are at work in the physical devices these dynamical systems describe. (Connectionist networks employ nonlinear activation functions: the new activation of a node is a nonlinear function of the node's current activation and its current inputs.) This mathematical structure corresponds physically not to the *intrinsic* physical structure of either the physical device or the physical states of the device, but rather to the device's overall pattern of *physical dispositions*—its full profile of potential temporal evolutions from one physical state to another. One important idea that emerges from connectionism is that this very mathematical structure—the structure of the physical device's physical potentiality-profile—can be exploited in nature's evolutionary design of cognitive architecture. Classical computational cognitive science, on the other hand, looks elsewhere for the kind of structure that it seeks to exploit in cognitive architecture—namely, to the *intrinsic* structure of the physical device, and/or to the intrinsic structure of current internal states of the device. This difference from classicism is important because of the much greater structural richness that can be exhibited by a physical device's physical potentiality-profile—the structure describable mathematically by the corresponding high-dimensional dynamical system. If that structure can be suitably exploited in the design of a cognitive engine—and if it does get exploited in nature's design of human cognizers—then this may help get past the limitations of classicism.

Explicit representations in a connectionist network are *activation patterns* over the network's nodes. The total occurrent cognitive state subserved by a network at a time (for short, the TCS) is realized *mathematically* by a point on the network's high-dimensional activation landscape; and this point, in turn, is realized *physically* by a total activation state of the network itself. Different cognitive components of a TCS need not be separately physically realized by activations over different nodes of the network; rather, every potential cognitive state—no matter how simple or complex in its overall representational content—might be physically realized by a fully distributed activation pattern.

Trained-up connectionist networks typically do information processing in a way that implicitly accommodates certain background information without explicitly representing it during the course of processing— information that is "in the weights," as connectionists like to say (rather than being explicitly represented via the activation patterns that occur during processing). From the dynamical-systems perspective, the automatic accommodation of this background information is a matter of the *contours on the activation landscape*: the landscape is so shaped that trajectories along it, from one TCS-realizing point to another, are appropriate to the relevant background information. Horgan and Tienson call such background information *morphological content*. The reason for this label is to capture the idea that the content is embodied in long-term structure, rather than in the short-term structure of occurrent physical states of the network. (The structure in question, of course, is not the network's intrinsic structure, but rather the high-dimensional topological structure of the network's physical potentiality-profile.) Perhaps such morphological content, subserved by high-dimensional landscape topography, can be directly exploited in the design of a cognitive engine—and *does* get directly exploited in nature's design of human cognizers—as a way of handling the problem of relevant background information, which makes so much trouble for classicism.

Learning, for connectionist networks, is a matter of following a trajectory through weight space until the network reaches a point in weight space at which its information processing is systematically appropriate to the content that needed to be learned. As the weights get progressively altered during learning, the network's activation landscape gets progressively *molded*: morphological content gets instilled into the landscape topography. Concurrently, the realization relation from TCSs to points on the activation landscape gets progressively *refined*: TCSs get repositioned on the landscape, and perhaps certain TCSs get realized on the landscape that were not initially realizable by the network at all (i.e., the cognitive agent becomes capable of explicitly representing information that it could not explicitly represent before). The upshot of learning is that temporal trajectories from one TCS-realizing point to another end up being systematically content appropriate, relative not only to the content of the explicit representations themselves but also to the content of the background morphological content.

In many extant connectionist models, learning occurs in a supervised way—for example, via external application of the "back propagation" algorithm. But perhaps there are internal weight-change mechanisms that can be grafted onto a neural network in such a way that the network's physical potentiality-profile—its profile of dispositions to evolve temporally from one point in *activation/weight* space to another—automatically and simultaneously subserves diachronic learning (in addition to synchronic information-processing). A temporal trajectory along the activation/weight landscape from any initial TCS-realizing point would simultaneously lead both (1) to a suitable new TCS-realizing point in *activation* space, and (2) to a suitable new point in *weight* space—a weight-space point subserving a new activation landscape whose topography morphologically embodies the newly learned information. Indeed, perhaps nature has discovered such internal weight-change mechanisms in the course of human evolution and has installed them as part of the innate structure of the human brain. If so, then the physical potentiality-profile of the human brain would subserve a high-dimensional activation/weight landscape that is so shaped that trajectories along it constitute not only (1) content-appropriate synchronic information-processing that is automatically sensitive to *current* background morphological content, but also (2) content-appropriate diachronic learning that automatically results in progressively better-molded activation landscapes that incorporate an increasingly richer background of morphological content.

Notice that we have not said anything about associative/statistical processing. Although neural networks certainly *can* be used to implement such processing, and although it is plausible that this is how many trained-up connectionist models actually do perform the relatively modular and constrained tasks they have been trained to perform, nothing in the ideas we have been sketching in this section limits neural networks to that kind of processing.

What one should be looking for is not a return to associationism, but rather a way to get beyond both associationism and the view that cognition is computation—a way to harness the ideas we have been sketching in an answer to the *"How Possibly?"* question—to which we now turn.

6.5.2 How the Mind Might Work Noncomputationally: Dynamical Cognition

It will be useful to address the question by conducting a thought experiment. Imagine a godlike being who sets herself the task of creating intelligent creatures much like humans who are to inhabit a planet much like Earth and are to have bodies much like ours. Since this goddess is a stand-in for evolution, we will call her Eva. She imposes various constraints upon herself concerning the physical resources she can employ in designing and creating these intelligent agents, including the following ones. (Some of these constraints could be relaxed in various ways without affecting the substance of the following discussion, but formulating them the way we do will simplify exposition and will make certain key points especially vivid.) First, the cognitive state-transitions are to be implemented in each humanoid via a neural network, with no more than some 10 to 100 billion nodes (roughly the number of actual neurons in actual human brains); the nodes in the network are to be fully connected to one another (although connections will be allowed to have zero connection-weights). Second, the neural network is to be discrete in various ways, so that its transitions from one total-activation state to another will be tractably computable. (For instance, the nodes update their activations in discrete time steps.) Third, she assigns in advance a fixed pool of nodes in the neural network as sensory nodes, and she establishes in advance certain hardwired input-connections from sensory organs to the sensory nodes; likewise, she establishes in advance another fixed pool of nodes as motor nodes, and she establishes in advance certain hardwired output-connections from motor-control nodes to muscles of the humanoid body. (Thus, she imposes in advance the way activation patterns over the sensory nodes will code various sensory stimulations of the body, and the way activation patterns over the motor nodes will code various motor-control instructions.) Fourth, she requires that each total cognitive state (TCS) instantiable by a humanoid creature will be realizable by only one total activation of the creature's neural network; thus, the realization relation from TCSs to total-activation states must be a realization *function*. Fifth, she requires that for each TCS instantiable by a humanoid creature, there will be a unique successor TCS that is instantiable; so cognitive transitions will be *deterministic*, and thus will conform to a cognitive-state transition *function*.

Suppose Eva approaches in two stages the task of designing and building an intelligent humanoid. In stage 1, she will assume a fixed body B of background information, which is to figure as morphological content in the cognitive state-transitions of the creature she is designing. This morphological content will not change as the creature's mental processes unfold. In stage 2, Eva will introduce into the creature the kind of learning that constitutes altered morphological content.

Let us focus for awhile on stage 1. The cognitive transition function (the CTF, for short) that Eva seeks to implement in the humanoid she is designing is not a *tractably computable* function. (It cannot be, as she realizes, since the Computational Theory of Mind cannot handle the relevance problem.) But she can easily conceive this CTF nonetheless, because of her own divine mental capacity: she conceives it in the form of an enormous, nonrecursively specifiable *list*. She holds the whole list before her divine mind at once. Each item on the list is a pair of TCSs $\langle S_i, S_i^* \rangle$, where the second element of the pair is the uniquely appropriate immediate cognitive successor to the first member.

Eva also holds before her divine mind another gigantic list: the set of pairs $\langle W_i, AL_i \rangle$, where W_i is a point in the weight space of the neural network N she is working with, and AL_i is the dynamical system (the activation landscape) describing the physical potentiality profile that N would possess if its connections had the weights specified by W_i. Call this list the *landscape function*, for the network N.

Eva's task of "cognitive engineering," at stage 1, is to search the landscape function to find a specific activation landscape AL_r of N, as determined by a specific weight setting W_r of N's connections, such that AL_r *subserves* the CTF she has in mind. In order to subserve the CTF, AL_r must be an activation landscape that satisfies the following constraint:

There is a (unique) *realization function* R, from the set of TCSs specified in the CTF into the set of points on AL_r, such that for each pair of TCSs $\langle S_i, S_i^* \rangle$ in the CTF, the temporal trajectory along AL_r that emanates at point $R(S_i)$ leads to a point P on AL_r such that

(1) $R(S_i^*) = P$, and

(2) there is no intermediate point Q, along the trajectory along AL_r that leads from $R(S_i)$ to P, such that for some TCS S_j in the CTF, $R(S_j) = Q$. (Although there can be intermediate points along the trajectory, they must not be points that realize TCSs. S_i^* is thus the immediate *cognitive* successor-state of S_i.)

Eva now achieves her cognitive-design goal by setting the weights on the connections of the network N to the weight values that jointly constitute point W_r in N's weight space. Under this weight setting, there is a class of total-activation states of the network—namely, those specified by the points on AL_r that are in the range of the function R—such that these total-activation states all have *precisely the right causal roles* vis-à-vis the humanoid's sensory inputs, vis-à-vis its behavioral outputs, and vis-à-vis one another that they need to have in order for them to be realizers of the TCSs to which they are assigned by the realization function R. Collectively these total-activation states really do *realize* the TCSs to which they are assigned by the realization function R, since they perform the causal jobs required of such realizing states. So the humanoid that Eva has thus designed will do what she wants it to do: its actual and potential temporal evolutions from one TCS to another will all conform to the CTF Eva started with—a cognitive transition function, recall, that is *not tractably computable*.

"But wait a minute!" someone might protest. "It was specified at the start that the neural network N is *discrete* in various ways, and that its temporal transitions from one total-activation state to another are tractably computable. How then could its *cognitive*-state transitions fail to be tractably computable too?" Well, in fact, this is perfectly possible mathematically: as long as the realization function R is *itself* not tractably computable, then there is no reason in principle why tractably computable state-transitions over total-activation states cannot realize state-transitions over TCSs that are *not* tractably computable. Tractable computability of state-transitions is not a feature that is automatically "transferred upward," via realization, from a lower theoretical level of description to a higher level. On the contrary: such transference via realization will happen only when the realization function itself meets certain constraints; what exactly these constraints are is an important and (we think) insufficiently discussed issue; but surely *one* such constraint is that realization itself must be tractably computable. Eva never imposed *that* resource constraint on herself. On the contrary, the realization function at work in *her* cognitive-engineering design will certainly *not* be tractably computable—precisely because what she is doing is finding a way to set up a neural network so that its tractably computable transitions over total-activation states will subserve a cognitive transition function that is *not* tractably computable.

It bears emphasis that the rich and subtle topological structure of the activation landscape AL_r figures centrally as the reason why there actually could *exist* a suitable realization function R, from the TCSs in the CTF to points on AL_r (corresponding to total-activation states of the neural network), such that under R, tractably computable updating of total-activation states subserves cognitive-state transitions that are *not* tractably computable. Eva's design for a cognitive agent thus accords with what Horgan and Tienson (1996, 154) called *The Fundamental Principle of Cognitive Design*:

> The high-dimensional topography of the activation landscape and the positioning of TCS-realizing points on that landscape are jointly just right to subserve content-appropriate cognitive transitions for the whole vast range of potential TCSs the cognitive system has the capacity to instantiate.

The cognitive transitions are appropriate not only to the explicit content of the TCSs, but also to the specific body B of total background information that Eva had in mind when she laid down the CTF in the first place. This background information is implicitly, morphologically, embodied in the contours of the activation landscape—contours that determine how the cognitive trajectories evolve from one TCS to another.

Let us now consider stage 2 of Eva's design project. The CTF she implemented in stage 1 was *synchronic* with respect to background information: that information was held fixed and constant rather than getting changed and updated during cognitive processing. But what she really seeks to implement, in the humanoid she is designing, is a *diachronic* cognitive-transition function (for short, a DCTF): one that incorporates content-appropriate transitions not only in total occurrent cognitive *states*, but also in the total background information. This DCTF, like the original synchronic CTF she implemented in stage 1, will be a transition function that is *not tractably computable*, and also not recursively specifiable. Eva, employing her divine mental capacity, brings before her mind the entire DCTF she seeks to implement, in the form of a gigantic list of specific cognitive transitions. Each item on the list is a pair of the form $\langle\langle S_i, B_j\rangle, \langle S_i^*, B_j^*\rangle\rangle$, where S_i and S_i^* are each a total occurrent cognitive state, and B_j and B_j^* are each a total body of background information. Thus, each entry $\langle\langle S_i, B_j\rangle, \langle S_i^*, B_j^*\rangle\rangle$ in Eva's list-specification of the DCTF says that if the cognitive agent is in TCS S_i and has total background information B_j, then the agent should next go into TCS S_i^* and have total background information B_j^*.

Once again Eva turns to the range of eligible high-dimensional dynamical systems, in order to find one that will subserve the DCTF she seeks to implement. Each of these dynamical systems is a *weight/activation* landscape: a landscape on which temporal trajectories progress from one point in weight-plus-activation space to another. These landscapes describe a range of physical potentiality-profiles that could be possessed by a physical internal-control system that Eva might install in the humanoid she is designing—where each eligible internal-control system consists of both (1) the neural network N she plans to install, and (2) some specific set of internal, physical, weight-change mechanisms. Using her divine mental capacities, she surveys the vast range of eligible dynamical systems, and she finds a weight/activation landscape WAL_r that *subserves* the DCTF she has in mind. In order to subserve the DCTF, WAL_r must be a weight/activation landscape that satisfies the following constraint:

There is a (unique) *realization function* R, from the set of items in the domain and range of the DCTF into the set of points on WAL_r, such that for each pair $\langle\langle S_i, B_j\rangle, \langle S_i^*, B_j^*\rangle\rangle$ in the DCTF, the temporal trajectory along WAL_r from point $R(\langle S_i, B_j\rangle)$ leads to a point P on WAL_r such that

(1) $R(\langle S_i^*, B_j^*\rangle) = P$, and

(2)   there is no intermediate point Q, along the trajectory along AL_r that leads from $R(S_i)$ to P, such that for some pair $\langle S_k, B_k\rangle$ in the DCTF, $R(\langle S_k, B_k\rangle) = Q$. (Although there can be intermediate points along the trajectory, they must not be points that realize items in the DCTF. $\langle S_i^*, B_j^*\rangle$ is thus the immediate *cognitive* successor-state of $\langle S_i, B_j\rangle$.)

Our thought-experimental goddess Eva is a stand-in for evolution. The blind forces of natural selection might have carried out the design task just described as stage 2. (There would not necessarily be a stage 1 along the way. We introduced stage 1 for expository purposes: it is easier to convey the whole picture by starting with the special case of a synchronic cognitive transition function.)

So the dynamical cognition framework for cognitive science provides an answer to the "How Possibly?" question. Admittedly, we have not put any flesh on the bones of the highly abstract answer just set forth, and we have not cited any extant models of cognitive processing (connectionist or otherwise) within cognitive science that clearly conform to the abstract picture of a noncomputational conception of cognition just described. But abstract answers to "How Possibly" questions can inform empirical theorizing, modeling, and experimentation by providing a general foundational framework—especially when the dominant foundational approach, namely, the conception of cognition as computation, appears to be so deeply inadequate.

The principal lesson to be learned from our discussion in the present section is this: there are types of structural complexity in nature that are richer than the intrinsic physical structure of the human brain and the intrinsic physical structure of occurrent states of the brain: namely, the structure of the brain's physical potentiality-profile. Such structure is describable mathematically, within the branch of mathematics known as dynamical systems theory. Nature's evolved design for human cognitive architecture might well exploit that rich structure, as a way of implementing (in brain activity) cognitive processes that (1) automatically accommodate vast amounts of holistically interconnected background information without explicitly representing that information during the course of processing, and (2) are too complex and subtle to conform to programmable rules.

The most general lesson to be learned from our overall discussion, in sections 6.4 and 6.5. as a whole, is that there is good reason to believe that human cognitive architecture *somehow* exhibits features (1) and (2). This lesson remains in place in any case, whatever one might think of the dynamical cognition framework. But it is nice to have in hand an answer to the "How Possibly?" question rather than none at all—whether or not one's available answer is the right one vis-à-vis human cognition.

The fact that human cognitive architecture exhibits features (1) and (2) fits hand-in-glove with a particularist conception of various kinds of normativity—and of semantic normativity specifically. Human cognition outstrips the capacities it would have if the computational paradigm were correct. It thereby has the capacity to master, and conform to, forms of normativity that are too complex and subtle to be systematizable by exceptionless general rules.

6.6 Summary

We now briefly summarize this chapter, with explicit attention to how the methodological points in section 6.1 have been honored.

The first objection to austere realism is that the ontological claims of austere realism seem utterly lunatic to common sense. We offered a debunking reply that puts particular emphasis on giving a *respectful* explanation of such a balking reaction: although the reaction is a certain sort of error, it is far from being a silly or stupid one. On the contrary, it is a very subtle and very understandable mistake—a competence-based performance error. Indeed, it is a kind of balking tendency that is likely to persist even if one accepts all that has been argued in the preceding chapters—somewhat as the Müller-Lyer visual illusion tends to persist even after one knows it is an illusion. *Of course* it sounds lunatic to claim that there are no tables, chairs, or people. For, there is a very strong and very persistent tendency to understand this claim the way one would understand it when typical IC semantic standards are in play; and under those standards, the claim is indeed screamingly false.

The second objection is that contextual semantics falls prey to the dilemma of either (i) embracing implausible content-relativism or (ii) committing itself to a hypothesis of massive equivocation within univocal-looking thought and language. To this we replied that the putative dilemma is a false one: on one hand, thoughts and statements governed by implicit contextual parameters normally are employed categorically rather than relativistically; on the other hand, variation in the contextually operative values of implicit contextual parameters is a much more fine-grained phenomenon than ordinary ambiguity. This weak form of synonymy is aptly called *différance*.

The third objection challenges us to provide a general and systematic account of IC semantic standards and of the dynamics of contextual variation in implicit parameter-values. In reply we argued that semantic normativity is very likely particularistic in nature, a conclusion that fits well with the apparent morals of the frame problem in cognitive science.

7 | Betting on the Blobject: The Choice among Austere Ontologies

The plan for this chapter is as follows. After some initial methodological remarks (section 7.1), we set out the blobjectivist position as a species of austere realism (section 7.2). Then, in section 7.3, we survey a range of potentially viable austere ontologies, including blobjectivism—all of which could be wedded to generic austere realism to yield a specific species of that genus position. (As we said in the introduction, the commonsense-driven road from simple realism forks once it reaches austere realism. The respective forks in the road lead to the various potentially viable alternative austere ontologies.) We urge that three principal alternatives look theoretically preferable to the other main competitor ontologies; blobjectivism is one of these three.

The theoretical attractions of blobjectivism would be negated, however, if this position cannot meet certain crucial requirements that any genuinely tenable version of austere realism must meet, including these: being internally coherent; accommodating the cosmos's spatiotemporal structural complexity; accommodating intentionality in language and thought; and accommodating semantic vagueness while repudiating ontological vagueness. In section 7.4 we explain why and how blobjectivism meets these requirements, and thus is a genuinely tenable philosophical view.

In section 7.5 we consider the comparative theoretical benefits and costs of blobjectivism and its two principal rivals. We argue that one of the rivals fails to meet a key minimal condition of adequacy, and thus falls out of the running. This leaves blobjectivism and one principal competitor position. These two views, we suggest, initially appear to fare roughly equally in relation to one another, when their respective benefits and costs (especially those involving matters of parsimony) are factored together. So blobjectivism ends up at least *tied for first place*, given this chapter's arguments—

not as good as ending up the lone winner, but surely a significant philosophical status nonetheless. Only two specific austere ontologies are left standing by the end of section 7.5 as the leading candidates for being the *right* ontology, and one of these is blobjectivism.

In section 7.6 we set forth a line of reasoning that we think goes some way toward tie-breaking and in favor of blobjectivism—an argument that we ourselves find plausible and appealing, but that we acknowledge is not decisive. (It is not decisive because reasonable people could disagree about the evidential strength of the considerations it appeals to.) Finally, in section 7.7 we briefly mention some further forms of argument in the recent metaphysical literature that ultimately might lead to a decisive victory for blobjectivism—although it is beyond the scope of the present text to take a stand on such arguments.

We will use the boldface convention only sparingly in this chapter. Often it will be clear enough in context that we mean to be using words like 'object' and 'property' in a DC manner, to make claims about ontology or to discuss competing hypotheses about ontology. So often the convention will not be necessary.

In this chapter we will assume the correctness of the generic semantic-cum-ontological position we call austere realism, since we have made a case for this position in the preceding chapters. Although we will often couch the discussion in terms of the comparative theoretical advantages and disadvantages of various austere ontologies, it should be kept in mind that each of these ontologies is being considered as a candidate for being the ontological component of the right version of austere realism.

7.1 Methodological Remarks

Up until now we have been engaged in a defense of austere realism. Now we focus on various species of the genus, including blobjectivism. We seek to show that on balance, blobjectivism fares very well in comparison to other candidate versions of austere realism.

A key theme in this chapter is therefore the importance of reflective equilibrium as a principle of theoretical reasoning in philosophy. One seeks out a theoretical position that appears to do better overall, in terms of comparative theoretical benefits and costs, than do viable alternative positions. Ideally, some single position will win out over all competitors. But narrow-

ing the field is a significant desideratum in its own right, even if the arguments readily available to reflective common sense do not suffice to yield a
single clear-cut winner.

We will maintain that reflective equilibrium, as carried out by appeal to
considerations available fairly directly to refined common sense, singles out
two candidate austere ontologies as preferable to the competitors—one of
these being blobjectivism. We will also maintain that refined common
sense has *some* additional reasons, in the process of reflective equilibration,
to favor blobjectivism—although perhaps not decisive reasons.

We acknowledge that even if one were to end up agreeing with us about
what the benefits and costs are of blobjectivism vis-à-vis its competitors,
one might nonetheless disagree about the net import of those benefits and
costs—one might conclude that, on balance, the various competing positions should be differently ranked than we ourselves will rank them. Such
balancing/equilibrating judgments are sometimes close calls, and reasonable people can differ. (In philosophy, we submit, disagreements in position often turn on just such differences among the disputants.)

We acknowledge too that ultimately, *wide* reflective equilibrium should
be brought to bear on the question of which austere ontology is the right
one. Various kinds of considerations other than those we invoke in the
present chapter probably should be stirred into the mix—some perhaps
emanating fairly directly from refined common sense itself, others perhaps emanating from scientific theorizing. (We will briefly mention some
potentially relevant considerations in section 7.7.) The hope is that wide reflective equilibrium can ultimately vindicate some single austere ontology
as the one that is most likely right, all things considered. Our own bet is
that this will be blobjectivism.

Considerations of comparative ontological parsimony will figure heavily
in the discussion below—and always within the general theoretical framework of austere realism. Given the semantic dimension of austere realism,
with its all-important distinction between direct correspondence and indirect correspondence, competing versions of austere realism should be
viewed as making competing claims about which kinds of statements are
true *under DC semantic standards*. For, it is only under DC standards that a
statement's ontic commitments count as genuine ontological commitments; that is, only under DC standards must a statement's posits be items
in the correct ontology in order for the statement to be true. Thus, the

question of comparative ontological parsimony arises for the competing claims *affirmed under DC semantic standards* that various different versions put forward.

Another factor that will figure importantly in the comparative cost-benefit evaluation, sometimes tending to exert theoretical pressures that are opposite to those exerted by parsimony considerations, is the need to secure the foundations of austere realism—that is, to render the generic assumptions of austere realism consistent with the specific austere ontology being advocated. The more austere the ontology, the more demanding is this foundational task. For instance, the blobjectivist version of austere realism must explain why and how the cosmos could harbor genuine spatiotemporal complexity and nonhomogeneity, even if the cosmos has no **parts**. All else equal, the version of austere realism that is most likely true will be the one that exhibits maximal ontological parsimony *consistently with the foundational claims of austere realism itself*.

7.2 Theses of Blobjectivism

We begin by setting out together the theses of blobjectivism, as a package-deal position about ontology and truth. This position incorporates the ontological theses of austere realism:

AO1. Metaphysical realism: There is a mind-independent, discourse-independent world.

AO2. Refined commonsense ontology: The right ontology excludes most of the posits of everyday belief and discourse and also excludes many of the posits of mature scientific theories.

Blobjectivism also incorporates the semantic theses of refined realism:

AS1. Correspondence conception of truth: Truth is correspondence between language and thought on one hand, and the world on the other.

AS2. Abundance of truth: Numerous statements and thought-contents involving posits of common sense and science are true—including numerous counting statements about such posits.

AS3. Refined construal of correspondence: Truth is semantic correctness under contextually variable semantic standards, and sometimes the contextually operative semantic standards require only indirect correspondence rather than direct correspondence.

AS4. Truth as indirect correspondence in most contexts: In most contexts of discourse and thought, including most contexts of scientific inquiry, truth (under the contextually operative semantic standards) is indirect correspondence rather than direct correspondence.

AS5. Refined construal of ontological commitment: When a thought or statement is governed by contextually operative semantic standards under which truth is indirect correspondence, the thought or statement is not ontologically committed to its posits.

In addition to the above ontological and semantic theses—those constituting austere realism—blobjectivism also embraces the following two, more specific, ontological theses:

BO1. Strong monism: There is really just one concrete particular, namely, the whole universe (the blobject).

BO2. Structural complexity: The blobject has enormous spatiotemporal structural complexity and enormous local variability—even though it does not have any genuine parts.

7.3   Ontology à la Carte

We will now provide a brief overview of some competing ontological positions, under the presupposition that a viable ontology must be austere. An austere ontology excludes numerous posits of common sense, and even of science—in particular, it eschews any ontologically vague objects or properties. We focus specifically on ontological positions concerning concrete particulars. Three candidate ontologies will emerge as leading contenders. One of these is blobjectivism.

The right ontology of concrete particulars, whatever it turns out to be, must meet several constraints. First, it must include no vague objects—no *slobjects* (as we call putative vague objects). Rather, any objects it countenances must be fully determinate and precise in all respects, including composition and spatiotemporal boundaries; that is, they must be *snobjects* (as we call them).[1] Second, the right ontology must provide a systematic and general answer to van Inwagen's special composition question (SCQ). Such an answer is needed in order to honor the nonarbitrariness of composition (NAOC) principle, which claims that it is not plausible to expect a bunch of disconnected facts or metaphysical surds as the basis of ontology.

Living organisms, of course, are slobjects. So, since slobjects are precluded, van Inwagen's own preferred ontology fails the first of these constraints, and is not eligible. (Recall that van Inwagen's ontology of physical beings includes only physical simples and living organisms.) What, then, are the principal eligible candidate ontologies? At a fairly coarse-grained level of description, there are three. First is what we will call *snobjective noncompositionalism*, which includes only snobjective simples and no composites.[2] A snobjective simple is an object that has no parts, and is also perfectly precise. Second is what we call *snobjective universalism*. This view is committed to composite snobjects that compose in an unrestricted way—that is, any bunch of snobjects jointly compose another snobject.[3] Third is blobjectivism, which countenances only one concrete particular (viz., the whole cosmos).

In effect, blobjectivism is a limit case of both snobjective noncompositionalism and snobjective universalism. For, it agrees with the former view in asserting that the right ontology includes no composite objects. And it agrees with the latter view in asserting that the right ontology includes the whole—that is, the entire cosmos.

All three ontological positions satisfy the requirement of repudiating vague objects. In addition, each also respects the requirement of providing a systematic and general answer to the special composition question, "When do several distinct objects compose an object?" To this question, snobjective noncompositionalism says "Never, because there are only simples." Snobjective universalism says "Always; snobjects compose without restriction." Blobjectivism says "Never, because there is only *one* real object, namely, the blobject."

Snobjective universalism is a somewhat generic ontological position, and several different species can be distinguished. One version would countenance only snobjective spatiotemporal *regions*. Being snobjective, these regions would be perfectly precise. (The simples would be minimal snobjective regions, viz., spatiotemporal *points*.) Another version would countenance only snobjective *nonregions*, snobjects that are not regions. Yet another version would countenance both kinds of snobjects.

Likewise, snobjective noncompositionalism is a generic position that has several different species. One variant would countenance only spatiotemporal points; another would countenance only simple snobjective nonregions; yet another would countenance both.

The versions of snobjective noncompositionalism and snobjective universalism that countenance snobjective nonregions are not at all plausible. For, it appears that entities falling under the rubric of snobjective nonregions simply are not posited, either in common sense or in science. *Simple* snobjective nonregions are evidently not posited, because scientists tell us that the "elementary particles" posited in physics are more like clouds than like little billiard balls, and thus are vague in certain respects (e.g., in their spatiotemporal boundaries). Snobjective *compound* nonregions are not posited either (let alone ones that compose in the completely unrestricted fashion hypothesized by universalism); rather, the kinds of compound objects posited in both science and in common sense are virtually always vague in various ways, for instance in the spatiotemporal boundaries and/or in their physical composition. Of course, the posits introduced in a particular discourse need not pick out genuine denizens of the **world** anyway—insofar as truth (for the given discourse) is indirect correspondence. But since snobjective nonregions are not even *posited* in science or in commonsense belief, such putative entities are simply not serious candidates for inclusion in the correct ontology.

So one is now left with three viable candidate ontologies for concrete particulars, two of which are specific versions of genus positions lately mentioned: (1) the version of snobjective noncompositionalism that countenances only spatiotemporal points (a view we will hereafter call *pointillism*); (2) the version of snobjective universalism that countenances only

Table 7.1
Candidates for a plausible austere ontology

(1) Snobjective noncompositionalism			(2) Snobjective universalism			(3) Blobjectivism
(a) regions	(b) nonregions	(a) and (b)	(a) regions	(b) nonregions	(a) and (b)	(3) the blobject

Table 7.2
Candidates for a plausible austere ontology

(1) Snobjective noncompositionalism			(2) Snobjective universalism			(3) Blobjectivism
(a) regions	(b) nonregions	(a) and (b)	(a) regions	(b) nonregions	(a) and (b)	(3) the blobject
(1a) OK	X	X	(2a) OK	X	X	(3) OK

snobjective spatiotemporal regions, including points, (a view we will here-after call *universalist snobjective regionalism*); and (3) blobjectivism.[4]

7.4 The Coherence and Tenability of Blobjectivism

Although blobjectivism is a viable candidate ontology insofar as one judges only by the criteria we stressed in section 7.3, any adequate ontology of concrete particulars must meet other requirements as well. In this section we set forth a number of such requirements, each of which looks initially challenging for blobjectivism to satisfy. We will argue that the package-deal position we call blobjectivism—which is a version of austere realism, and thus incorporates austere realism's semantic theses—can indeed meet these additional requirements. In the course of so arguing, we will elaborate somewhat upon the blobjectivist position itself.

7.4.1 Spatiotemporal Complexity I: Jello-world

The cosmos exhibits enormous spatiotemporal structural complexity and nonhomogeneity; hence, any adequate ontology must accommodate this fact. But one might initially think that there can be no coherent and tenable account of the world's structural complexity that does not suppose that the right ontology includes a multiplicity of objects, some of which bear the relation of parthood to other objects. One might think that this is so, however austere the correct ontology might turn out to be, in the sense of repudiating ordinary posits of common sense and even science. We claim otherwise. We begin by offering a thought experiment, designed to make it intuitively plausible that blobjectivism is both coherent and tenable. A way of thinking about spatiotemporal complexity without ontological part-hood will emerge naturally from the thought experiment, and then will be described more abstractly in the next subsection.

Imagine a world consisting entirely of gunkish, jello-ish, stuff. Suppose that this jello-stuff is physically continuous, at all degrees of magnification. Suppose too that it exhibits local variation (both spatially and temporally) in features like color, transparency, density, and the like. Now, because the jello is physically continuous, it seems not only intelligible but even some-what natural, commonsensically, to say that the stuff itself is a *single partless object*—and that any talk of parts would be a mentally imposed "conceptual carving" of this partless jello.

Suppose, then, that there could be such stuff. (This supposition is not question-begging in the present dialectical context, because the supposition seems intuitively natural and apt, at least prima facie. We are pursuing the idea, to see whether it can be sustained rather than leading to blatant incoherence.) Local variation is not a matter of instantiation of certain properties by *parts* of the jello, because it has no parts (by supposition). Rather, it is a matter of the jello itself instantiating *in spatiotemporally local ways* various properties and relations—that is, it involves certain complex *manners* of instantiation by the jello, namely, spatiotemporally local manners of instantiation.

Given that the jello-world does not really have any parts, what would be an appropriate way to describe how various features are instantiated by the jello in various spatiotemporally local manners? One natural-looking way would be to introduce a linguistic/conceptual framework that posits certain kinds of discrete entities and attributes various features to them. For instance, the framework might posit points and/or regions, and then attribute various properties (e.g., specific degrees of transparency or density, or specific shades of color) to these putative entities. This descriptive framework would be apt because it would provide a way to track and describe the various aspects of real local spatiotemporal variability exhibited by the jello-world. There would be systematic correspondence between certain statements couched in this discourse, on the one hand, and how things really are with the jello-world, on the other hand. Nonetheless, the posited points and regions would not be denizens of the jello-world itself, because this world is one which, ex hypothesi, lacks genuine parts. Thus, the operative language–world correspondence would be indirect, in the sense that the task of specifying how various properties are locally instantiated within the jello-world is accomplished by means of a descriptive/conceptual framework whose posits—namely, spatiotemporal points and regions —are mere constructs of the framework itself and are not genuine parts of the world being described. (That world has no real parts, by supposition.)

The jello-world might occasionally exhibit quite abrupt local spatial or temporal variations, in the degree to which various magnitudes are locally instantiated. Some such variations would be naturally trackable by means of still further posits in one's descriptive/conceptual framework—for instance, bodies, events, and processes. In the case of dramatic local spatial transitions from high density and opacity on one hand to low density and transparency on the other hand, it would be natural to speak of certain kinds of bodies in the jello—for example, lumps. Likewise, the jello-world might occasionally exhibit variation of a kind that is locally abrupt both spatially and temporally, and is naturally trackable by means of posits like events and processes—for example, local congealings. Systematic patterns of local spatiotemporal variation—that is, specific patterns among spatio-temporally local ways that the jello-itself instantiates various properties—might well be trackable by means of generalizations involving these further posits—for instance, the generalization "Congealings generate lumps." Again, discourse employing posits like lumps and congealing-events would systematically track how things really are with the jello—how it really does vary spatiotemporally in its local instantiation of magnitudes like density, transparency, color, and the like—even though it does not have any real parts. And again, such tracking would constitute an indirect kind of language–world correspondence—indirect because the posited entities would be linguistic/conceptual constructs that are not denizens of the part-less jello-in-itself.

Color, transparency, density, and the like need not be among the funda-mental properties and magnitudes instantiated locally by jello-stuff. It might turn out instead that other magnitudes of a theoretically more basic kind are locally instantiated by this partless world and that "macroproper-ties" like color and transparency are supervenient upon, and explainable in terms of, lawful regularities involving these basic properties. Yet these basic regularities too might employ posits like points, regions, and particles—again as a way of facilitating the articulation of how the basic magnitudes are locally instantiated by the partless jello.

So a descriptive/conceptual framework that posits various kinds of parts, and makes claims employing those posits, would be quite natural even if the world being described were one which, like our hypothetical jello-world, did not really have any genuine parts at all. Such talk would track genuine local spatiotemporal variation with respect to how magnitudes are instantiated by the jello-stuff. There would be substantial and systematic—albeit somewhat indirect—language–world correspondence. Such correspondence, we suggest, would be a very plausible candidate for truth. After all, the posits would be playing the role of enabling one to say how the partless jello-stuff instantiates magnitudes spatiotemporally lo-cally. In terms of ontology, however, there would be no real parts at all.

Rather, the jello-stuff itself would be the only concrete particular, and thus the only real instantiator of properties; and it would instantiate properties in various spatiotemporally local ways.

In light of these remarks about the hypothetical jello-world, it begins to appear a conceptually coherent possibility that the actual world we humans inhabit, in all its glorious complexity and local spatiotemporal variation, does not have any real parts. Indeed, this is an attractive-looking ontological framework for physics, especially if one focuses on broadly field-theoretic formulations of physical theory. The ontological framework construes the entire cosmos as a physical field which, although it certainly exhibits local variation, does not really have parts.[5] Various physical magnitudes are instantiated not by *parts* of the field (say, spatiotemporal points and/or spatiotemporal regions), but rather by the field *itself*. The field instantiates magnitudes in a variety of different manners—namely, spatiotemporally local manners of instantiation.

Likewise, it now emerges as a conceptually coherent possibility that numerous posit-wielding statements of physical theory are true even if the posits are mere constructs of the theoretical framework and are not genuine denizens of reality. It is possible (1) that for the actual world, as for the hypothetical jello-world, posit-wielding statements couched in the language of physics track genuine local spatiotemporal variation with respect to how physical magnitudes are instantiated, (2) that this tracking relation constitutes truth for such statements, and nevertheless (3) that the actual world does not really contain any parts. If so, then the truth of such statements is a matter of indirect language–world correspondence, since the posits (e.g., space-time points and regions, as putative parts of the physical field that is the cosmos) enable one to say how things are physically with the cosmos without actually designating real entities themselves.

Since statements in physics-level discourse could be true even if the world does not really have parts, the same goes for statements of other kinds—statements employing terms and concepts of the "special sciences," and statements of ordinary nonscientific discourse. After all, it is very plausible that all truths about our world are supervenient on physics-level truths—that the physically describable facts determine all the facts.[6] Thus, insofar as the relevant truths of physics already involve indirect correspondence, in general this should also be so for truths of higher-level discourse, truths that supervene on physics-level truths. Here too, language and thought would be tracking real local spatiotemporal variation in the blob-ject. And in general, the operative language–world correspondence relation now would be even more indirect than in physics: the contextually operative semantic standards would conspire with **reality** in more complex, more subtle, and more holistic ways to render statements semantically correct (i.e., true).

Take, for instance, a statement like "In summer of 2006, Israel was conducting a massive bombing campaign against Hezbollah in southern Lebanon." Certainly there are genuine, mind-independently real, physical variations of the blobject that are tracked by this statement, even on the supposition that the blobject lacks real parts—for example, the kinds of physical variations that correspond to talk of explosions. But the statement also presupposes a rich and complex network of intertwined concepts (nation, religious group, campaign, bomb, war, airplane, etc., etc.); these concepts figure in a broad fabric of interconnected statements. According to the ontological/semantic picture now being suggested, such statements typically would figure collectively in complex, somewhat holistic, indirect-correspondence relations to the mind-independent world. Individual statements would often count as semantically correct (i.e., true), under contextually operative semantic standards, even though they employ posits (e.g., Israel, Lebanon, Hezbollah) that do not designate genuine denizens of **reality**.

The upshot of the preceding discussion is that blobjectivism appears to be a conceptually coherent, and theoretically tenable, philosophical position concerning matters of ontology and semantics. Ontologically, the actual world could be like the hypothetical jello-world, a physical blobject that lacks real parts, and yet still exhibits genuine structural complexity—that is, genuine variability in how magnitudes are locally, spatiotemporally instantiated. Semantically, part-positing discourse could often be true nonetheless—with its truth being indirect language–world correspondence, consisting in semantic correctness under contextually operative semantic standards that do not require those part-posits to be "furniture of the world."

The question we have been addressing is whether blobjectivism has the conceptual resources to make sense of the cosmos's spatiotemporal structural complexity. It might be objected that the jello-world thought experiment actually *begs* this question, by specifying a putative scenario in a way that presupposes the very point at issue—namely, the claim that it makes sense to talk about a partless object exhibiting spatiotemporal structural complexity. But the charge of question-begging is out of place in the present dialectical context. The point of the thought experiment is that (1) it is intuitively fairly natural to say that a mass of physically continuous jello-stuff would not have any mind-independently real parts (and thus that applying part-talk to it would be mere "conceptual carving"), and (2) that this intuitive idea evidently can be intelligibly retained while yet acknowledging the jello-stuff's spatiotemporal complexity and variability. The key idea is to eschew instantiation of magnitudes by *parts*, in favor of the jello-stuff's own instantiation of magnitudes *in spatiotemporally local ways*. We will elaborate this idea in section 7.4.2.

Before doing so, and to further underscore both the apparent conceptual coherence of blobjectivism and its theoretical tenability, we will briefly consider, and reply to, three initially plausible objections. (The replies can be brief because they will largely echo replies given above to similar objections against the generic position of austere realism.)

First objection: Blobjectivism is a lunatic view because it runs so radically contrary to both ordinary beliefs and scientific beliefs about the world. One simply cannot take seriously the claim that there really is only a single concrete thing rather than the multiplicity of things that both science and common sense say there are. Numerous claims about such things—about tables, chairs, persons, molecules, quarks, and the like—are literally true, and not merely "contextually sanctioned." So blobjectivism is not a credible philosophical position.

Reply: This same objection can be leveled against *any* austere ontology, and we have already addressed it at some length in section 6.2 of chapter 6. Here we will just briefly restate a portion of that more extensive reply. The semantic component of blobjectivism says that truth—genuine, literal truth—is semantic correctness under contextually operative semantic standards.[7] It also says that in most real-life contexts of thought and assertion, including contexts of scientific inquiry, the contextually operative semantic standards operate in such a way that the part-posits of the discourse need not link up to **entities**—and hence that truth, in such discourse contexts, is indirect correspondence. Thus, blobjectivism significantly accommodates common sense and scientific beliefs by classifying them as quite literally true.

Furthermore, the semantic component of blobjectivism also provides the resources to explain why the ontological component of blobjectivism sounds so extremely odd, even lunatic. For, the semantic component says that blobjectivism's ontological claims are made under very unusual, limit-case, semantic standards—standards requiring direct correspondence. Although the ontological claims are indeed true under these DC semantic standards, such limit-case standards are very rarely employed in human thought/discourse, even in science. (Their principal use is in ontological inquiry within philosophy.) So the ontological claims are bound to sound odd and even lunatic, given that language and concepts are almost never employed under DC semantic standards. Since this oddness is thus explainable by means of the semantic component of blobjectivism itself—explainable as a competence-based performance error (cf. sections 6.2.1 and 6.2.2 of chapter 6)—the oddness should not count strongly against the tenability of blobjectivism. As one might put it, package-deal blobjectivism renders ontological blobjectivism much more tenable than it would be on its own.

Second objection: According to blobjectivism, very little can be said positively about the blobject under DC semantic standards. One can say, negatively, that it does not have parts. But evidently one cannot say much at all, positively, about how things are with the blobject. Thus, according to blobjectivism **the world** is indescribable by, and thus is unknowable by, humans; it is noumenal, in Kant's sense. Why believe in noumenal **reality** at all?

Reply: Blobjectivism does not entail that **the world** is indescribable and unknowable by humans. On the contrary, humans can indeed say—and can indeed know—how things are with **the world**. In particular, they can know how fundamental physical-magnitude properties are locally, spatiotemporally instantiated by the blobject. True, in order to say how things are with the blobject with respect to the local spatiotemporal instantiation of physical magnitudes, it is very useful to employ language that employs certain part-posits (e.g., spacetime points, and/or spacetime regions)—language governed by semantic standards that are not limit-case, DC standards (since the blobject has no real parts). But one nevertheless manages, by speaking this way, to say how things are with the blobject itself—how those physical magnitudes get instantiated, spatiotemporally locally.

Third objection: Surely it is very implausible that systematic, tractably specifiable truth conditions for posit-employing discourse could be formulated in language that eschews all such posits and talks only about the blobject and its attributes.

Reply: It is indeed implausible that there are truth conditions of the kind in question. But, given the general conception of truth as semantic correctness under contextually operative semantic standards, there simply need not be (and very probably are not) those kinds of truth conditions— conditions that would amount, in effect, to systematic paraphrases of all true statements into statements that would bear a direct-correspondence relation to the mind-independent world. What is required, rather, is that the semantic standards be masterable by humans—that is, internalizable as a component of human linguistic and conceptual competence. But this latter requirement could very well be satisfiable even if statements that conform to IC semantic standards are not systematically translatable into statements that eschew all part-posits and are true even under limit-case, direct-correspondence semantic standards. (See chapter 6, sections 6.4 and 6.5.)

7.4.2 Spatiotemporal Complexity II: Local Manners of Instantiation

Several probing questions have been posed about blobjectivism by John Tienson (2002) and will be addressed in the course of the present chapter. He asks, inter alia, for an ontological analysis of the spatiotemporal complexity of the blobject. The analysis would need to accommodate spatiotemporal complexity within the austere ontology of blobjectivism, thereby deflecting the suspicion that blobjectivism "deconstructs" itself through ontological commitments that are incompatible with its own core theses. In this subsection we will elaborate a version of blobjectivism that provides such an ontological analysis and that seems to us plausible and credible. The task of the blobjectivist ontological analysis is to explain the spatiotemporal complexity of the blobject without positing any concrete, spatiotemporally located **parts**.

Our proposed ontological analysis of spatiotemporal complexity will resort to a paraphrase technique (involving adverbial constructions) for eliminating apparent ontological commitments. The reader should keep the following three points well in mind, however. First, in general when a judgment or statement employing posits of common sense or science is semantically correct (i.e., true) because the contextually operative semantic standards require only *indirect* correspondence to **the world**, the content of the given judgment or statement need not be paraphrasable by some statement that is correctly affirmable under semantic norms that require *direct* correspondence to **the world**. Once the ontological foundations of indirect correspondence are secure, we maintain, the demand for paraphrasability can and should be repudiated. Even so, securing those foundations does require ontological analysis; and for this *specific* theoretical purpose, paraphrase strategies will have a key role to play.[8]

Second, the proposed paraphrases need not be outright *synonymous* to the statements for which they go proxy under ontological analysis. What is needed for purposes of ontological analysis is a statement, governed by DC semantic standards, that picks out the same range of possible worlds (maximal **world**-instantiable properties) as does the statement that it paraphrases. Such sameness of truth conditions does not entail synonymy.

Third, in claiming that statements employing certain adverbial constructions provide *ontological* analyses of spatiotemporal complexity, we are maintaining that the relevant adverbial constructions directly reflect certain aspects of **reality**—namely, spatiotemporally local **manners of instantiation**. Statements employing the relevant adverbial constructions will thus be employed under DC semantic standards, and thereby will carry ontological commitment. (That these statements are being employed under DC standards is a matter of our stipulation. But of course, whether or not the statements are *true*, as thus employed, is not a matter of stipulation at all, but depends on what the right ontology is.) Blobjectivism, in the version now being proposed, claims that the right ontology includes not only (i) **the blobject** (as the only concrete particular), (ii) **properties** instantiable by **the blobject**, and (iii) **instantiation** itself, but also includes (iv) a whole panoply of spatiotemporally local **manners** of instantiation.

So let us turn to the matter at hand. Concerning our contention that the blobject has structural complexity even though it does not have any parts, Tienson asks two questions:

(Q1)   Doesn't **complexity** require **properties** and **relations**?

(Q2)   What has those **properties** and **relations** that make for the complexity of the blobject?

And concerning our more specific contention that the blobject has *spatiotemporal* complexity, he asks a further question:

(Q3)   Doesn't spatiotemporal **complexity** require space-time **locations** (**points** and/or **regions**) at which **properties** and **relations** are **instantiated**?

Our answer to question (Q1) is affirmative. Our answer to question (Q2) is this: since the blobject is the only concrete particular, it is the only available concrete instantiator of properties and relations. But now, of course, question (Q3) looms large. The natural-seeming way to understand spatiotemporal complexity is in terms of the instantiation of properties and relations by various different *space-time* **locations**. Question (Q3) challenges us to provide an ontological analysis that accommodates genuine spatiotemporal complexity *without* appeal to space/time locations.

We propose to meet this challenge by way of a familiar theoretical technique for avoiding ontological commitments—namely, paraphrasing discourse that appears to posit certain tendentious entities into discourse that employs *adverbial constructions* to avoid positing such entities. (This approach was already intimated in our discussion of the hypothetical jello-world in section 7.4.1.) Consider these two statements, for example:

(a) Smith has a loud laugh.

(b) Smith laughs loudly.

Since statement (a) is paraphrasable by statement (b), the former evidently does not carry ontological commitment to any such putative entity as Smith's laugh. Rather, statement (a), like statement (b), is true just in case Smith instantiates *in a loud manner* the property *laughing*—and thereby instantiates the more specific property *laughs loudly*. (In treating the paraphrase (b) as a construal of statement (a) under which (a) does not really posit such a putative entity as Smith's loud laugh, one thereby treats (b) as positing a certain *manner* of instantiation of the property *laughing*—viz., the *loudly* manner.)[9]

Consider, then, certain properties that are putatively instantiated by putative spatiotemporal points or regions, as expressed in claims like this:

(c) Mass M is instantiated at region R.

On the ontological analysis we propose, such a claim is to be understood metaphysically by way of this adverbial paraphrase:

(d) The property *mass M* is instantiated R-ishly by the blobject.

The idea is that a property like *mass M* can be instantiated by the blobject *in spatiotemporally local ways*. This blobjectivist ontological analysis eschews spatiotemporal locations and instead appeals to spatiotemporally local manners in which properties get instantiated by the blobject. These manners of instantiation are the ontological counterparts of adverbial constructions like the one in statement (d).[10]

Relations are to be handled similarly, by generalizing the proposed ontological analysis. Thus, a statement like

(e) Region R_1 is denser than region R_2

is to be paraphrased this way:

(f) The relation *denser-than* is instantiated (R_1, R_2)-ishly by the blobject.

The blobjectivist ontological analysis eschews locations as instantiators of relations and instead appeals to spatiotemporally binary (in general, spatiotemporally *n*-ary) manners in which relations are instantiated by the blobject. These are the ontological counterparts of adverbial constructions like the one in statement (f).[11] Thus, even though the blobject lacks any concrete parts, it does have spatiotemporal complexity—by virtue of the many spatiotemporally specific manners in which various ontologically precise properties and relations are instantiated by the blobject itself.[12]

7.4.3 Mental Intentionality: Vague Content without Ontological Vagueness

Tienson has posed further foundational questions for blobjectivism—questions that really arise not only for blobjectivism but for other versions of austere realism as well. These pertain to the ontological status of the contextually variable semantic standards that supposedly govern language and thought.

Because we regard mental intentionality as ontologically prior to intentionality in language, mental intentionality will figure centrally in our answers to Tienson's questions about semantic normativity. Before addressing those questions (in section 7.4.4), we need to explain how we propose to accommodate mental intentionality within blobjectivist ontology. The version of blobjectivism we are now elaborating incorporates intentional mental **properties**. We will pose and address several questions about them, beginning with this one:

(A) How can intentional mental **properties** be **instantiated** if there are no **people**?

Our answer, dictated by what we said in section 7.4.2, is that intentional mental properties are instantiated in spatiotemporally local ways, by the blobject. Thus, mental intentionality is incorporated into blobjectivist ontology, even though people and/or other kinds of thinkers are eschewed.[13]

Since ontological vagueness is impossible for properties just as much as for objects, intentional mental properties cannot be ontologically vague— that is, vague with respect to how they are instantiated. Hence this question:

(B)   How can intentional mental **properties** be ontologically *precise* (as blobjectivism requires)?

This question seems especially pressing in light of the fact that mental intentional *content* is almost always vague. Moreover, question (B) arises even for an ontology that departs from blobjectivism by including precise space/time locations as eligible instantiators of **properties**; for **properties** would still have to be ontologically precise (as would locations).[14]

In order to address question (B), it will be helpful to distinguish two kinds of ontological vagueness for putatively vague properties. (For ease of exposition in citing illustrative examples, assume for the moment that there are precise locations.) The first is vagueness with respect to the *range* of instantiation. For example, if there were such a property as baldness, then this property would be vague with respect to the range of its instantiation vis-à-vis various candidate cases. The second kind is vagueness with respect to *locally specific* instantiation. For example, even in a particular case where the predicate 'bald' clearly applies, there would still be vagueness with respect to the precise location at which the putative property baldness is instantiated in the given case—because of the vagueness of spatiotemporal boundaries for putative instantiators like persons and their heads. Question (B) thus bifurcates into two questions:

(B1)   How can intentional mental **properties** be ontologically precise with respect to range of **instantiation**?

(B2)   How can intentional mental **properties** be ontologically precise with respect to locally specific **instantiation**?

It will turn out that intentional mental properties are indeed ontologically precise in the requisite ways, even when their intentional content is vague.

Our answer to question (B1) goes as follows. At any moment the overall *phenomenal character* of one's total mental state (i.e., what the state is like) is fully precise. This total mental state is a *phenomenologically* precise complex mental property. Normally, such a property is complex, being a composite of various *constituent* mental properties, each of which is itself phenomenologically precise. The total mental property often includes a constituent mental property whose phenomenal character is a specific *phenomenology of intentionality*—for instance, the phenomenologically precise "what it's like" of *thinking that p* (on a particular occasion).[15] Instantiating such a phenomenologically precise property *constitutes* instantiating an *intentional* mental property—namely, a phenomenologically precise *determinant* of the determinable kind *thinking that p*. This determinant intentional property— that is, this phenomenologically precise *way* of thinking that p—is itself predicable by means of the predicate 'is thinking that p'.[16] Since the determinant property is phenomenologically precise, it is thereby precise with respect to range of instantiation—even if its intentional content is vague.

Concerning question (B2), our answer is this.[17] For any two properties P_1 and P_2, let P_1 be a *minimal supervenience base* for P_2 just in case (i) P_2 supervenes on P_1, and (ii) there is no constituent-property P_3 of P_1 such that P_2 supervenes on P_3. Suppose, then, that physical property Φ is instantiated R-ishly by the blobject, and that Φ is a minimal supervenience base for a phenomenologically precise intentional mental property Ψ. (The **R-ish** manner of instantiation is *precise*, of course.) Then Ψ too is instantiated R-ishly by the blobject. Thus, Ψ is precise with respect to specific instantiation—even if its intentional content is vague.

To summarize: Intentional mental properties are instantiated by the blobject itself, in spatiotemporally local manners. Determinant properties expressible by intentional mental predicates are phenomenologically precise (despite normally having vague intentional content), and thereby are precise with respect to range of instantiation. Also, a determinant intentional mental property Ψ gets instantiated in the same spatiotemporally local manner as does the physical property Φ that is its minimal physical base (for a specific local instantiating of Ψ by the blobject); so, since any minimal physical supervenience base for Ψ always gets instantiated in a *precise* spatiotemporal manner, Ψ itself thereby is always precise with respect to specific local manner of instantiation (even when Ψ has vague intentional content). In short, intentional mental properties are ontologically precise while also having vague content, and are instantiated (in precise spatiotemporally local ways) by the blobject itself.

7.4.4 The Ontological Status of Semantic Normativity

We contend that truth is often *indirect* correspondence between thought or language and **the world**—where indirect correspondence is construed as semantic correctness under contextually operative semantic standards. Tienson raises questions pertaining to the ontological analysis of this semantic thesis, questions involving the ontological status of semantic normativity itself. He asks,

(Q4)   Is it sufficient for blobjectivism that there be norms in the descriptive sense, or does blobjectivism require **objective norms**?

Also, since semantic normativity is prima facie a matter of the semantically correct use of concepts by people, he asks,

(Q5)   How can there be norms/**norms** and concepts/**concepts** if there are no people?

Let us begin with question (Q4). We take it that what Tienson calls "descriptive norms" are closely related to what are often called *conventional* norms. Although the semantic normativity of public language surely depends in part upon conventional norms (e.g., the conventional use of certain inscriptions and sounds to play specific word-roles), convention evidently plays no role in the ontologically fundamental kind of intentionality—namely, the primary intentionality of thought.[18] So blobjectivism needs a kind of semantic normativity that does not depend upon, or emerge from, conventionally accepted norms—and is instead prior to the conventional aspects of semantic normativity in public language. The key question is whether this primary, nonconventional form of semantic normativity is **real**.

As we acknowledged in section 7.4.3, there are phenomenally precise, intentional, mental **properties**.[19] Thus there is genuine mental **intentionality**. Partly *constitutive* of intentional mental properties, we maintain, is this feature: they *normatively regulate* affirmation/denial practice, in thought and in language.[20] Since it is an inherent feature of intentional mental properties to be normatively regulative in this way, mental **intentionality** is, by its very nature, semantically **normative**.

Concerning question (Q5), our answer is parallel to what we said earlier in reply to question (Q3) and draws upon our discussion in section 7.4.2. Intentional mental properties, whose intentional content is semantically normative, are instantiated by the blobject in spatiotemporally local ways.

These intentional properties, despite typically having vague intentional content, are ontologically precise, as explained in section 7.4.2: they are precise both with respect to *range* of instantiation and with respect to locally specific *manner* of instantiation.

In sum: The version of blobjectivism here described does posit genuine semantic **normativity**, which it takes to be built into the very nature of the intentional mental properties whose instantiation constitutes intentionality. But it does without **people**, by affirming that intentional mental properties are really instantiated—in spatiotemporally local manners—by the blobject itself.

7.4.5 Dialectical Interlude

In closing Section 7.4, let us point out that much of what we have said would remain relevant and applicable even if one were to embrace an ontological/semantic position that includes precise spatiotemporal locations but otherwise is like ours. Given our argument in chapter 2 against the possibility of ontological vagueness and our argument in chapter 4 against fence-straddling realism, there still could not be **people**; for, these putative entities would be *vague* in certain respects—for instance, with respect to their diachronic spatial boundaries, and with respect to their synchronic physical composition. So, the instantiators of intentional mental properties presumably would be spatiotemporally precise **regions** rather than putative **people**, and thus Tienson's question (Q5) would still arise. Moreover, the intentional properties themselves would still need to be ontologically precise and questions (B1) and (B2) about the ontological status of semantic normativity would still need addressing. Our discussion in sections 7.4.3 and 7.4.4 would still be applicable, mutatis mutandis, apart from this one change: instead of intentional mental properties being instantiated in precise spatiotemporal local ways by the blobject, these properties would be directly instantiated by precise spatiotemporal regions themselves.

7.5 Comparative Cost-Benefit Evaluation

In section 7.3 three candidate austere ontologies emerged as theoretically more preferable than various others that were canvassed there. The three leaders were pointillism, universalist snobjective regionalism, and blobjectivism. Viewed solely in terms of what they say about concrete particulars, these three candidates can be ordered with respect to comparative ontological parsimony. The simplest is blobjectivism; it maximizes ontological parsimony by countenancing just one real concrete object, the blobject. Less parsimonious is pointillism, since it countenances all those point-objects. (Some might argue that pointillism is not significantly worse off than blobjectivism on the score of parsimony in positing concrete particulars, since pointillism repudiates the blobject itself while also repudiating any composite objects. But pointillism will fall out of the competition for other reasons, as shall be explained presently.) Still less parsimonious is universalist snobjective regionalism, since it countenances not only all the same point-objects, but also a completely unrestricted mereological hierarchy of snobjective region-objects as well.

All else equal, comparative ontological parsimony in the positing of concrete particulars is a powerful theoretical reason to prefer one ontological theory to another. And in some respects, at least, all else *is* equal insofar as these three candidate ontologies are concerned. For one thing, the need to complicate semantics as a counterweight to ontological austerity is faced by all three candidates; they all repudiate vague objects, and hence they all need a semantic picture according to which truth, for vast portions of human discourse, both scientific and nonscientific, is indirect correspondence. Furthermore, the notion of indirect correspondence, already needed for so much discourse, extends naturally to statements that posit spatiotemporal points and/or snobjective spatiotemporal regions—statements specifying which physical-magnitude values are instantiated "at" points or regions. The only object that needs to exist, in order for such statements to be *true* under IC semantic standards, is the blobject itself, instantiating physical magnitudes in spatiotemporally local ways.

But there is more to consider, for purposes of comparative cost/benefit evaluation, than parsimony with respect to concrete particulars. In one significant way, pointillism fares much worse than the other two views:

Table 7.3

Parsimony rankings	Blobjectivism
	Pointillism
	Universalist snobjective regionalism

namely, it cannot plausibly accommodate the **instantiation** of mental **properties**. (Providing such ontological accommodation is crucial because **instantiated** mental **properties** are needed in order to secure the ontological foundations of austere realism—specifically, in order to make room within austere ontology for semantic normativity. So we argued in sections 7.4.3 and 7.4.4.) Universalist snobjective regionalism can treat phenomenologically precise mental properties as instantiated by precise nonpointillist regions—namely, regions that also instantiate physical properties that constitute minimal supervenience bases for the mental ones. Blobjectivism can do something analogous, replacing the precise regions as the instantiators by spatiotemporally precise **manners** of instantiation by the blobject itself. Both approaches honor ordinary thinking about when and where mental properties are instantiated and ordinary counting practice concerning how often a given mental property gets instantiated.

Pointillism, however, would have to say that mental properties are instantiated by spatiotemporal **points** (since these are the only available concrete particulars to serve as instantiators, according to pointillism). And this would mean that mental properties are instantiated *vastly* more often than they are normally thought to be. For, consider a case where the minimal supervenience base for the instantiation of a given mental property M comprises what universalist snobjective regionalism would count as a nonminimal spatiotemporal region and what blobjectivism would count as a nonminimal spatiotemporally local manner of instantiation. For pointillism, this supervenience base would consist of the simultaneous instantiation, by nondenumerably many spatiotemporal points, of various physical-magnitude properties. (The relevant points would be just the ones that, according to universalist snobjective regionalism, collectively constitute the pertinent region.) The pointillist evidently would have to say that *every single one* of these nondenumerably many points instantiates mental property M; after all, it would be arbitrary to treat some as M-instantiators but not others, given that each point's instantiating the physical magnitudes it does is part of the minimal supervenience base for M's being locally instantiated. But having to say that is so wildly counterintuitive, and so utterly ad hoc theoretically, that it counts as a very serious deficit of pointillism vis-à-vis its two competitors, blobjectivism and universalist snobjective regionalism. Pointillism, we conclude, falls out of the running.

So the competition is now between blobjectivism and universalist snob-jective regionalism. All else equal, as we said, comparative parsimony favors a more parsimonious ontology over a less parsimonious one—and blobjec-tivism obviously fares better on this score, provided that one is considering only concrete particulars. But of course, comparative parsimony depends not just on what the two ontologies say about concrete particulars, but also on what they say about other aspects of ontology. And in this regard, the scales tip back the other way. For, universalist snobjective regionalism evidently can get by with just straightforward **instantiation** of properties and relations—with the instantiators being spatiotemporal **regions**. Blob-jectivism, on the other hand, needs to posit not only instantiation itself but also a whole host of spatiotemporally local **manners** of instantiation.

We ourselves favor blobjectivism. So it would be very nice, at this dialec-tical juncture, to provide an overwhelmingly plausible argument for the claim that, all things considered, blobjectivism clearly trumps universalist snobjective regionalism on the score of comparative overall ontological parsimony. Unfortunately, we do not have such an argument to offer. Rather, we acknowledge that one very reasonable-looking stance would be that the two competing views are roughly on a par in terms of parsimony: blobjectivism gets by with one concrete particular, at the price of a whole host of spatiotemporally local **manners** of property instantiation; univer-salist snobjective regionalism gets by with instantiation simpliciter, at the price of spatiotemporal **regions** that compose without restriction; and the upshot is that the parsimony-related benefits and costs of the one view essentially just offset those of the other view.

But even if the contest remains a tie, given only what has been said so far in this book, the fact remains that blobjectivism has emerged as a view that needs to be taken very seriously indeed. We have argued in chapters 1–6 for the generic ontological/semantic position we call austere realism, and we have argued so far in the present chapter that blobjectivism is one of only two leading competitors for being the right version of austere realism—the other one being universalist snobjective regionalism. To be one of just two finalists still left standing is no shabby outcome, for a phi-losophical position that naive common sense is apt to consider self-evidently absurd!

Moreover, this apparent tie situation is an important philosophical con-clusion in itself. Not only is there a strong case for austere realism as a generic ontological-cum-semantic position, but there are two specific versions of it that are theoretically preferable to other versions and are prima facie on roughly equal footing insofar as comparative ontological parsimony is concerned: blobjectivism and universalist snobjective regionalism.

7.6 Considerations Favoring Blobjectivism

Although we cannot offer an argument that decisively establishes the theoretical superiority of blobjectivism over universalist snobjective regionalism, we do think that there are considerations that nondecisively favor blobjectivism. These involve aspects of parsimony again—aspects over and above those considered above. We will set forth these considerations in the present section, in the hope that our readers will find them evidentially relevant (even if not decisive) in support of blobjectivism. Once again, we acknowledge that reasonable people can disagree about the degree of evidential support, positive or negative, that accrues to a given theory from various specific features the theory possesses. We also acknowledge that the whole subject of the differing aspects of ontological parsimony, and their comparative evidential weight, deserves systematic philosophical scrutiny in its own right—something well beyond the scope of the present book.

A familiar metaphysical distinction is between what is actual and what is merely possible. (And of course there are various kinds of possibility, too—e.g., nomological, metaphysical, conceptual.) An ontological position might be fairly liberal in the range of possibilities it posits, while yet being comparatively conservative in the range of possibilities that it treats as actual. The latter kind of theoretical stinginess, we suggest, is itself a form of ontological parsimony; we will call it *modal* parsimony.

Another familiar metaphysical distinction is between those aspects of reality that are ontologically fundamental on one hand and those that are supervenient on the fundamental aspects.[21] An ontological position might be fairly liberal in the range of supervenient aspects it posits (e.g., properties whose instantiation would be supervenient upon the instantiation of ontologically fundamental properties), while yet being comparatively conservative in the range of posited items it treats as ontologically fundamental (e.g., as ontologically fundamental properties or objects). The latter kind of metaphysical stinginess, we suggest, is yet another form of ontological parsimony; we will call it *subvenience* parsimony. (The term 'subvenience' has come into philosophical parlance as a counterpart to 'supervenience'.)

There is third form of ontological parsimony that results jointly from the modal dimension and the subvenience dimension. Suppose there is an ontological position that is fairly liberal in the full range of possibilities it posits and treats as *actual*, and likewise is fairly liberal in the full range of *ontologically fundamental* possibilities it posits, but nonetheless is comparatively conservative in the range of possibilities it treats as *both actual and ontologically fundamental*. We suggest that this too is a significant form of ontological parsimony; we will call it *deep* parsimony. (This label is intended to capture the idea of modal parsimony at the ontologically fundamental level; we do not at all mean to suggest that other forms of parsimony are merely superficial.)

Return now to blobjectivism versus universalist snobjective regionalism (for short, US regionalism), with an eye toward comparative ontological parsimony. As noted already, in some respects there is rough parity between the two: blobjectivism posits only one concrete particular but also posits numerous spatiotemporally local modes of property instantiation, whereas US regionalism posits only property instantiation simpliciter but also posits a plethora of precise spatiotemporal regions that compose without restriction. Nevertheless, this rough parity arguably gets broken in favor of blobjectivism, once one factors the lately noted forms of parsimony into the mix.

To elaborate: According to US regionalism, all those posited regions are *actual*; they are all present within the actual world. They are also *ontologically basic*; they are subvenient entities, rather than supervening upon a sparser fundamental ontology that includes only some of the regions but not all of them. On the other hand, it is very plausible, given the broad contours of contemporary scientific theorizing both in physics and in the special sciences, that a scientifically adequate blobjectivist metaphysic of the actual world would treat comparatively few properties, and comparatively few spatiotemporally local instantiation-manners, as both actual and ontologically basic. (Even if the right blobjectivist metaphysic of the actual world were to countenance numerous "gerrymandered" properties that are actually instantiated by the blobject in numerous "gerrymandered" local manners of instantiation, most of these gerrymandered properties and instantiation-manners would be supervenient rather than ontologically basic.) Thus, blobjectivism scores higher than US regionalism, in terms of comparative degree of deep ontological parsimony.

So the initial apparent parity between the two views, in terms of comparative ontological parsimony, now evidently gets broken in favor of blobjectivism. The right cost-benefit comparison in terms of *overall* ontological parsimony, we submit, is between (i) US regionalism's compositionally unrestricted plethora of precise regions *all of which are actual and ontologically fundamental*, and (ii) blobjectivism's unrestricted plethora of spatiotemporally local instantiation modes, most of which are *not* both actualized and ontologically fundamental. This is not an even tradeoff after all, because the blobjectivist alternative does better in terms of the aspect of theoretical simplicity we are calling deep ontological parsimony.

We will close this section by mentioning a line of thought that is different in formulation from our appeal to deep ontological parsimony, but which we suspect taps into a very similar underlying idea. A common intuitive reaction to mereological schemes that allow unrestricted composition is that any such scheme really constitutes merely a way of "conceptually carving" reality, rather than constituting the right ontology of the world. A closely related idea is that the vast majority of the composite entities posited by such a scheme would be *artificially gerrymandered* "conceptual carvings," rather than being genuine components of the mind-independent, discourse-independent world; these conceptual carvings simply would not reflect nature's own "joints." This line of thought is one that many find intuitively powerful, despite its metaphorical formulation. What it taps into, we suggest, is the genuine and important insight that, ceteris paribus, ontologies allowing unrestricted composition fare far worse, in terms of deep ontological parsimony, than those that do not.

7.7 Prospects for a Decisive Victory for Blobjectivism

Although we leave at this our tentative defense of blobjectivism over competing austere ontologies, let us close by remarking that there may well be other arguments available that could tip the scales much more decisively in favor of blobjectivism. Especially worthy of mention here is the work of Jonathan Schaffer (2007, forthcoming). Schaffer (forthcoming, sec. 2.4) argues this way, for instance: (1) infinitely divisible matter ("gunk") is metaphysically possible; (2) if the one whole is metaphysically basic, then gunk is metaphysically possible; (3) if the many parts are metaphysically basic, then gunk is not metaphysically possible; hence (4) the whole is metaphysically basic. He also argues that the phenomenon of entanglement in quantum mechanics fits best with an ontology in which the whole is metaphysically basic. And he offers a number of further arguments for this conclusion.

Assessing such arguments is beyond the scope of the present book, and to some extent (e.g., in the matter of quantum entanglement) is beyond the competence of the present authors. But we do recommend such arguments to the reader for serious consideration.

Schaffer himself advocates what we earlier called a layered ontology: although he holds that the one whole is metaphysically basic, he also holds that the right ontology includes "the many parts." He also evidently espouses fence-straddling realism concerning the objects posited by common sense—the view that (1) rejects ontological vagueness, (2) claims that there are nonvague objects that fall under the vague categories of common sense, and (3) claims that there are vastly many more such objects than would accord with everyday counting practices.[21]

But in chapter 4 we argued against the viability of a layered ontology that incorporates commonsense objects, and we also argued against fence-straddling realism. Given those arguments, commonsense objects and properties must be excluded from ontology altogether—not just from the ontologically basic level, but entirely. Moreover, although precise snobjective regions would not be excluded by such arguments, it seems there would be very little theoretical *need* for them if "the one whole" (as Schaffer calls it) is really ontologically basic. So if indeed the one whole is metaphysically basic, then it is also metaphysically exclusionary: the right ontology is blobjectivism. At the present moment, the prospects for a decisive dialectical victory for blobjectivism are encouraging.

7.8 Summary

Blobjectivism is a coherent and tenable position. It incorporates an ontological analysis of spatiotemporal complexity that eschews genuine **parts** in favor of spatiotemporally local **manners of instantiation**. It incorporates an ontological analysis of mental intentionality that (i) eschews **persons** and (ii) delivers vague content without ontological vagueness. It incorporates an ontological analysis of semantic normativity that grounds it in the reality of intentional mental **properties**, instantiated by **the blobject** in precise spatiotemporally local **manners**.

On balance, considerations of comparative overall ontological parsimony seem to us to favor blobjectivism vis-à-vis its most viable-looking austere competitors. But we admit that it is not at all obvious how best to assess the ultimate upshot of the comparative costs and benefits of these competing views—including the costs and benefits that accrue to various different aspects of parsimony, such as modal parsimony and subvenience parsimony. This is an issue on which reasonable people can reasonably differ, pending further additional considerations that might tip the scales more decisively.

7.9 Conclusion

The bulk of this book—six of its seven chapters—has been devoted to articulating and defending austere realism. This was done by way of the dialectic of reflective common sense in chapters 1–4, together with further positive arguments in favor of austere realism in chapter 5 and replies to objections in chapter 6. A reader certainly could embrace austere realism, and could accept our case in support of it, without necessarily embracing the specific version of austere realism we ourselves advocate, namely, blobjectivism. Austere realism is a key way station on the road to blobjectivism—and an important philosophical destination in its own right.

In the final chapter we argued that once austere realism is in place, there are really only three viable-looking austere ontologies of concrete particulars that can plausibly be wedded to it: (1) an ontology of concrete spatiotemporal points (pointillism), (2) an ontology of precise spatiotemporal regions that compose without restriction (universalist snobjective regionalism), and (3) blobjectivism. We argued that blobjectivism fares better than the other two in terms of comparative overall theoretical benefits and costs—but we acknowledged that the comparison between blobjectivism and universalist snobjective regionalism is a close call.

Two key themes throughout the book have been the need to respect common sense and the idea that truth is very often an indirect form of correspondence between thought/language and the world. Numerous commonsense beliefs are really true, according to austere realism, even though

the right ontology does not include items answering to the positing apparatus these beliefs deploy. Their truth is a matter of indirect correspondence
to the mind-independent world, which means that they are not actually
ontologically committed to their posits.

Common sense about matters of ontology and semantics also gets well
respected by austere realism and by blobjectivism—although here the story
is somewhat complicated. Common sense initially tends to confuse itself
when it goes reflective about matters of ontology and semantics. Continued and persistent commonsense reflection on these matters, however,
leads common sense to repudiate simple realism in favor of austere realism.
Blobjectivism then emerges not as the crazy position it initially seems to
be, but instead as the ontological-cum-semantic position that has perhaps
the best overall chance of being right.

Notes

Introduction

1. The expression Mr. Blobby is sometimes used by children in order to express a disrespectful attitude with respect to somebody who is too fat and who may also be called Fatso or Fatty, implying that he has got no shape in the sense that robust athletic types do have a muscular shape. For monistic aspects of blobjectivism, see Potrč 2003.

2. We thank David Chalmers for his suggestion to use the term 'blobjectivism', as well as for the suggestion about our book's title.

3. This is not to say that the original statement is strictly equivalent in meaning to the proposed paraphrase; we do not think it is. In our view, statements about posits need not be synonymous to any claims about positing-uses of thought constituents or language constituents in order for the former statements to be free of ontological commitment to entities called "posits." This is just a special case of our contention—to be articulated and defended in later chapters—that truth is often indirect correspondence. As shall be seen, this contention will be applicable to many uses of philosophical discourse itself—including talk of "posits."

2 Problems for Simple Realism

1. Some candidate ontologies include many more, and also many fewer, kinds of concrete entities than are normally posited in common sense and in science. See the discussion of "snobjective universalism" in chapter 7.

2. Another practice standard that is also in play, and is associated with the status principle we called the Difference Condition, is the following *Predecessor/Successor Requirement*: If one assigns an initial status to some item in a sorites sequence, then one is thereby committed to assignments of that same status to all predecessors of that item in the sequence, and one's judgmental/affirmatory practice must conform to this commitment; likewise, if one assigns the polar-opposite status to some item in the sequence, then one is thereby committed to assignments of that same

polar-opposite status to all successors of that item, and one's practice must conform to this commitment. This requirement, the ISA Prohibition, and the CSA Prohibition are all three mutually obeyable.

3. Are there other plausible cases, apart from vagueness and apart from semantic normativity more generally, in which practice is normatively governed by mutually unsatisfiable requirements or principles? We would say yes—although the cases that come to mind are subject to philosophical dispute. For instance, we would claim that there are genuine moral dilemmas—situations in which an agent is subject to several mutually unsatisfiable moral obligations, none of which have defeasibility conditions that are met in the circumstances, and all of which therefore remain in force. (In such cases, remorse is a rationally appropriate attitude concerning one's failure to meet one of the obligations; often one also is morally required to do something by way of addressing the unmet obligation—such as making reparations, offering an apology, etc.) We also would claim that there can be epistemic dilemmas (as one might call them)—situations in which an agent is subject to several mutually unsatisfiable epistemic norms; all of which remain in force in the circumstances. For instance, arguably it is rational to accept both quantum mechanics and general relativity, on the grounds of the enormous predictive accuracy and explanatory power of these two theories, even though they are known to be logically incompatible with one another; yet accepting them both goes contrary to the epistemic norm prohibiting the joint acceptance of theories known to be logically incompatible.

4. Supervaluationism construes truth simpliciter as truth under all "permissible interpretations"—there being multiple permissible interpretations, each of which "precisifies" the statement's vague vocabulary in a specific way. A vague statement is true simpliciter iff it is true under all permissible interpretations, is false simpliciter iff it is false under all permissible interpretations, and otherwise is neither true nor false. The locus classicus for this approach is Fine 1975.

5. The reason we characterize strong logical incoherence in terms of *rampant* commitment to contradictions is that there are systems of logic and semantics—so-called "paraconsistent" systems—that allow limited commitment to contradictions. Some philosophers have proposed paraconsistent treatments of vagueness—e.g., Hyde (1997).

3 Contextual Semantics: Truth as Indirect Correspondence

1. One way to capture the special self-involvingness of a "centered" possible world is to construe it as a maximal world-involving property instantiable by *oneself* (cf. Lewis 1983a). Such an approach would need to be modified somewhat to fit with austere realism, which eschews persons as items in the correct ontology. We will return to this matter in chapter 7, where we propose an account of how mentality is instantiated that comports with blobjectivism, the specific version of austere realism we advocate.

2. Nominalistic approaches to direct correspondence would attempt to eschew appeal to properties and relations. Our discussion throughout this book is nonnominalistic. A nominalist might attempt to recast our discussion into some favored nominalistic format.

3. Some metaphysical schemes would eschew states of affairs and seek to make do with just the objects and (nominalism aside) the properties and relations. But here we are positing states of affairs, if only for simplicity of exposition. Those who would repudiate them might attempt to recast our discussion into some favored ontological format.

4. Quine himself, of course, balked at the idea that *predicative* constituents of sentences are ontologically committed to properties and relations. But again, here we are conducting the discussion nonnominalistically.

5. There also might be limit cases in which the truth of a thought or sentence is not a matter of correspondence at all—i.e., not a matter of which centered possible world is the actual world. More below on such cases.

6. Putnam (1981, 1983); Dummett (1976); Rorty (1979, 1982); Goodman (1978).

7. Contextual semantics is also uncommitted about whether coarse-grained contextual variation extends to any coarse-grained category of semantic standards other than either DC or IC standards. Horgan believes that there is at least one additional such category, which could be called *expressivist* standards. Here the contextually appropriate use of the truth predicate is a form of appraisal that is not purely semantic but instead rests upon certain further, nonsemantic, normative standards together with a minimalistic use of the truth predicate that conforms with schema (T). Horgan favors such a view of truth attributions to moral judgments and statements, together with an expressivistic construal of moral judgments and statements themselves (cf. Horgan and Timmons 2000, 2006). But we will not pursue these themes in the present book. The theses of contextual semantics we set forth in the present section do not mention this further coarse-grained category (but do not preclude it either).

8. The metaphor of a spectrum is really too simple and unidimensional, but it serves the present expository purposes.

9. The semantic standards governing such statements still can count as IC standards, however—albeit limit-case IC standards in which the contribution of **the world** to the statement's semantic correctness is nil. In the limit case, IC standards require only vacuous or degenerate "correspondence," because the semantic standards do all the work themselves to guarantee semantic correctness. Vacuous "correspondence" obtains no matter what **the world** is like.

10. Contextual semantics is not officially committed to the claim that there are analytic existence claims, however, either in pure mathematics or elsewhere. Someone

might accept contextual semantics as we formulate it, and moreover might accept full-fledged austere realism concerning concrete particulars, while also claiming (1) that pure mathematics is normally governed by DC semantic standards, and (2) that the right ontology includes **numbers** and other mathematical **objects**.

11. Should one say that different semantic standards prevail at the various different positions on the spectrum just described, or should one say instead that a single set of IC standards is operative at all positions except the limit case where DC standards prevail? (A single body of IC standards might, after all, impose very different semantic-correctness requirements on various kinds of discourse involving different types of posits—including even making some existence claims, e.g., in pure mathematics, analytically true.) This will depend on how one individuates semantic standards—something that we ourselves think can vary depending on context. We return to this matter in section 3.4.2 below.

12. Although it is convenient here for expository purposes to speak as though Beethoven himself belongs to the correct ontology, we are not committed to this. Indeed, we are committed to denying it—because if persons were real then they would be vague in their synchronic composition and their temporal boundaries, but ontological vagueness is impossible.

13. Horgan argues against epistemically reductionist construals of truth like those of Putnam 1981, 1983 and Wright 1987, 1992 in Horgan 1991, 1995b, 1996.

14. This leaves it open whether or not contextually operative semantic standards typically sanction as true *all* instances of schema (T). In connection with vagueness, doubts can be raised about instances of (T) in which the statement replacing 'P' is a vague predication involving a borderline case (e.g., a statement predicating 'bald' of someone who is a borderline case of baldness).

15. Contextual semantics, as it has so far been worked out, focuses more on truth than on meaning.

16. Our intention is to treat the difference between 'ontological' and 'ontic' with respect. That is, we show respect in the face of what Heidegger calls ontological difference. It is startling to realize how disrespectful mainstream ontology is in these matters. (See Potrč and Strahovnik 2004a.)

17. At any rate, these candidates are all highly good ones *if indeed the right ontology contains precise spatiotemporal regions*. In chapter 7 we argue against such an ontology and in favor of blobjectivism. But we think that the blobjectivist can still retain the underlying spirit of the claim to which the present note is appended—even though the claim would need some reformulating (in terms of spatiotemporally local manners of instantiation of properties by the blobject). We return to this point briefly in chapter 7.

18. We say *largely* a direct-correspondence manner because the metalevel positing of various kinds of truth-bearers (e.g., thoughts, sentences, etc.) perhaps should be construed in a way that involves only ontic, and not ontological, commitment to such posits.

19. See, for instance, Cohen 1987, 1999; DeRose 1995, 1999; and Lewis 1983b, 1996.

20. On freedom and determinism, see, for instance, Horgan 1979; Graham and Horgan 1994; and Heller forthcoming. On mental causation, see, for instance, Horgan 1989, 1998a; Graham and Horgan 1994; Menzies 2003; Maslen 2005; and Maslen, Horgan, and Habermann forthcoming.

21. Concerning the concept of knowledge, however, let us register our dissatisfaction with the extant versions of contextualism we have seen. Often, advocates of contextualism about knowledge claim that the posing of a Cartesian radical-deception scenario automatically and inevitably drives the implicit parameters to a maximally demanding setting under which ordinary knowledge-claims all go false. This seems too crude. DeRose (2004) has tried to remedy this problem, by claiming that disputed knowledge-claims all lack truth value in a context where different conversationalists are deploying different parameter-settings for the concept *knowledge*. This too seems too crude.

22. Note the contextually operative setting of the implicit individuation-parameter for the notion "semantic standards." Semantic standards are being individuated in a coarse-grained manner in claim (1), as is contextually appropriate.

23. Note the contextually operative setting of the individuation-parameter for the notion "semantic standards." Semantic standards are being individuated in a fine-grained manner in claim (2), as is contextually appropriate.

24. Moreover, as noted above, the term 'meaning' itself is evidently governed by semantic standards with contextually variable parameters: although the term is frequently used in the coarse-grained way just described, it can sometimes be used in such a manner that the phrase 'change in meaning' tracks more fine-grained semantic differences.

25. We ourselves would say the same thing about *propositions*: for instance, one and the same proposition can be asserted on two different occasions, even if different semantic parameter-settings are operative in the two contexts. It is the same proposition across the two contexts, but this proposition exhibits an identity-preserving difference—a *différance*—from one context to the other. But philosophers typically use the word 'proposition', which is much more a philosophical term of art than are 'meaning' or 'concept', in a way that makes no room for the phenomenon of *différance* for propositions. Indeed, philosophical fans of contextualism often use proposition-talk this way: they often express their contextualism by saying that a single sentence can express different propositions, depending on contextual factors.

Because of this widespread philosophical usage, we try in this book to avoid proposition-talk almost completely. (For interesting recent challenges to the standard usage of 'proposition' and the assumptions embodied in such usage, see MacFarlane 2005, forthcoming.)

26. Putnam tries to argue from conceptual relativity to the conclusion that metaphysical realism is false—that there is no such thing as a mind-independent, discourse-independent, world. However, as our discussion in the present section will make clear, we ourselves see no incompatibility between conceptual relativity (as here explicated) and metaphysical realism. For more on this theme, see Horgan and Timmons 2002.

27. For expository convenience, we have formulated these two principles in a way that makes them specifically about just the one case of Carnap and the Polish logician. But such principles can also be formulated more abstractly to apply to cases of conceptual relativity in general. Of course, it need not always be the case that each of the persons in affirmatory conflict is actually making a *true* statement (under the given person's own way of using concepts that are susceptible to conceptual relativity); for, the affirmed statement might happen to be false even under the speaker's own way of using the relevant concepts.

28. These remarks are further supported by reflecting on the attempt to accommodate the phenomenon of conceptual relativity in Lynch 1998, 91–93. Lynch appears to accept a version of what we are calling the relativized content view (although the text is not completely unambiguous about this), and in order to make sense of the principle of affirmatory conflict, he claims that the statements made by Carnap and the Polish logician are in conflict in the sense that *"if these propositions were relative to the same scheme, they would be inconsistent"* (ibid., 93). But this sort of conflict is merely counterfactual; it does not constitute or explain the *actual* affirmatory conflict that is present in the claims that are actually made by Carnap and the Polish logician. Yet once one embraces a relativized content view about the claims in question, one seems forced to make a move like Lynch's in trying (unsuccessfully) to accommodate the idea that there is genuine affirmatory conflict in the actual claims being made in the Carnap–Polish logician case.

29. Parallel remarks apply to the example of the differing uses of 'entity' and 'The Ontology Discussion Group' in section 3.4.2 above—one usage by the room-scheduling supervisor and the other by the disgruntled metaphysican from the philosophy department.

30. In principle, this kind of fine-grained contextual variation could operate even under coarse-grained semantic standards of the DC kind. For, it could amount to implicit restriction in the range of quantification, even though the only items eligible to be quantified over at all are **objects** and **properties**.

31. See especially the essays "Truth and 'Correspondence'," "Grammar and Existence: A Preface to Ontology," and "Some Reflections on Language Games" in Sellars 1963, and chapter 4 of Sellars 1968.

32. An important difference between Wright and the approach embraced here is that we vigorously eschew epistemic reductionism, whereas Wright (1992) remains officially neutral about it; furthermore, his book can be read as supportive of the contention that truth, in any discourse, is the epistemically characterizable attribute he calls superassertibility. Horgan (1995b, 1996) applauds Wright's generic position but argues against an epistemically reductionist version of it.

4 Austere Realism: Overcoming Simple Realism's Problems

1. One reason we call our position transvaluationism is to emphasize that it is not a species of what Williamson (1994, 165) calls *nihilism*—the view that "vague expressions are empty; any vaguely drawn distinction is subverted." Another reason is to emphasize the need for a "transvaluation of all truth values," so to speak—i.e., the need to transcend the impossible goal of finding some logically coherent, semantically correct, collective assignment of semantic statuses to all the statements in a sorites sequence. The proper goal for a semantics of vagueness, as we have emphasized already, is to provide an adequate account of the normative standards governing semantically correct *affirmatory practice*.

2. Perhaps transvaluationism can even be implemented by standard two-valued logic, employed in a way that respects in practice the weak logical incoherence of vagueness. Concerning the accommodation of vagueness, Quine (1995, 57) remarks, "What I call my desk could be equated indifferently with countless almost coextensive aggregates of molecules, but I refer to it as a unique one of them, and I do not and cannot care which. Our standard logic takes this ... in stride, imposing a tacit fiction of unique though unspecifiable reference."

3. As John Tienson once remarked to Horgan.

4. Perhaps pure mathematics can be conducted without vague concepts. Perhaps some forms of mathematical physics can be too—especially field theories that dispense with notions like 'particle' in favor of magnitudes that take on precise numerical values at precise field-locations. But most sciences employ vague concepts galore.

5. One might think that items falling under the object categories of ordinary thought and discourse can still be included in the right ontology, provided (1) these objects are ontologically precise rather than ontologically vague, and (2) there are many *more* of them in the correct ontology than would conform to ordinary counting-practices. We consider this suggestion in section 5.5 of chapter 5, and we argue that it cannot work.

6. Brian McLaughlin, in conversation, has suggested that the version of iterated supervaluationism in McGee and McLaughlin 1995 accommodates our own view that there is logical incoherence in vagueness. Several features of their treatment are relevant here. First, they introduce a metalinguistic 'definitely' operator, appendable to the truth predicate. Second, they claim that the pretheoretic notion of truth bifurcates into two distinct notions with respect to vagueness, which they express as 'true' and 'definitely true', respectively. Third, they maintain that the former notion obeys the *disquotation principle*, which "tells us that any adequate understanding of truth ought to give us the [Tarskian] (T)-sentences and (F)-sentences" (ibid., 214), whereas the latter notion obeys the *correspondence principle*, which "tells us that the truth conditions for a sentence are established by the thoughts and practices of the speakers of a language, and that a sentence is true only if the nonlinguistic facts determine that these conditions are met" (ibid.). McLaughlin's claim is that, in effect, this approach treats the pretheoretic notion of truth as a logically incoherent amalgam of the two distinct truth-notions that he and McGee express as 'true' and 'definitely true' respectively. But even if they are right that the notion of truth needs to be thus bifurcated, we maintain that the logical incoherence of vagueness cuts deeper. As we are about to argue, logical incoherence is still present within iterated supervaluationist treatments of vagueness—including theirs, despite its explicit distinction between two notions of truth.

7. In chapter 5 we will argue that contextual semantics is theoretically preferable to various other semantic approaches that might get wedded to austere realism.

5 The Ascendance of the Austere: Further Arguments for Austere Realism

1. It bears emphasis, in connection with the argument just given, that an iterated supervaluationist treatment of the semantics of some word or concept does not by itself preclude semantic sharp boundaries that arise by virtue of the whole infinite metalinguistic hierarchy in which each metalanguage M_i gets a supervaluationist semantics in the next-higher metalanguage M_{i+1}. For instance, here is an iterated supervaluationist way of laying down semantics for the predicate 'Zenoid', a predicate that applies to certain real numbers. (The construction to be described is reminiscent of Zeno.) The first-order metalanguage M_1 stipulates that in any permissible interpretation of the predicate 'Zenoid', (i) any real number less than 100 belongs to the extension of 'Zenoid', and (ii) any real number greater than 400 does not belong to this predicate's extension; nothing else is said in M_1 about this predicate (which effectively allows permissible interpretations to specify any sharp boundary between 100 and 400, as far as M_1 itself is concerned). The second-order metalanguage M_2 stipulates that in any permissible interpretation I* of the predicate 'permissible interpretation of the predicate 'Zenoid'', (i) any real number less than 150 belongs to the extension of 'Zenoid' under any interpretation I of 'Zenoid' that belongs to I*, and (ii) any real number greater than 350 does not belong to the extension of 'Zenoid'

under any interpretation I of 'Zenoid' that belongs to I^*. Nothing else is said in M_2 about the first-order metalinguistic predicate 'permissible interpretation of the predicate 'Zenoid' '—which, as far as M_2 is concerned, effectively allows permissible interpretations of this higher-order predicate to specify any class of first-order interpretations each of whose member-interpretations specifies a sharp boundary for 'Zenoid' between 150 and 350. This sequence of stipulations is iterated "Zeno-style" up through the hierarchy of metalanguages *ad infinitum*: the successive lower values increase by increments of half the preceding increment (100, 150, 175, 187.5, ...), while the successive higher values decrease by the same increments (400, 350, 325, 312.5, ...). The upshot is that the overall, iterated supervaluational, semantic hierarchy fixes definite semantic statuses for all statements of the form "Real number r is Zenoid." Such a statement is true for any real number less than 200; is false for any real number greater than 300; and is neither true nor false for any real number that is greater than or equal to 200 and less than or equal to 300. (Likewise, mutatis mutandis, for the pertinent statements within each metalanguage that employ semantic predicates like 'is a permissible interpretation of the predicate 'Zenoid' '.) The moral is that the machinery of iterated supervaluationism does not *by itself* prevent statements in sorites sequences from having determinate semantic statuses; rather, some additional semantic factor is needed. (Accordingly, an expression's having iterated supervaluational semantics does not suffice for vagueness; the predicate 'Zenoid' is not vague.) Our claim is that the additional factor is the following, in the case of vagueness: semantically correct judgmental/affirmatory practice is normatively governed by mutually unsatisfiable status-principles.

2. The possibility remains open that for *some* forms of thought/discourse governed by IC semantic standards, the specific IC standards operative in certain contexts are ones under which there is no conceptual gap between semantic correctness and some form (possibly idealized or beefed up) of warranted affirmability. Our suspicion is that it will be hard to concoct any convincing example that is not subject to counterexample. But even if a convincing case could be offered, we claim, it would be the exception that proves the rule. The rule is that what is semantically correct under IC semantic standards (or under DC semantic standards) does not coincide completely with what is warrantedly assertible, ideally warrantedly assertible, or superassertible.

3. See Lynch 2004, 2005, 2006.

4. Maybe this is too simple. Lynch might want to say that in order to capture the full essence of truth, one needs a specification of the various kinds of discourse domains there are, and of certain constitutive requirements on what counts as an allowable realizing-property relative to each of these domains. But the point we make in the text would still hold.

5. The doubts persist even if one includes, among the general principles, ones that lay down constitutive requirements (relative to any given discourse domain D) on what counts as an allowable realizing-property relative to D. See the preceding note.

6. See, e.g., Merricks 2001. Merricks argues, via considerations different from those we have invoked in this book, that there are no statues, rocks, chairs, or stars. He also maintains that affirmative claims about such posits are systematically false, even though they are often semantically appropriate in a non-truth-constituting way.

6 Objections to Austere Realism

1. We do not necessarily want to lean heavily on the analogy with the Müller-Lyer illusion here. That example does put one kind of meat on the bones of the idea of a competence-based performance error. We will be describing *another* kind of meat now, leaving it open how much our account does or does not parallel the Müller-Lyer case. However, for the relation between optical illusion and phenomenology, specifically in Brentano's work, see Potrč 2002a, 2002c.

2. Indeed, we ourselves talk that way some of the time in setting forth our account of contextual semantics—as when we say, "Truth is semantically correct affirmability *under contextually operative semantic standards.*" Here we should emphasize that we regard the contextual-semantics story as applicable to virtually all the concepts and terms usable to *tell* the story, and in particular to the concept *truth*. Although the explicitly relativistic usage of 'true' is a legitimate usage, very often—indeed, typically—one does not use 'true' in a relativistic way. On the contrary, one uses it categorically, from within a stance in which one not only accepts certain specific semantic-correctness standards as contextually operative, but one lets them govern one's truth ascriptions too—the familiar (though not inevitable, on our view) "schema T" usage of 'true'.

3. This is a specific philosophical usage of 'really'—not the only one that might be appropriate in philosophical contexts, to be sure, and one that is different from *most* uses of 'really'. This specific usage is employed to overtly signal a shift into a mode of thought/discourse governed by DC semantic standards.

4. See Reicher 2002, and Horgan's reply to Reicher in Horgan 2002.

5. On particularism concerning moral normativity, the locus classicus is Dancy 1993; see also Dancy 2004, and Potrč's commentary on Dancy's views in Potrč 2004b. On quasi-particularism, with particular attention to epistemic normativity, see Potrč 2000. For more on particularism concerning semantic normativity, see Horgan and Potrč 2006a, forthcoming.

6. See Barnard and Horgan forthcoming; Horgan 2002; Horgan and Potrč 2006a; Potrč and Strahovnik 2004b; Horgan and Tienson 1996.

7. Thanks to Mark Timmons for suggesting this phrase.

8. In earlier writings we have sometimes used the expression 'quasi-particularism' for what we are now calling softly generalist particularism. See, for instance, Barnard and

Horgan forthcoming; Horgan and Potrč 2006a; Potrč 2000. But it now appears to us that 'quasi-particularism' is overly concessive to those who would apply the label 'particularism' only to an extreme version of the position.

9. The way the answer is explained here employs a thought experiment that was not invoked in Horgan and Tienson 1996, but in an early version was invoked in Horgan and Tienson 1992.

7 Betting on the Blobject: The Choice among Austere Ontologies

1. The terms 'slobject', 'snobject', and 'blobject' were introduced in Horgan 1991, with due credit to Barry Loewer, who coined the first two in conversation with Horgan. An overview of ontological choices is given in Potrč 1999a.

2. Van Inwagen uses the term 'nihilism' for the view that there are only simples and no composites. But we do not adopt his terminology here because it has unduly pejorative connotations.

3. 'Universalism' is van Inwagen's term for the view that any bunch of real objects jointly compose another real object. One potential form of snobjective universalism would eschew simples and would claim instead that every snobject has other snobjects as proper parts. On this view, snobjects are composed of what David Lewis called "atomless gunk" (e.g., Lewis 1991, 4). For reasons of simplicity we will not explicitly discuss the gunkist form of snobjective universalism. If our reasoning below is sound, then blobjectivism is theoretically preferable to both forms of snobjective universalism.

4. Might there be a distinction to be drawn between a nonregional blobject and a blobjective region? We doubt that any such distinction would make clear sense, in part because we find very plausible the following claim: it is a conceptual truth concerning the notion of *region* that any extended region has other regions as proper parts. This would make the blobject a nonregion.

5. At any rate, on this picture the cosmos does not have any *spatiotemporal* parts. One might construe the cosmos as consisting of several distinct but *superimposed* fields, each of which extends spatiotemporally throughout the universe and none of which has spatiotemporal parts; and one might treat these fields as separate "parts" of the cosmos. But for simplicity, we will ignore this possibility in the text. It yields a picture much like ontological blobjectivism, even though it claims there are several concrete particulars rather than just one, because these distinct entities are *all* blobjects, superimposed with one another.

6. We leave open the question of the modal strength of supervenience relations between the facts describable in the language of physics and facts describable in the language of the special sciences or ordinary discourse. Presumably such supervenience relations are *at least* nomically necessary, and perhaps some or all of them

are necessary in a stronger way than that—e.g., metaphysically necessary, or conceptually necessary.

7. The term 'literal', like many in ordinary language, is governed by contextually variable semantic parameters. *One* use of 'literal' that is occasionally contextually appropriate is to shift the language-game into DC semantic standards—perhaps while simultaneously denying that a given statement is true under *those* standards. But from the perspective of contextual semantics, this is certainly not the only correct use of 'literal', and not an especially common one. More commonly, the term functions to do things like distinguish metaphorical from nonmetaphorical uses of language, or distinguish truth (under the contextually operative semantic standards) from near truth (under those same standards).

8. Our thanks to David Sosa for a question that prompted the present paragraph.

9. From the perspective of blobjectivism, the example of statements (a) and (b) really pertains to the ontic rather than to ontology (in the terminology of contextual semantics). The lesson of the example is that although statement (a) is ontically committed to Smith, it is not ontically committed to Smith's laugh. But according to blobjectivism, statements (a) and (b) do not carry *ontological* commitment to Smith either. There is no such **individual** as Smith, and there are no such (vague) **properties** as *laughing* or *laughing loudly*. Rather, statements (a) and (b) are true by virtue of *indirect* correspondence to **the world**.

10. We are not committed to claiming that statements (c) and (d) are synonymous, and we doubt that they are. But they do have the same truth conditions—truth conditions that do not require the cosmos to have proper parts.

11. In note 17 of chapter 3 we mentioned that blobjectivism needs to reformulate the idea that in the case of an experientially posited item, there are numerous good candidates in **the world** for being the region occupied by that item. The reformulation is this: there are numerous spatiotemporally precise manners of instantiation that are good candidates for being the manner in which the blobject instantiates properties that commonsense thought and belief attribute to the posited item.

12. Although the idea that locations instantiate properties and relations might very well be more fundamental *psychologically* than the idea that properties and relations are instantiated by the cosmos in spatiotemporally local ways, our adverbialist answer to Tienson's question (Q3) commits us to claiming that the latter idea is more fundamental *ontologically* than the former. The order of being (as Sellars called it) need not coincide with the order of conceiving—just as it need not coincide with the order of knowing. (Thus, if someone wants to argue that the idea of spatiotemporal manners of instantiation makes no sense unless one supposes that there are spatiotemporal **locations** in the right ontology, it will not suffice just to claim that the notion of location is psychologically more fundamental than the notion of spatiotemporal manner of instantiation. The inadequacy of such a line of argument is

especially vivid in light of the fact that location-positing claims can perfectly well be true, according to blobjectivism, under *IC* semantic standards.)

13. Given our arguments against ontological vagueness in chapter 2 and against fence-straddling realism in chapter 4, people and other kinds of thinkers must be eschewed even if one admits *precise* concrete **parts** into ontology. For, material beings such as **people**, if there were any, would be ontologically vague.

14. It bears emphasis that question (B) arises for any ontological position that denies ontological vagueness but embraces intentional mental **properties**. Thus, it is not by any means a question only faced by blobjectivism. Although our answer to question (B) will not invoke locations, it will be readily adaptable by an ontological position that posits nonvague locations and/or other kinds of nonvague spatiotemporal particulars as putative **parts** of **the world**.

15. See Horgan and Tienson 2002 and Horgan, Tienson, and Graham 2004. These two papers argue that phenomenally constituted intentionality is the most fundamental kind of mental intentionality and is constitutively independent of the experiencing subject's causal or historical relations to a wider environment; they also argue that "externalistic" intentionality, involving constitutive externalistic factors that contribute to reference fixing for certain thought-constituents (e.g., thought-constituents purporting to refer to concrete particulars or to natural kinds), is a product of such externalistic factors together with the more fundamental, phenomenally constituted form of intentionality. For intentionality of phenomenology in Brentano, see Potrč 2002a.

16. For present purposes we can remain neutral about whether the determinable kind associated with the predicate 'is thinking that *p*' is itself a **property**. But prima facie, this predicate looks to be vague with respect to range of applicability—which would mean that it cannot express a genuine **property**. Compare: since the predicate 'is red' is vague with respect to range of applicability, there cannot be such a property as redness; but there still can be color properties that are *precise determinants* of the determinable kind expressed by 'is red'.

17. Our thanks to Richard Grandy for pointing out to us that the original answer we proposed to question (B2) committed us to **regions**—a realization that prompted us to propose the answer given in the present paragraph.

18. This is not to deny that certain aspects of thought involve convention—for instance, when one "thinks in English," or when one thinks *about* matters of convention. But on our view, the primary, phenomenally constituted form of mental intentionality is prior to, and is a prerequisite for, these convention-involving aspects of thought.

19. Are there **concepts**, perhaps as constituents of **contents** that themselves perhaps are constituents of intentional **properties**? Blobjectivism per se can remain neutral

about this question, which pertains to the ontological structure of intentional **properties**.

20. Semantically correct affirmation/denial practice does *not* cleanly sort all potential thought-contents and statements into categories like truth (semantic correctness), falsity (semantic incorrectness), indeterminacy, etc. For, intentional content is typically *vague*, and vagueness precludes any determinate overall assignment of such semantic statuses to thought-contents and statements arranged in a sorites sequence.

21. Although we use the unvarnished term 'supervenient' for convenience of exposition, we really mean supervenience that is explainable rather than sui generis—what Horgan (1993a) called "superdupervenience." Brute, unexplainable, interlevel relations of metaphysical necessitation would be ontologically fundamental themselves, even if they rendered some phenomena supervenient on others. Likewise for brute, unexplainable, interlevel relations of *nomic* necessitation. Arguably, features of the world that are supervenient only in virtue of brute necessitation would be no less ontologically fundamental than the supervenience-base features themselves.

22. We say he *evidently* espouses fence-straddling realism on the basis of casual conversations he had with Horgan at the 2006 Arizona Ontology Workshop in Tucson. We do not wish to attribute this view to him definitively.

References

Barnard, R., and T. Horgan. 2006. "Truth as Mediated Correspondence." *Monist* 89, no. 1: 28–49.

Benacerraf, P. 1973. "Mathematical Truth." *Journal of Philosophy* 19: 661–679.

Carnap, R. 1950. "Empiricism, Semantics, and Ontology." *Revue Internationale de Philosophie* 11: 20–40.

Cohen, S. 1987. "Knowledge, Context, and Social Standards." *Synthese* 73: 3–26.

Cohen, S. 1999. "Contextualism, Skepticism, and the Structure of Reasons." *Philosophical Perspectives* 13: 57–89.

Crimmins, M. 1998. "Hesperus and Phosphorus: Sense, Pretense, and Reference." *Philosophical Review* 107: 10–48.

Dancy, J. 1993. *Moral Reasons*. Oxford: Blackwell.

Dancy, J. 2004. *Ethics without Principles*. New York: Oxford University Press.

DeRose, K. 1995. "Solving the Skeptical Problem." *Philosophical Review* 104: 1–52.

DeRose, K. 1999. "Contextualism: An Explanation and Defense." In *The Blackwell Guide to Epistemology*, ed. J. Greco and E. Sosa. Oxford: Blackwell.

DeRose, K. 2004. "Single Scoreboard Semantics." *Philosophical Studies* 119: 1–21.

Dummett, M. 1976. "What Is a Theory of Meaning? (II)." In *Essays in Semantics*, ed. G. Evans and J. McDowell, 67–137. Oxford: Oxford University Press.

Field, H. 1986. "The Deflationary Conception of Truth." In *Fact, Science and Morality*, ed. D. MacDonald and C. Wright. Oxford: Blackwell.

Fine, K. 1975. "Vagueness, Truth, and Logic." *Synthese* 30: 265–300.

Fodor, J. 1983. *The Modularity of Mind*. Cambridge, Mass.: MIT Press/A Bradford Book.

Fodor, J. 2001. *The Mind Doesn't Work That Way: The Scope and Limits of Computational Psychology*. Cambridge, Mass.: MIT Press/A Bradford Book.

Goodman, N. 1978. *Ways of Worldmaking*. Indianapolis: Hackett.

Graham, G., and T. Horgan. 1994. "Southern Fundamentalism and the End of Philosophy." *Philosophical Issues* 5: 219–247.

Heller, M. Forthcoming. "How to Be a Contextualist about Free Will."

Horgan, T. 1979. "'Could', Possible Worlds, and Moral Responsibility." *Southern Journal of Philosophy* 17: 345–358.

Horgan, T. 1986a. "Psychologism, Semantics and Ontology." *Noûs* 20: 21–31.

Horgan, T. 1986b. "Truth and Ontology." *Philosophical Papers* 15: 1–21.

Horgan, T. 1989. "Mental Quausation." *Philosophical Perspectives* 3: 47–76.

Horgan, T. 1991. "Metaphysical Realism and Psychologistic Semantics." *Erkenntnis* 34: 297–322.

Horgan, T. 1993a. "From Supervenience to Superdupervenience: Meeting the Demands of a Material World." *Mind* 102: 555–586.

Horgan, T. 1993b. "On What There Isn't." *Philosophy and Phenomenological Research* 50: 693–700.

Horgan, T. 1994. "Robust Vagueness and the Forced-March Sorites Paradox." *Philosophical Perspectives* 8, *Logic and Language*: 159–188.

Horgan, T. 1995a. "Transvaluationism: A Dionysian Approach to Vagueness." *Southern Journal of Philosophy* 33 (Spindel Conference Supplement): 97–125.

Horgan, T. 1995b. "Critical Study of Crispin Wright, *Truth and Objectivity*." *Noûs* 29: 127–138.

Horgan, T. 1996. "The Perils of Epistemic Reductionism." *Philosophy and Phenomenological Research* 66: 891–897.

Horgan, T. 1998a. "Kim on Mental Causation and Causal Exclusion." *Philosophical Perspectives* 11: 165–184.

Horgan, T. 1998b. "The Transvaluationist Conception of Vagueness." *Monist* 81: 313–330.

Horgan, T. 2000. "Facing Up to the Sorites Paradox." In *Proceedings of the Twentieth World Congress of Philosophy*, volume 6: *Analytic Philosophy and Logic*, ed. A. Anamori, 99–111. Charlottesville, Virginia: Philosophy Documentation Center.

Horgan, T. 2001a. "Causal Compatibilism and the Exclusion Problem." *Theoria*: 95–116.

Horgan, T. 2001b. "Contextual Semantics and Metaphysical Realism: Truth as Indirect Correspondence." In *The Nature of Truth*, ed. M. P. Lynch, 67–95. Cambridge, Mass.: MIT Press/A Bradford Book.

Horgan, T. 2002. "Replies." *Grazer Philosophische Studien* 63: 303–341.

Horgan, T., and M. Potrč. 2000a. "Blobjectivism and Indirect Correspondence." *Facta Philosophica* 2: 249–270.

Horgan, T., and M. Potrč, eds. 2000b. *Vagueness and Meaning. Acta Analytica* 23. Dettelbach: Röll Verlag.

Horgan, T., and M. Potrč. 2002. "Addressing Questions for Blobjectivism." *Facta Philosophica* 2: 311–321.

Horgan, T., and M. Potrč, eds. 2003. *Vagueness. Acta Analytica* 29. Dettelbach: Röll Verlag.

Horgan, T., and M. Potrč. 2006a. "Particularist Semantic Normativity." *Acta Analytica* 21, no. 1: 45–61.

Horgan, T., and M. Potrč. 2006b. "Abundant Truth in an Austere World." In *Truth and Realism: New Debates*, ed. P. Greenough and M. P. Lynch, 137–161. Oxford: Oxford University Press.

Horgan, T., and M. Potrč. 2007. "Contextual Semantics and Particularist Normativity." In *Challenging Moral Particularism*, ed. M. Lance, M. Potrč, and V. Strahovnik. London: Routledge.

Horgan, T., M. Potrč, and J. Tienson, eds. 2002. *Origins: The Common Sources of the Analytic and Phenomenological Traditions. Southern Journal of Philosophy* (Spindel Conference Supplement).

Horgan, T., and J. Tienson. 1992. "Cognitive Systems as Dynamical Systems." *Topoi* 11: 27–43.

Horgan, T., and J. Tienson. 1996. *Connectionism and the Philosophy of Psychology.* Cambridge, Mass.: MIT Press/A Bradford Book.

Horgan, T., and J. Tienson. 2002. "The Intentionality of Phenomenology and the Phenomenology of Intentionality." In *Philosophy of Mind: Classical and Contemporary Readings*, ed. D. Chalmers, 520–533. New York: Oxford University Press.

Horgan, T., J. Tienson, and G. Graham. 2004. "Phenomenal Intentionality and the Brain in a Vat." In *The Externalist Challenge*, ed. R. Schantz, 297–317. Berlin: Walter de Gruyter.

Horgan, T., and M. Timmons. 2000. "Nondescriptivist Cognitivism: Framework for a New Metaethics." *Philosophical Papers* 29: 121–153.

Horgan, T., and M. Timmons. 2002. "Conceptual Relativity and Metaphysical Realism." *Philosophical Issues* 12: 74–96.

Horgan, T., and M. Timmons. 2006. "Cognitivist Expressivism." In *Metaethics after Moore*, ed. T. Horgan and M. Timmons, 255–298. Oxford: Oxford University Press.

Horwich, P. 1990. *Truth*. Oxford: Blackwell.

Horwich, P. 1998. *Truth*, second edition. Oxford: Oxford University Press.

Hyde, D. 1997. "From Heaps of Gaps to Heaps of Gluts." *Mind* 106: 440–460.

Lewis, D. 1972. "Psychophysical and Theoretical Identifications." *Australasian Journal of Philosophy* 50: 249–258.

Lewis, D. 1980. "Mad Pain and Martian Pain." In *Readings in the Philosophy of Psychology*, vol. 1, ed. N. Block, 216–222. Cambridge, Mass.: Harvard University Press.

Lewis, D. 1983a. "Attitudes De Dicto and De Se." In his *Philosophical Papers*, volume I, 133–159. Oxford: Oxford University Press.

Lewis, D. 1983b. "Scorekeeping in a Language Game." In his *Philosophical Papers*, volume I, 233–249. Oxford: Oxford University Press.

Lewis, D. 1991. *Parts of Classes*. Oxford: Basil Blackwell.

Lewis, D. 1996. "Elusive Knowledge." *Australasian Journal of Philosophy* 74: 549–567.

Lewis, D. 1999. "Many, but Almost One." In his *Papers in Metaphysics and Epistemology*, 164–182. Cambridge: Cambridge University Press. First appeared in *Ontology, Causality and Mind: Essays in Honour of D. M. Armstrong*, ed. J. Bacon, K. Campbell, and L. Reinhardt, 23–37. New York: Cambridge University Press.

Lynch, M. P. 1998. *Truth in Context: An Essay on Pluralism and Objectivity*. Cambridge, Mass.: MIT Press/A Bradford Book.

Lynch, M. P. 2002. "The Truth in Contextual Semantics." *Grazer Philosophische Studien* 63: 173–195.

Lynch, M. P. 2004. "Truth and Multiple Realizability." *Australasian Journal of Philosophy* 82: 384–408.

Lynch, M. P. 2005. "Functionalism and Our Folk Theory of Truth: Reply to Cory Wright." *Synthese* 145: 29–43.

Lynch, M. P. 2006. "ReWrighting Pluralism." *Monist* 89, no. 1: 63–84.

MacFarlane, J. 2005. "Making Sense of Relative Truth." *Proceedings of the Aristotelian Society* 105: 321–339.

MacFarlane, J. Forthcoming. "Semantic Minimalism and Nonindexical Contextualism." In *Context Sensitivity and Semantic Minimalism: Essays on Semantics and Pragmatics*, ed. G. Preyer and G. Peter. Oxford: Oxford University Press.

Maslen, C. 2005. "A New Cure for Epiphobia: A Context-Sensitive Account of Causal Relevance." *Southern Journal of Philosophy* 43: 131–146.

Maslen, C., T. Horgan, and H. Habermann. Forthcoming. "Mental Causation." In *The Oxford Handbook of Causation*, ed. H. Beebee, C. Hitchcock, and P. Menzies. Oxford: Oxford University Press.

McGee, V., and B. McLaughlin. 1995. "Distinctions without a Difference." *Southern Journal of Philosophy* 33 (Spindel Conference Supplement): 203–251.

Menzies, P. 2003. "The Causal Efficacy of Mental States." In *Physicalism and Mental Causation: The Metaphysics of Mind and Action*, ed. S. Walter and H. D. Heckmann, 195–223. Exeter: Imprint Academic.

Merricks, T. 2001. *Objects and Persons*. Oxford: Oxford University Press.

Peacocke, C. 1992. *A Study of Concepts*. Cambridge, Mass.: MIT Press/A Bradford Book.

Potrč, M. 1993. *Phenomenology and Cognitive Science*. Dettelbach: Röll Verlag.

Potrč, M. 1999a. "What's Cooking? World à la Carte." In *Metaphysics in the Post-Metaphysical Age*, ed. U. Meixner and P. Simons, 116–122. Kirchberg am Wechsel: Austrian Ludwig Wittgenstein Society.

Potrč, M., ed. 1999b. *Connectionism and the Philosophy of Psychology. Acta Analytica* 22. Dettelbach: Röll Verlag.

Potrč, M. 2000. "Justification Having and Morphological Content." *Acta Analytica* 24: 151–173.

Potrč, M. 2002a. "Intentionality of Phenomenology in Brentano." In (2002). *Origins: The Common Sources of the Analytic and Phenomenological Traditions. The Southern Journal of Philosophy, Spindel Conference Supplement*, ed. T. Horgan, M. Potrč, and J. Tienson, 231–267.

Potrč, M. 2002b. "Non-arbitrariness of Composition and Particularism." *Grazer Philosophische Studien* 63: 197–215.

Potrč, M. 2002c. "Phenomenal Green and the Optical Paradox." In *Philosophical Perspectives*, ed. T. Tapio Korte and J. Räikkä, 83–97. Turku: Department of Philosophy.

Potrč, M. 2002d. "Transvaluationism, Common Sense and Indirect Correspondence." *Acta Analytica* 29: 97–114.

Potrč, M. 2003. "Blobjectivist Monism: Repulsive Monism: One Dynamic BLOB and No Principles." In *Monism*, ed. A. Baechli and K. Petrus, 125–155. Frankfurt: Ontos Verlag.

Potrč, M. 2004a. *Dinamična filozofija* [Dynamical philosophy]. Ljubljana: ZIFF.

Potrč, M. 2004b. "Particularism and Resultance." *Acta Analytica* 33: 163–187.

Potrč, M., and V. Strahovnik. 2004a. "Metaphysics: Ultimate and Regional Ontology." *Informacion Filosofica* 1: 21–45.

Potrč, M., and V. Strahovnik. 2004b. *Practical Contexts*. Frankfurt: Ontos Verlag.

Potrč, M., and V. Strahovnik. 2005. "Meinongian Scorekeeping." *Meinong Studies* 1, 309–330. Frankfurt: Ontos Verlag.

Putnam, H. 1981. *Reason, Truth, and History*. Cambridge: Cambridge University Press.

Putnam, H. 1983. *Realism and Reason: Philosophical Papers*, volume 3. Cambridge: Cambridge University Press.

Putnam, H. 1987. *The Many Faces of Realism*. La Salle: Open Court.

Putnam, H. 1988. *Representation and Reality*. Cambridge, Mass.: MIT Press/A Bradford Book.

Putnam, H. 1991. "Reply to Terry Horgan." *Erkenntnis* 34: 419–424.

Putnam, H. 2004. *Ethics without Ontology*. Cambridge, Mass.: Harvard University Press.

Quine, W. V. O. 1960. *Word and Object*. Cambridge, Mass.: MIT Press.

Quine, W. V. O. 1995. *From Stimulus to Science*. Cambridge, Mass.: Harvard University Press.

Reicher, M. 2002. "Ontological Commitment and Contextual Semantics." *Grazer Philosophische Studien* 63: 141–155.

Richard, M. 2006. "Context, Vagueness, and Ontology." In *Truth and Realism: New Debates*, ed. P. Greenough and M. P. Lynch, 62–74. Oxford: Oxford University Press.

Rorty, R. 1979. *Philosophy and the Mirror of Nature*. Princeton: Princeton University Press.

Rorty, R. 1982. *Consequences of Pragmatism*. Minneapolis: University of Minnesota Press.

Sainsbury, M. 1990. "Concepts without Boundaries." Inaugural Lecture, King's College, London. Reprinted in *Vagueness: A Reader* ed. R. Keefe and P. Smith (Cambridge, Mass.: MIT Press/A Bradford Book, 1996).

Schaffer, J. 2007. "From Nihilism to Monism." *Australasian Journal of Philosophy* 85, no. 2: 175–191.

Schaffer, J. Forthcoming. "Monism: The Priority of the Whole."

Sellars, W. 1963. *Science, Perception, and Reality*. London: Routledge and Kegan Paul.

Sellars, W. 1968. *Science and Metaphysics*. London: Routledge and Kegan Paul.

Soames, S. 1999. *Understanding Truth*. Oxford: Oxford University Press.

Sorenson, R. A. 1988. *Blindspots*. Oxford: Blackwell.

Szubka, T. 2002. "Truth as Correct Assertibility: An Intermediate Position?" *Grazer Philosophische Studien* 63: 157–171.

Thomasson, A. 2007. *Ordinary Objects*. Oxford: Oxford University Press.

Tienson, J. 2002. "Questions for Blobjectivism." *Facta Philosophica* 2: 301–310.

Timmons, M. 1999. *Morality without Foundations*. New York: Oxford University Press.

Unger, P. 1980. "The Problem of the Many." *Midwest Studies in Philosophy* 5: 411–467.

van Fraassen, B. C. 1980. *The Scientific Image*. Oxford: Oxford University Press.

van Inwagen, P. 1990. *Material Beings*. Ithaca, N.Y.: Cornell University Press.

Walton, K. 1990. *Mimesis as Make-Believe*. Cambridge, Mass.: Harvard University Press.

Williamson, T. 1994. *Vagueness*. London and New York: Routledge.

Williamson, T. 2002. "Horgan on Vagueness." *Grazer Philosophische Studien* 63: 273–285.

Woodbridge, J. 2005. "Truth as Pretense." In *Fictionalism in Metaphysics*, ed. M. Kalderon, 134–177. Oxford: Oxford University Press.

Wright, C. 1987. *Realism, Meaning, and Truth*. Oxford: Blackwell.

Wright, C. 1992. *Truth and Objectivity*. Cambridge, Mass.: Harvard University Press.

Index